The Tennessee Gardener's Guide

The Tennessee Gardener's Guide

BY
WALTER GLENN & LARK FOSTER

1-24-98

Beth,
Tennessee Gardening...
good for Body & Soul
and good luck in your
New home!
Lark

COOL SPRINGS PRESS
FRANKLIN, TENNESSEE

FIRST EDITION PUBLISHED 1996. SECOND EDITION PUBLISHED 1997

FIRST PRINTING 1997
PRINTED IN THE UNITED STATES OF AMERICA
02 01 00 99 98 97 96   10 9 8 7 6 5 4 3 2

GLEEN, WALTER
    THE TENNESSEE GARDENERS GUIDE BY
WALTER GLENN AND LARK FOSTER

    p.   cm
INCLUDES BIBLIOGRAPHICAL REFERENCES AND INDEX
ISBN 1-888-608-38-2
1. GARDENING -- TENNESSEE. 2. GARDENING -- SOUTHERN STATES
I. FOSTER, LARK. II. TITLE`
635.9 -- dc20
GLE / FOS

Published by
Cool Springs Press
118 FOURTH AVENUE SOUTH
FRANKLIN, TENNESSEE 37064

On the Cover (Clockwise from top left):
American Yellowood, American Holly, Japanese Wisteria, Pansy

D E D I C A T I O N

*W*E WOULD LIKE TO DEDICATE this book to the memory of our longtime friend and fellow horticulturalist Geddes "Plupy" Douglas, Jr. "Plupy," as he was affectionately called, was a second-generation horticulturalist. His father, Geddes Douglas, Sr., owned and operated a nursery and landscape company in Nashville for many years.

The Douglas family has been an inspiration to our families' involvement in gardening and we feel blessed to be able to take this opportunity to acknowledge the Douglas influence on our family and on gardeners in Tennessee.

A WORD TO THE READER

*O*VER THE LAST TWENTY-FIVE YEARS, I have seen the world
of gardening change and expand dramatically. When Dad and I started
our landscape and gardening business, we did it because of our respect
and love for things that grow and a desire to help people fully appreciate the wonders of gardening and landscaping. These goals are still
real today. As our business has expanded, we have been blessed with
the opportunity to make many friends. Also, we have made friendships
over the years through our lawn and garden radio programs. It was
during the radio program some years ago that we began to realize that
a pattern was developing in the questions from our listeners. It became
clear that many of the calls were about the same trees and shrubs and
about similar landscaping problems. This was echoed by our garden
center customers, as was a common reluctance on the part of many
gardeners to try new varieties. Also, we have had numerous requests
that we write a book about the plants in our area and how to properly
care for them. For these reasons, we have written *The Tennessee Gardener's
Guide*. If it helps capture the imagination of the reader and leads to a
deeper appreciation of the world outside, this book will be a success.

Lark Foster, Franklin, Tennessee April, 1996

"*M*ANKIND HAS BEEN commissioned by his Creator to be a
gardener." From the beginning of Genesis, the Lord planted a garden
in Eden then created man as its gardener, to tend and care for it. I
believe that because man was created to be a gardener, that it is gardening that will be the building block for mankind's peaceful, loving,
fulfilling existence during our stay on this Earth. Think about it!
Gardening is an essential activity to mankind's existence. Gardening is
a common experience that transcends age, race, gender, nationality
and spiritual differences.

It is my hope and prayer that *The Tennessee Gardener's Guide* will provide our readers with useful information about plants for their own corner of paradise. We wish our readers excitement and joy about their
calling as gardeners—not as a task, but as a privilege. My daughters,
Vicki, Lark and Robin, my son Howard, and my wife, Betty, are blessed
to share our corner of the garden in Tennessee with our readers. We
feel blessed and our hope is that our readers will be blessed also.

Walter Glenn, Franklin, Tennessee April, 1996

CONTENTS

Gardening Checklist for the Tennes Seasons

WINTER

✔ Water container plants, perennial beds and evergreens as needed if we experience a "dry" season.

✔ Clean and sharpen lawn mowers and hand tools as needed for Spring.

✔ Keep birdfeeders full of birdseed and supply a water source for our feathered friends.

✔ Prune fruit trees and later flowering shrubs. Spray with dormant oil.

✔ Trim branches of quince, forsythia and other spring-flowering plants to force blooms indoors. Crush or split stems before arranging in "deep" vase.

✔ Force bulbs (amaryllis and paperwhites) for easy indoor fragrance and color. Great gift idea!

✔ Prune evergreens and utilize boughs for holiday decor and place in containers outdoors for filler.

SPRING

✔ Prune Winter damaged limbs of trees and shrubs as needed.

✔ Remove heavy mulch from around your roses and perennials.

✔ Early Spring apply a crabgrass preventer to lawns as needed.

✔ Fertilize cool season lawns with a slow-release food (consider one containing a weed killer if needed).

✔ Plant trees, shrubs, roses, perennials, Summer bulbs, vines, fruits, berries, cool season grasses and just about anything!

✔ Start a compost pile.

✔ Mark overcrowded bulb beds so you can divide this Summer.

✔ When planting bulbs and perennials, create labels . . . it will make next Spring's identification of them a lot easier.

Gardening Checklist for the Tennes Seasons

SUMMER

✔ Now is the time to successfully kill or plant Bermuda Grass.

✔ Continue to water plants as needed during extreme heat.

✔ Deadhead annuals, perennials, and flowering shrubs to encourage more blooms.

✔ Consider applying a (Summer oil) horticultural spray to control insects on shrubs, groundcovers and even perennials. (Avoid extreme temperatures!)

✔ Mulch to help conserve the moisture around plants and help to control weeds which compete for moisture.

✔ If the weather is wet . . . apply lime-sulphur fungicide on lilacs, crape myrtles, zinnias and phlox.

FALL

✔ Pull up frost-biten annuals and replace with cheery pansies, kale, cabbage or even Mexican sage.

✔ Consider planting some fall perennials besides just "mums" . . . try Japanese anenomes, asters, artemisias, ornamental grasses!

✔ Clean up beds removing spent blooms and dead foliage on perennials.

✔ Plant trees, shrubs, perennials, lawns and bulbs.

✔ Apply in LATE Fall a lawn food that contains a weed killer for cool season lawns.

✔ Create a journal of successes and failures from the past year in your garden and refer to it next year to avoid the same mistakes.

Lawns

"*S*HOW ME A GOOD-LOOKING, healthy, green lawn and I'll show you a lawn on a program." I've been known to recite this phrase many times over when asked how to have a green lawn.

My opening comment emphasizes the idea that to have a good-looking lawn, you need to make a commitment. This doesn't mean you have to obligate yourself to signing a contract with a lawn service. You do, however, need to make a personal commitment to taking a program approach. You need to be consistent in fertilization and seasonal weed control as required by your choice of turf. Speaking of choice, the variety of landscapes across Tennessee insures many regional choices when it comes to turf selection.

Some folks in West Tennessee simply adore the attributes of a lush hybrid Bermuda lawn. On the other hand, in Middle Tennessee, we are constantly answering the question, "How can I get rid of this Bermuda in my lawn and flower garden?"

CHAPTER ONE

There are cool season and warm season grasses that all have a place in the landscape. There are options for sunny conditions and even solutions for a shaded lawn. The bottom line is, nothing sets off or frames the overall look of your home like a pristine green lawn.

It will certainly pay to have a healthy lawn, and as I say, you'll get healthier, too, with the garden aerobics of doing the "program" yourself!

Bermuda Grass

Cynodon dactylon

This warm season grass becomes dormant during the Winter and greens up during mid-Spring. As temperatures increase, the growth of the Bermuda increases. This grass is very tolerant of drought and loves hot, moist growing conditions.

WHEN TO PLANT:

In Tennessee, you need to seed after the 15th of May to insure that the nights are warm enough for Bermuda to germinate effectively. Refrain from planting after the 15th of July.

WHY YOU PLANT:

If the soil in your yard is less than perfect (shallow or rocky), Bermuda is a good choice to begin your lawn. After it is established, Bermuda provides a rich green color and requires minimal care.

WHERE YOU PLANT:

For the best results, plant Bermuda in full sun. You can grow Bermuda in partial shade, but your stand will not be as lush and full.

HOW YOU PLANT:

1) For a new lawn, first determine the soil pH. The ideal range of pH is from 6-7. If your soil falls below this level, a lime application will raise the pH level.

2) Determine the square footage of the area that you will seed.

3) Apply the seed in an amount equal to 1 pound per 1,000 square feet.

4) Broadcast a starter fertilizer to promote growth.

5) Straw your new yard lightly at a rate equal to 1/2-1 bale per 1,000 square feet (or 40 bales per acre).

Sprigging: When planting Hybrid Bermuda, such as 328, 419

Tifton, or Tiffway, it must be propogated by spreading cut-up stolons on the new surface and lightly covering them with 1/2" of sand or soil. Fertilize and lime according to the common bermuda instructions. Stolons may be obtained by shredding Hybrid Bermuda sod. Use 1-2 bushels of shredded stolons per 1,000 square feet. Stolons may be drilled into the lawn area.

WHEN YOU WATER:

After seeding, soak your new yard equal to 1" of rainfall. To determine the proper amount, place a bucket within range of your sprinkler and when the bucket contains 1" of water, you have watered sufficiently. Repeat this process every three days until the seed germinates. Once the seed germinates, water as needed to maintain the health of the lawn. A moisture meter will help in this process. In the case of stolons, water the same as above initially, but daily watering must continue in amounts sufficient to keep the surface wet. This may take several waterings per day. Once the stolons are firmly rooted (observe new growth), watering can be less frequent.

HOW/WHEN YOU PRUNE:

Mowing can begin after the new lawn has reached 2" in height. Bermuda should be cut to a level of 1-2".

HOW/WHEN YOU FERTILIZE:

After Bermuda has been established, feed every four weeks with a complete time-release fertilizer. You will need to cease this feeding after August, but apply a winterizer/fertilizer during October to promote a healthy Bermuda lawn the following growing season.

ADDITIONAL ADVICE FOR PROPER CARE:

Black Seed Smut, Winter Dead Spot, Army Worms, and Sod Webworms are common enemies of Bermuda, but the aggressiveness of Bermuda usually keeps these troubles at bay. Through the recommended feeding, you will promote a healthy lawn, which is the best preventive control of these problems. And we would suggest that you also raise your mower level in late Summer and early Fall. This will keep your lawn from scorching and promote extra foliage growth that will help protect the grass roots from freezing during the Winter.

"More seed,

more grass" is

not the correct

plan for

planting grass.

Always follow

recommended

rates.

Bluegrass, Kentucky
Poa pratensis

This is cool season grass with turf-type growth habits, finely textured, and tolerant of closer mowing than the Tall Fescues.

WHEN TO PLANT:
For the best results, plant in early Spring or in the Fall.

WHY YOU PLANT:
If you want a grass that will stay green in the cooler months and a lawn you can trim close, choose this colorful grass. When the term "barefoot lawn" was coined, it was Bluegrass that they had underfoot.

WHERE YOU PLANT:
If you want a lawn of 100 percent Bluegrass, we hope you live in East Tennessee, but you may be successful elsewhere if your lawn is partially shaded. This partial shade can be obtained in your yard even if you don't have trees. Simply plant Tall Fescue with your Bluegrass.

HOW YOU PLANT:
1) For a new lawn, first determine the soil pH. The ideal range

of pH is from 6-7. If your soil falls below this level, a lime application will raise the pH level.

2) Determine the square footage of the area that you will seed.

3) Apply the seed in an amount equal to 3 pounds per 1,000 square feet.

4) Broadcast a starter fertilizer to promote growth.

5) Straw your new yard lightly at a rate equal to 1/2-1 bale per 1,000 square feet (or 40 bales per acre). And there is no need to rake the straw, just let it decompose into the lawn.

Note: If you are overseeding a lawn, broadcast 4-5 pounds of seed per 1,000 square feet.

WHEN YOU WATER:

Water heavily when you establish a new Bluegrass lawn. As a guide, try to water at a rate of 1" of rain per watering. Place a bucket near your sprinklers until the water measures 1" and be sure to move sprinklers over the entire lawn. Follow these practices religiously until the new grass emerges. Once the lawn is initially established, water frequently at lighter rates. For mature lawns, water at a rate equal to 1" of rain per week.

HOW/WHEN YOU PRUNE:

When your lawn reaches 2-3", mow 1/3 of the grass growth. Bluegrass will tolerate a lower cutting level, but this higher level will stimulate deeper root growth and a healthier lawn.

HOW/WHEN YOU FERTILIZE:

To insure a healthy lawn, we suggest the following feeding schedule:

March—Apply a crabgrass preventer that contains lawn fertilizer. Distribute at the rate recommended on the bag.

April—Apply lawn fertilizer combined with a broadleaf weed control such as Trimec.

September—Now is the time to apply a starter fertilizer / winterizer formula.

November—Repeat your April application.

ADDITIONAL ADVICE FOR PROPER CARE:

Your Bluegrass lawn may fall victim to the following insects and diseases: Leaf Spot, Dollar Spot, Japanese Beetle Grubs, and Sod Webworms. If you notice these problems, or if you have an increase in mole activity, you may want to apply a soil insecticide. Brown Patch may occur during the Summer, but it can be controlled by applying a Daconil fungicide every 1-3 weeks, depending on the severity of the problem. To insure that your soil pH level is at the proper level of 6-7, test your soil every 2-3 years. Apply lime if the level is incorrect. For proper advice, or if you have any questions, consult your local lawn and garden center.

Fescue, Creeping Red
Festuca rubra

Creeping Red Fescue is a very finely textured turf-type grass. It spreads by rhizomes, blends well with Bluegrass, and is quite tolerant to shade.

WHEN TO PLANT:
As is the case with other grasses, Creeping Red Fescue should be planted in the Fall. Spring planting is the second choice.

WHY YOU PLANT:
Creeping Red Fescue is ideal for lawns which are primarily shaded.

WHERE YOU PLANT:
It performs best in partial to full shade. It is suggested that Creeping Red Fescue be mixed with Bluegrass for an effective, shade tolerant grass seed combination.

How you plant:

1) For a new lawn, first determine the soil pH. The ideal range of pH is from 6-7. If your soil falls below this level, a lime application will raise the pH level.

2) Determine the square footage of the area that you will seed.

3) Apply the seed in an amount equal to 3 pounds per 1,000 square feet.

4) Broadcast a starter fertilizer to promote growth.

5) Straw your new yard lightly at a rate equal to 1/2-1 bale per 1,000 square feet (or 40 bales per acre). And there is no need to rake the straw, just let it decompose into the lawn.

Note: If you are overseeding a lawn, broadcast 4-5 pounds of seed per 1,000 square feet. Drop the rate to 3 pounds per 1,000 sq. ft. for new lawns.

When you water:

Water heavily when you establish a new Bluegrass lawn. As a guide, water at a rate of 2″ of rain per week. Place a bucket near your sprinklers until the water measures 2″ and be sure to move sprinklers over the entire lawn. Follow these practices religiously until the new grass emerges. Once the lawn is initially established, water frequently at lighter rates. For mature lawns, water at a rate equal to 1″ of rain per week.

How/When you prune:

When your lawn reaches 2-3″, mow 1/3 of the grass growth. Creeping Red Fescue will tolerate a lower cutting level, but this higher level will stimulate deeper root growth and a healthier lawn.

How/When you fertilize:

To insure a healthy lawn, we suggest the following feeding schedule:

March—Apply a crabgrass preventer that contains lawn fertilizer. Distribute at the rate recommended on the bag.

April—Apply lawn fertilizer combined with a broadleaf weed control such as Trimec.

September—Now is the time to apply a starter fertilizer / winterizer formula.

November—Repeat your April application.

ADDITIONAL ADVICE FOR PROPER CARE:

Creeping Red Fescue is more resistant to Brown Patch than Bluegrasses. However, it goes more dormant in the Summer than Bluegrass.

Fescue, Tall

Festuca alta

This variety is the most widely used turf grass in Tennessee. KY-31 is an old standard by which new cultivars are judged. The new Tall Fescues exhibit more turf-type qualities by rhizomes, are more drought resistant, and display vigorous growth. Some names by which the new cultivars are marketed are: Rebel I, Rebel II, Rebel III, Bonanza, Arid, Anthem, and many more.

WHEN TO PLANT:

This old standard is best planted in the Fall, however it can be sown in the early Spring, as well.

WHY YOU PLANT:

Tall Fescue performs best in the cool seasons of Spring and Fall and stays green throughout the Winter. Summer is tough on Fescue, but if sufficient moisture is present to cool the grass, it will remain green and healthy.

WHERE YOU PLANT:

Tall Fescue is suitable for both sun and shade. It even tolerates poor soil conditions, but prefers a soil pH of 6-7, where Tall Fescue will thrive and provide a beautiful lawn.

HOW YOU PLANT:

1) For a new lawn, first determine the soil pH. The ideal range of pH is from 6-7. If your soil falls below this level, a lime application will raise the pH level.

2) Determine the square footage of the area that you will seed.

3) For new lawns, apply seed in an amount equal to 4-6 pounds per 1,000 square feet.

4) Broadcast a starter fertilizer to promote growth.

5) Straw your new yard lightly at a rate equal to 1-2 bales per 1,000 square feet (or 40 bales per acre).

Note: If you are overseeding a lawn, broadcast 6-8 pounds of seed per 1,000 square feet.

WHEN YOU WATER:

Water heavily when you establish a new lawn. As a guide, try to water at a rate of 1" of rain per week. Place a bucket near your sprinklers until the water measures 1", and be sure to move sprinklers over the entire lawn. Follow these practices religiously until the new grass emerges. Once the lawn is initially established, water frequently at lighter rates.

Note: For older, more established lawns, you will need to water enough to make up for any rain deficit that is below 1" per week.

HOW/WHEN YOU PRUNE:

Once your new grass has reached a height of 2", you may mow. After the lawn has been established, cut 1/3 of the growth when it reaches a height of 2-3". For a well-manicured and healthy lawn, bag excessive clippings.

HOW/WHEN YOU FERTILIZE:

To insure a healthy lawn, we suggest the following feeding schedule:

March—Apply a crabgrass preventer that contains lawn fertilizer. Distribute at the rate recommended on the bag.

April—Apply lawn fertilizer combined with a broadleaf weed control such as Trimec.

September—Now is the time to apply a starter fertilizer / winterizer formula.

November—Repeat your April application.

ADDITIONAL ADVICE FOR PROPER CARE:

Brown Patch may occur during the summer, but it can be controlled by applying a Daconil fungicide application every 1-3 weeks, depending on the severity of the problem. To insure that your soil pH is at the proper level of 6-7, test your soil every 2-3 years. Apply lime if the level is incorrect. For proper advice, or if you have any questions, consult your local lawn and garden center.

Ryegrass
Lolium

Ryegrasses are like their parent cereal grain grasses. They are quick to germinate, aggressive, and fast growing. Under good growing conditions, Ryegrass may need mowing more than once per week.

WHEN TO PLANT:

Ryegrass can be planted during the Spring, Summer, or Fall.

WHY YOU PLANT:

Rye, a fine-textured grass, is used primarily to overseed Bermuda, Bluegrass, or Fescue to provide green color throughout the cold months.

WHERE YOU PLANT:

Rye is not picky about where it grows. It will prosper in a variety of soil conditions and it does not care whether it is in full sun or partial shade.

How you plant:

1) For a new lawn, first determine the soil pH. The ideal range of pH is from 6-7. If your soil falls below this level, a lime application will raise the pH level.

2) Determine the square footage of the area that you will seed.

3) For new lawns, apply the seed in an amount equal to 5-8 pounds per 1,000 square feet for annual Ryegrass. For perennial Ryegrass, apply seed at 6-8 pounds per 1,000 square feet.

4) Broadcast a starter fertilizer to promote growth.

5) Straw your new yard lightly at a rate equal to 1/2-1 bale per 1,000 square feet (or 40 bales per acre).

Note: If you are overseeding a lawn, broadcast 8-10 pounds of seed per 1,000 square feet.

When you water:

Water heavily when you establish a new lawn. As a guide, try to water 2-3 times per week at a rate of 1/2-1" of rain per watering. Place a bucket near your sprinklers until the water measures 1/2-1", and be sure to move sprinklers over the entire lawn. Follow these practices religiously until the new grass emerges. Once the lawn is initially established, water frequently at lighter rates.

Note: For older, more established lawns, you will need to water enough to make up for any rain deficit that is below 1" per week.

How/When you prune:

Rye is a fast-growing grass, so you may need to mow more than once per week. When you mow, try to remove only 1/3 of the grass height while maintaining a mown height of 2".

How/When you fertilize:

We recommend that you follow the following fertilizer schedule to protect your Rye lawn:

March—Apply a crabgrass preventer that contains lawn fertilizer. Follow application instructions stated on the bag.

April—Broadcast a broadleaf weed control with a lawn fertilizer, following application instructions on the bag.

September—Apply a starter fertilizer/winterizer formulation per bag instructions.

November—Repeat your April application.

ADDITIONAL ADVICE FOR PROPER CARE:

The most common problem for Rye is "Melting Out," which is caused by applying too much seed. It is important that proper seed application recommendations are followed. Drought is the other significant concern for Rye, but consistent watering will prevent this problem.

Zoysia
Zoysia spp.

This is the 'Cadillac' of lawn grasses and my choice of grass for the Tennessee area. It is a medium-textured grass that forms a very dense turf. Zoysia has upright growth and is slower growing than most turf grasses, meaning it requires less frequent mowing. The dense growth pattern crowds out any weed invasion.

WHEN TO PLANT:

Plant by sprigging, plugging, or sodding from late Spring through late Summer.

WHY YOU PLANT:

Zoysia is drought tolerant and has "barefoot" qualities, making it the top of the line for full-sun lawns in the South.

WHERE YOU PLANT:

Plant in full sun, although sodding is sometimes successful in light shade areas. Zoysia is tolerant of average soil conditions, but responds quite dramatically in well-draining soil.

How you plant:

Test your soil. Zoysia prefers a pH of 6-7, but will tolerate a 5.5 pH range. Broadcast lawn starter fertilizer and lime if test confirms they are required.

Zoysia may be started by one of three methods:

1) Sprigging: Shred up the sod to provide chopped roots and stolons. Broadcast the stolons over the surface of a finely tilled "seed bed". Do this at at a rate of 1-2 bushels of stolons per 1,000 square feet of lawn area. Cover the stolons lightly with 1/4" of sand or soil. Roll to press and firm the seed bed. Water thoroughly and keep surface moist by watering at least twice per day until new growth appears.

2) Plugging: Cut the sod into 2"x 2" plugs. Plant in a seed bed on 1 foot centers. Soak well and water daily until new growth appears. Zoysia that is plugged in established lawns usually takes 3-5 years to cover and take over.

3) Sodding: Prepare and firm the seed bed as described. Lay the sod, (green side up)! *Note: In sodding, rolling will not assure a level lawn.* Make sure the lawn is level prior to sodding. Rolling helps to press the sod firmly in place and speeds up the rooting. Immediately soak the sod after placement. Continue to water daily until new growth appears.

When you water:

After plugging, soak your new yard equal to 1" of rainfall. To determine the proper amount, place a bucket within range of your sprinkler and when the bucket contains 1" of water, you have watered sufficiently. Repeat this process every three days until the growth begins. Once the growth begins, water as needed to maintain the health of the lawn. A moisture meter will help in this process. In the case of stolons, water the same as above initially, but daily watering must continue in amounts sufficient to keep the surface wet. This may take several waterings per day. Once the stolons are firmly rooted (observe new growth), watering can be less frequent.

HOW/WHEN YOU PRUNE:

Mowing can begin after the new lawn has reached 2″ in height. Zoysia should be cut to a level of 1-2″.

HOW/WHEN YOU FERTILIZE:

After planting, fertilize every four weeks with a complete, slow-release lawn food.

ADDITIONAL ADVICE FOR PROPER CARE:

Black Seed Smut, Winter Dead Spot, Army Worms, and Sod Webworms are common enemies of Zoysia, but the aggressiveness of Zoysia usually keeps these troubles at bay. Through the recommended feeding, you will promote a healthy lawn, which is the best preventive control of these problems. And we would suggest that you also raise your mower level in late Summer and early Fall. This will promote extra foliage growth that will help protect the grass roots from freezing during the Winter.

Notes:

Ground Covers

WHEN GARDENERS DISCUSS ground covers, low maintenance is always a hot topic. Through the years we have been constantly asked to recommend a plant that is low maintenance, and invariably we have turned to ground covers to satisfy that need.

Ground covers are an excellent choice if you need a plant to cover a large, hard-to-maintain area, such as a slope or steep embankment. You may also want to consider a ground cover if you have an area that tends to harbor weeds and you are tiring of the seasonal task of mulching, mulching, and more mulching. Also, these ground covers will add a new look to your total landscaping plan.

We are fortunate here in Tennessee to have many types of ground covers for both sun and shade conditions. There are some plants listed in this chapter that you may have never considered as a ground cover or for a large mass planting. The choices vary from dark green foliage to flowering plants, from plants that grow rapidly, to slow creepers. All have been very effective in achieving a bold and solid look that works quite well and makes a statement in the landscape.

Always remember, when first attempting a ground cover bed, be sure to apply some form of weed preventer until the ground cover has a chance to really take off and spread. We know how gardeners want that perfect look as soon as planting is complete, but this can take a season or two. We promise it will happen, and it will be worthwhile in the long run.

We have always liked this little poem about us "Instant Gratification Gardeners":

Ivy
The first year it sleeps
The second year it creeps
The third year it leaps!

What this simply says is: it will take a year or two for these plants to get their roots firmly settled in and established. Once that has happened, step back and watch 'em grow! Your patience will be rewarded.

Ajuga
Ajuga reptans

Ajuga's foliage is what really sets it apart. It consists of fleshy, somewhat oval, waxy leaves 2-4" long that form a low, thick mat. The plant spreads readily by stems rooting on contact with the soil, making it a hardy performer.

WHEN TO PLANT:
Plant in Spring or Fall, as soil conditions allow.

WHY YOU PLANT:
Ajuga is used for its low-growing, fast-spreading habits and its large, attractive leaves. Brilliant blue flower spikes in Spring make it very appealing.

WHERE YOU PLANT:
Place in full sun to partial shade areas in rich, moist soil.

HOW YOU PLANT:
Prepare ground cover beds by working in ample organic compost or peat moss to 4" in depth. Use starter fertilizer after planting. Mulch and water with a liquid root stimulator fertilizer.

WHEN YOU WATER:
For new plantings, use a hand-held, open-ended hose, watering plants directly. Do this until the plant's roots are established, generally one growing season or when new growth is evident. Light, frequent watering is preferred over heavy watering. When in doubt, check soil wetness with a moisture meter before watering.

HOW/WHEN YOU PRUNE:
Ajuga is an aggressive ground cover that spreads relatively quickly. If the plant's runners invade unwanted areas, just cut them back.

Like many ground covers, Ajuga can spread almost before you know it, so it is a good idea to inspect new growth frequently.

HOW/WHEN YOU FERTILIZE:
During the Spring, apply a granular, slow-release balanced fertilizer. It should be lightly scratched into the soil close to the newest plant growth. Be sure to water-in the fertilizer.

ADDITIONAL ADVICE FOR PROPER CARE:
No serious problems noted with Ajuga, so enjoy its unique leaves, while keeping an eye on its growth habits.

Deadnettle
Lamium

This delicate little ground cover's looks are deceiving. Lamium is very hardy, while the small heart-shaped leaves are very dainty and come in all sorts of variegated shades of cream, silver, green and white. The plants can have several growth habits from 4-6" high and several bloom colors from a pure white to a clear pink. The blooms are quite small, however, and bloom on a stem with clusters similar to a Snapdragon's flowers. This plant spreads well, yet it never gets out of hand. Another great benefit for a shady spot is the semi-evergreen foliage.

WHEN TO PLANT:
As is the case with most perennial ground covers, Lamium would benefit from being planted in early Spring or Fall. If maintained properly, Lamium could be planted almost anytime it is available.

WHY YOU PLANT:
This particular plant provides great contrast to other plants

because of its beautiful foliage. Lamium also tolerates deep shade, and unlike ivy and vinca minor, the foliage is not as dark so it is able to show off in low-light areas. Another reason for planting Lamium is for the evergreen foliage and the sweet little clusters of blooms that are enjoyable in the Summer.

WHERE YOU PLANT:
Anywhere in a shady garden or underneath a tree's canopy is ideal for this ground cover. This variety's ability to tolerate extreme shade to partial sun makes it very desirable. Planting around the base of taller plants works well, yet planting among rocks or stepping stones can also be very effective.

HOW YOU PLANT:
Lamium is easy to transplant, whether you choose starter plants or large containers purchased from the garden center. Begin by digging the planting hole approximately twice the size of the rootball. Add peat moss or organic humus and blend it with the soil you have removed. Then add some of the blended soils back into the hole and place the plant into the hole. As you place the plant, gently loosen the roots, then backfill to the point where the top of the rootball is even with the existing soil level. Mulch lightly and water-in thoroughly.

WHEN YOU WATER:
Since this variety calls for shady conditions, it will not dry out as quickly as some full sun perennial ground covers. When in the first season of growth, watering two times a week is sufficient, and two to three times a month will be fine (unless we experience drought conditions) for the following years.

How/When you prune:

This plant needs little pruning, but by late Summer you may want to trim the spent bloom stalks. If the early Spring foliage has Winter damage, you may choose to groom old Winter growth to make way for new growth.

How/When you fertilize:

Lamium enjoys at least two good feedings per year: one in March/April and another in August/September. With both feedings, a granular slow-release balanced fertilizer is advised. This should be scratched in lightly around the newest growth of the plant, being careful not to work it in directly at the center or base of the plant. Always water well after feeding.

Additional advice for proper care:

You may also feed throughout the growing season (two to three times a month) with a water-soluable fertilizer. A high phosphorus fertilizer will promote the roots and bloom potential.

Euonymus
Fortunei coloratus

Some folks call this Winter Creeper Euonymus. It matures at 6-10" in height. It is an evergreen vine characterized by its striking purple to burgundy leaves during the Fall and Winter. Euonymus is a multiple-use plant that can either be a ground cover or a vine. It is very adaptable to a wide range of planting conditions.

When to plant:

For best results, plant during the Spring or Fall, as soil conditions allow.

WHY YOU PLANT:

Euonymus is used as a ground cover where fast growth and minimum maintenance are desired. An evergreen, Euonymus will provide some color in the garden even in the coldest days of Winter.

WHERE YOU PLANT:

Plant in an area that is sunny to partly shady.

HOW YOU PLANT:

1) Dig a hole twice the width and as deep as the container.

2) Remove from container and position in prepared hole.

3) Add a liquid starter fertilizer.

4) Backfill with a medium soil mix.

5) Apply a weed preventer such as Treflan.

6) Mulch to a depth of 1-2".

7) Water very well.

WHEN YOU WATER:

Water as needed to maintain the plant's health. A soil moisture meter will assist in determining when and how much to water.

HOW/WHEN YOU PRUNE:

Your own personal tastes are the only reasons to prune Euonymus.

HOW/WHEN YOU FERTILIZE:

Fertilize in the Spring with a well-balanced, slow-release granular fertilizer. We also recommend a supplemental Summer feeding to maintain optimum health.

ADDITIONAL ADVICE FOR PROPER CARE:

You may encounter Euonymus Scale. This problem is not considered dangerous to the life of the plant and can be cured easily after consulting your garden center. Otherwise, water well and enjoy!

Ivy, English
Hedera helix

English Ivy is Tennessee's most popular ground cover. English Ivy is the traditional ground cover that adorns many beautiful landscapes and homes. If you notice a ground cover uniformly covering the foundation of a home, it is likely to be English Ivy. One reason it is so popular is that it has many uses. It does well in heavy shade, although it will adapt to sunny conditions without much problem.

WHEN TO PLANT:
Transplant Spring through early Fall, as soil conditions allow.

WHY YOU PLANT:
English Ivy is planted for its traditional ground cover qualities and the ease in establishing it. It is also used to cover walls and trees, giving it a regal feeling of formal gardens from the past.

WHERE YOU PLANT:
Can be planted in full sun, but prefers partial to full shade areas. Try utilizing in mixed seasonal containers and urns to cascade over the sides for an overall lush look.

HOW YOU PLANT:
Plant by rooted cuttings or 4" to 1-gallon size container plants. Space rooted cuttings 6" to 1 foot apart. Space 4" pots 1 to 2 feet apart. Space 1-gallon containers 2 to 3 feet apart. Prepare ground cover beds by working in ample organic compost or peat moss to 4" in depth. Use starter fertilizer after planting. Mulch and water with a liquid root stimulator fertilizer.

WHEN YOU WATER:
For new plantings, use a hand-held, open-ended hose, watering plants directly. Do this until the plant's roots are established, generally one growing season, or when new growth is evident.

Light, frequent watering is preferred over heavy watering.
When in doubt, check soil wetness with a moisture meter
before watering.

HOW/WHEN YOU PRUNE:
You will want to prune English Ivy with shears as needed to
maintain growth in desired areas.

HOW/WHEN YOU FERTILIZE:
Fertilize in the Spring with a well-balanced, slow-release granular fertilizer. We also recommend a supplemental Summer feeding to maintain optimum health. Be sure to water-in well.

ADDITIONAL ADVICE FOR PROPER CARE:
Common diseases and insects include Bacterial Leaf Spot,
Powdery Mildew, Aphids and Mites. Vigorous growing English
Ivy usually overcomes any pests. However, buildup of mites or
scale can be a problem that you may want to discuss with your
lawn and garden center.

Juniper, Creeping
Juniperus horizontalis

*One of the popular ground covers, Creeping Juniper matures to 1-2 feet in
height and 4-5 feet in width. Cultivars of this low-growing evergreen vary in
colors and textures. 'Blue Rug' is bluish, 'Prince of Wales' is light green with
layering branches, and 'Blue Chip' and 'Blue Summer' are maroon in Winter
and display a layering growth pattern.*

WHEN TO PLANT:
Plant year-round as soil conditions permit.

WHY YOU PLANT:

This variety is used in mass plantings and as ground cover. It is often used on embankments for soil stability. It is a dense ground cover that offers consistent growth and color.

WHERE YOU PLANT:

The Creeping Juniper is very adaptable to a variety of soils from sandy, light soil to heavier, clay soil. But it should be planted in an area that receives full sunlight.

HOW YOU PLANT:

1) Dig a hole twice the width and as deep as the container.
2) Remove from container and position in prepared hole.
3) Add a liquid starter fertilizer.
4) Backfill with a medium soil mix.
5) Apply a weed preventer such as Treflan.
6) Mulch to a depth of 1-2".
7) Water very well.

WHEN YOU WATER:

For new plantings, use a hand-held, open-ended hose, watering plants directly. Do this until the plant's roots are established, generally one growing season, or when new growth is evident. Light, frequent watering is preferred over heavy watering. When in doubt, check soil wetness with a moisture meter before watering.

Note: *The Creeping Juniper will withstand hot, dry weather. However, like all plants, it responds well to good care.*

HOW/WHEN YOU PRUNE:

Prune only to contour the size and shape. The Creeping Juniper may be trimmed year-round, but early Spring is best.

HOW/WHEN YOU FERTILIZE:

Fertilize in the Spring with a well-balanced, slow-release granular fertilizer. We also recommend a supplemental Summer feeding to maintain optimum health. Be sure to water-in well.

ADDITIONAL ADVICE FOR PROPER CARE:

Common diseases and insects include Juniper Blight, Branch Die-Back, and Spider Mites, each of which may become serious. Watch for declining foliage color, particularly during the Fall and Winter months, and call your local garden center to address these problems correctly.

Pachysandra
Pachysandra terminalis

Pachysandra is a perennial evergreen ground cover for shady locations. It has oval leaves, 2-4" in length, that grow in clusters at the top of upright stems. This plant may not be as exciting as many other ground covers, but its redeeming quality is its aggressive growth in full shade conditions.

WHEN TO PLANT:
For best results, plant in the Spring or Fall.

WHY YOU PLANT:
This plant is used as a ground cover in large shady areas and is one of our most effective shade-loving ground cover options for difficult to cover areas, such as embankments where erosion is a problem. An added benefit is that it will provide some color throughout the Winter.

WHERE YOU PLANT:
This unusual plant needs to be planted in full shade.

HOW YOU PLANT:
1) Dig a hole twice the width and as deep as the container.
2) Remove from container and position in prepared hole.

3) Add a liquid starter fertilizer.

4) Backfill with a medium soil mix.

5) Apply a weed preventer such as Treflan.

6) Mulch to a depth of 1-2".

7) Water very well.

WHEN YOU WATER:

Water as needed to maintain health. A soil moisture meter will be a great benefit.

HOW/WHEN YOU PRUNE:

Unless your personal taste dictates it, Pachysandra never needs pruning.

HOW/WHEN YOU FERTILIZE:

Fertilize in the Spring with a well-balanced, slow release granular fertilizer. We also recommend a supplemental Summer feeding to maintain vigorous growth.

ADDITIONAL ADVICE FOR PROPER CARE:

Scale is sometimes a problem, but it is not considered life threatening. Consult your garden center for proper advice.

Snow on the Mountain

Aegopodium podagraria variegatum

When referring to Snow on the Mountain, it is easy to get sentimental. The foundation of my grandmother's house was totally engulfed in this white and green foliaged plant. Its memory is vivid because it made such a strong visual impact on me. Snow on the Mountain grows to 12-18" in height, but really covers the ground in width. It has rose-shaped leaves that appear to be covered with snow that is just beginning to melt, revealing light green foliage below. It is a wonderful ground cover!

WHEN TO PLANT:
Plant in the Spring or Fall, as soil conditions permit.

WHY YOU PLANT:
This plant is an easily grown ground cover that provides accent color to the landscape, particularly around home foundations. It can be planted in a variety of soil conditions.

WHERE YOU PLANT:
Snow on the Mountain prefers full sun to shade in slightly acid, to acid, moist and humus soils. In West Tennessee, Snow on the Mountain should be planted in full shade, since it prefers cool and moist conditions.

HOW YOU PLANT:
Loosen the roots of plants grown in pots...thoroughly! Prepare a wide, shallow hole three-fourths as deep and twice as wide as the root ball. Make a mix of 1/3 soil, 1/3 coarse sand, and 1/3 peat moss, organic humus, or commercial planting mix. Pack firmly around sides of root ball. Add 1-3" of mulch on top, staying clear of the crown of the plant. Then water well with a root stimulator fertilizer. *Note: Avoid planting when soil is frozen 1" deep, or muddy.*

WHEN YOU WATER:
For newly planted shrubs, use a hand-held, open-ended hose, watering plants directly. Do this until the shrub's roots are established, generally one growing season, or when new growth is evident. Light, frequent watering is preferred over heavy watering. When in doubt, check soil wetness with a moisture meter before watering.

HOW/WHEN YOU PRUNE:
Very little pruning is needed. After the first hard frost you may simply rake or remove the season's foliage, clean up, and lightly mulch for the Winter.

HOW/WHEN YOU FERTILIZE:
Fertilize lightly by broadcasting a complete granular fertilizer in early Spring.

ADDITIONAL ADVICE FOR PROPER CARE:
Snow on the Mountain has the added benefit of lacking any serious disease problems. After years of pleasure, this plant would be receptive to dividing and sharing with friends and family. Use a spade and simply lift up shallow clumps of the plant and fill the hole with a commercial grade topsoil. Within a season, the plant will completely cover the bare areas.

Vinca-Periwinkle

Vinca minor

This evergreen ground cover sends out trailers that root and spread rapidly. It holds an outstanding green color in the cold of Winter, and shows off blue flowers during mid-Spring. What is more peaceful than large shade trees surrounded by forest green ground cover dotted with soft blue flowers?

WHEN TO PLANT:
Plant this popular plant in the Spring, Summer or Fall.

WHY YOU PLANT:
Many of us have large shaded areas where it is difficult to grow anything. Vinca prospers in these areas and spreads rapidly. An evergreen, Vinca will provide some color even in the coldest Winters.

WHERE YOU PLANT:
Plant your Vinca in a shady, moist area.

HOW YOU PLANT:
1) Dig a hole twice the width and as deep as the container.

2) Remove from container and position in prepared hole.

3) Add a liquid starter fertilizer.

4) Backfill with a medium soil mix.

5) Apply a weed preventer such as Treflan.

6) Mulch to a depth of 1-2".

7) Water very well.

WHEN YOU WATER:

Water as needed. If you will use a soil moisture meter, your watering habits will be more consistent and your results will show it.

HOW/WHEN YOU PRUNE:

Vinca is virtually maintenance free. Trimming is only necessary if your personal taste dictates it.

HOW/WHEN YOU FERTILIZE:

Fertilize in the Spring with a well-balanaced, slow-release granular fertilizer. We also recommend a supplemental Summer feeding to maintain the plant's growth.

ADDITIONAL ADVICE FOR PROPER CARE:

Vinca is almost disease and insect free. Scale may occur, but it is not considered life threatening to the plant. Consult your garden center for proper advice.

Notes:

Ornamental Grasses

"*B*EAUTY IS IN THE EYE OF THE BEHOLDER" is a time-honored phrase that provides commentary about these plants that have been considered weeds by some and Ornamental Grasses by others. In the past, these grasses were referred to as perennials, but their growing popularity now warrants their own category and classification, called Ornamental Grasses.

As gardeners are showing more interest in native plants, Ornamental Grasses are a natural choice. These carefree plants offer a variety of selections from the large Pampas Grass, to smaller blue tufts of Oat Grass, to striped variegated grasses, to blood-red color grasses and many combinations of large to small fruiting panicles, or plumes. Ornamental Grasses trigger memories of the seashore and they denote permanency with their tenacious ability to withstand wind, sun, and drought conditions.

There are even wild varieties of grasses that have their place in the landscape. An example from personal experience is Sedge grass, which has invaded many pastures and fields in

C H A P T E R   T H R E E

Tennessee, including mine. It has been mowed down repeatedly in the past, but now it is left alone and it provides enjoyment throughout the Winter season.

If you have a wet or dry site, there is an Ornamental Grass that will serve the needs of the Tennessee gardener. Grasses may not be everyone's choice, but the number of admirers of Ornamental Grasses is growing. Take a look at the options available and you may find yourself getting hooked!

Blue Clump Fescue
Festuca glauca

This is another blue-colored Ornamental Grass option. Blue Clump Fescue has icy blue leaves, 10" tall, which retain their color through the heat of the Summer. During the early Summer, Blue Clump Fescue displays buff-colored flowers on 15" stalks. This Ornamental Grass forms 10-12" wide clumps, making it ideal for use as a border or as an edging plant.

WHEN TO PLANT:
Since Blue Clump Fescue is container-grown, it can be planted Spring through Fall, as long as the soil is not frozen or too wet.

WHY YOU PLANT:
The icy blue blades that retain their color throughout the heat of the Summer make this an interesting choice for a border or even as a ground cover.

WHERE YOU PLANT:
Plant in full sun or in partial shade, but you must plant in an area that drains well.

HOW YOU PLANT:
1) Dig a hole twice the width and as deep as the container.
2) Remove from container and position in prepared hole.
3) Add a liquid starter fertilizer.
4) Backfill with a medium soil mix.
5) Apply a weed preventer such as Treflan.
6) Mulch to a depth of 1-2".
7) Water very well.

WHEN YOU WATER:
After your first week of heavy watering to jump start your new plant, a soil moisture meter will be a help in assisting you in your watering habits.

HOW/WHEN YOU PRUNE:

This species needs very little pruning, but you need to remove Winter damage in the Spring.

HOW/WHEN YOU FERTILIZE:

Fertilize in the Spring with a well-balanced, slow-release granular fertilizer. We also recommend a supplemental Summer feeding to maintain the plant's health.

ADDITIONAL ADVICE FOR PROPER CARE:

Scale is a problem, but it can be taken care of with very little effort, after consulting your garden center. Water as needed, and you will have a wonderful plant.

Blue Oat Grass

Helictotrichon sempervirens

Blue Oat Grass matures at 1-2 feet in height. It forms a dense rounded mound which has showy, silver-blue blades. During Summer, striking pale blue flowers are displayed on long, arching stalks, which become straw-colored with time.

WHEN TO PLANT:

For best results, plant any time during the Spring through Fall season, as soil conditions permit.

WHY YOU PLANT:

If we experience a prolonged drought, you will be glad you have this grass in your landscaping plan. The fact that it is almost care free adds to its desirability. The stiff, showy, blue blades will rise 1-2 feet in height, and in warmer climates, this grass will remain an evergreen.

WHERE YOU PLANT:

Plant in full sun with good drainage.

HOW YOU PLANT:
1) Dig a hole twice the width and as deep as the container.
2) Remove from container and position in prepared hole.
3) Add a liquid starter fertilizer.
4) Backfill with a medium soil mix.
5) Apply a weed preventer such as Treflan.
6) Mulch to a depth of 1-2".
7) Water very well.

WHEN YOU WATER:
Water as needed to maintain the health of the plant, but remember this plant is very drought resistant! A soil moisture meter will assist you in determining when and how much to water.

HOW/WHEN YOU PRUNE:
In April, or before any new growth appears, you need to prune back as close as 3-5" to the ground.

HOW/WHEN YOU FERTILIZE:
Use a well-balanced, slow-release granular fertilizer in the Spring to stimulate growth. You may choose to provide a supplemental feeding in the Summer.

ADDITIONAL ADVICE FOR PROPER CARE:
Water well during extreme drought and your Blue Oat Grass will provide years of enjoyment.

Fountain Grass
Pennisetum alopecuroides

The Fountain Grasses are well-named, as their narrow leaves form graceful clumps of broadly arching foliage. Above these rise stems carrying foxtail-like flower plumes. P. setaceum is a popular grass that is drought-tolerant and adorned throughout the Summer with great numbers of copper-pink to purplish spikes.

WHEN TO PLANT:
Fountain Grass can be planted at any time, Spring through Fall, as long as the soil is not frozen or too wet.

WHY YOU PLANT:
Fountain Grass lends a unique appearance to the landscape and offers variety in how it is used. It works quite well as an anchor for the ends of an annual planting area, and it is quite suitable as a single specimen within the landscape. When multiples are planted together in a group, the effect can be striking, especially in windy conditions when the leaves move gracefully with the wind.

WHERE YOU PLANT:
Fountain Grass requires full sun for optimum growth, however, average to good soil is suitable for this plant.

HOW YOU PLANT:
1) Dig a hole twice the width and as deep as the container.
2) Remove from container and position in prepared hole.
3) Add a liquid starter fertilizer.
4) Backfill with a medium soil mix.
5) Apply a weed preventer such as Treflan.
6) Mulch to a depth of 1-2".
7) Water very well.

WHEN YOU WATER:
Pennisetum requires regular watering for vigorous growth, while the close relative, P. setaceum, will perform well with moderate to light watering. Make use of a soil moisture meter to assist you in proper watering habits.

HOW/WHEN YOU PRUNE:
Fountain Grass requires no regular pruning within the growing season, however, it should be cut back to ground level in early Spring before new growth begins.

HOW/WHEN YOU FERTILIZE:

Fertilize in the Spring with a well-balanced, slow-release granular fertilizer. We also recommend a supplemental Summer feeding to maintain the plant's health.

ADDITIONAL ADVICE FOR PROPER CARE:

Fountain Grass is relatively trouble-free and has no serious
problems.

Japanese Blood Grass
Imperata cylindrica rubra

*This Ornamental Grass has outstanding blood-red blades growing to nearly
2 feet in height. It has slow, spreading, underground stems which form clumps
10-12" wide. Japanese Blood Grass is very effective when planted in groups.
The best foliage color is displayed in the Fall.*

WHEN TO PLANT:

Plant during the Spring through Fall season, as long as the soil
is not frozen or too wet.

WHY YOU PLANT:

Japanese Blood Grass is planted for its blood-red blades that
grow to nearly 2 feet and its contrast with other landscaping
choices. You may choose to use it as a ground cover or in a
mass grouping. A very interesting choice!

WHERE YOU PLANT:

Japanese Blood Grass performs just as well in partial shade as in
full sun.

HOW YOU PLANT:

1) Dig a hole twice the width and as deep as the container.
2) Remove from container and position in prepared hole.
3) Add a liquid starter fertilizer.

4) Backfill with a medium soil mix.

5) Apply a weed preventer such as Treflan.

6) Mulch to a depth of 1-2".

7) Water very well.

WHEN YOU WATER:

For new plantings, use a hand-held, open-ended hose, watering plants directly. Do this until the plant's roots are established, generally one growing season, or when new growth is evident. Light, frequent watering is preferred over heavy watering. When in doubt, check the soil's wetness with a moisture meter before watering. A moisture meter is a "must" for gardening peace of mind.

HOW/WHEN YOU PRUNE:

Cut back during March or April, before new growth appears. You should cut back as close as 3-5" to the ground. No pruning is necessary during the growing season.

HOW/WHEN YOU FERTILIZE:

Fertilize in the Spring with a well-balanced, slow-release granular fertilizer. We also recommend a supplemental Summer feeding to maintain the plant's health.

ADDITIONAL ADVICE FOR PROPER CARE:

This plant is virtually disease and pest free. Water at the specified rate and you will have a great addition to your landscape.

Maiden Grass

Miscanthus sinensis gracillimus

Maturing to a height of 6 feet, this Ornamental Grass forms a clump of finely textured silver-green blades, 1/2" in width. It becomes a golden bronze color during the Winter. In Fall, the leaves are topped with large, fan-shaped,

delicate silver-white blooms. Maiden Grass is most striking when the sun
streams through the multiple tall blades.

WHEN TO PLANT:

Hold off your urge to plant in the Winter and wait until the
Spring thaw to plant. Maiden Grass can be planted anytime during the Spring through Fall season, as long as the
soil is not frozen or too wet.

Horse sense

WHY YOU PLANT:

For the gardener who is looking for season-long
color, texture change, or contrast, Maiden Grass is

is stable

an appropriate choice.

WHERE YOU PLANT:

thinking coupled

If you have the need to block the view of your
neighbor's garbage cans, Maiden Grass is an excellent choice as a screening grass. Additionally, it can

with the

be used effectively as an interesting specimen, or
single plant, in a sunny area of your lawn.

ability to say

HOW YOU PLANT:

1) Dig a hole twice the width and as deep as the
container.

"nay."

2) Remove from container and position in prepared
hole.

3) Add a liquid starter fertilizer.
4) Backfill with a medium soil mix.
5) Apply a weed preventer such as Treflan.
6) Mulch to a depth of 1-2".
7) Water very well.

WHEN YOU WATER:

Water on a regular basis until the grass is established. Your local
garden center has water meters available to test the moisture
content of the soil. After the plant is more established, reduce
your watering to maintain the health of the grass.

HOW/WHEN YOU PRUNE:

Cut back only during the Spring before new growth emerges. We recommend you do this in March. You may cut the grass as close as 3-5" to the ground.

HOW/WHEN YOU FERTILIZE:

Fertilize in the Spring with a well-balanced, slow-release granular fertilizer. We also recommend a supplemental Summer feeding to maintain the plant's health.

ADDITIONAL ADVICE FOR PROPER CARE:

Maiden Grass is basically disease and insect free. Just keep it well watered and you will have a new garden friend that will provide years of enjoyment.

Mondo Grass

Ophiopogon japonicus

Mondo Grass forms dense clumps of 1/8" wide leaves that arch into mounds of dark green foliage. It is similar to Liriope, but without the flowering spikes. Mondo Grass is one of our best choices for a border or edging plant, since it grows uniformly without pruning to an appropriate height and width.

WHEN TO PLANT:

Since it is container-grown, Mondo Grass can be planted anytime during the Spring through Fall seasons, as long as soil conditions are not frozen or too wet.

WHY YOU PLANT:

In areas where you wish a "lawn look" without the maintenance, choose Mondo Grass. This dark green plant will grow in clumps that are composed of very small leaves or blades. It is well-suited for use as a bordering device as well as a general ground cover. It is a true garden and landscape workhorse.

WHERE YOU PLANT:

This grass is not picky about where it is planted. It performs well in areas that range from sun to partial shade.

HOW YOU PLANT:

1) Dig a hole twice the width and as deep as the container.
2) Remove from container and position in prepared hole.
3) Add a liquid starter fertilizer.
4) Backfill with a medium soil mix.
5) Apply a weed preventer such as Treflan.
6) Mulch to a depth of 1-2".
7) Water very well.

WHEN YOU WATER:

Water generously at the time of planting to properly establish the grass. Then water as needed to maintain health. A soil moisture meter will be a great benefit.

HOW/WHEN YOU PRUNE:

Personal taste is really the only consideration in the pruning of Mondo Grass.

HOW/WHEN YOU FERTILIZE:

Fertilize in the Spring with a well-balanced, slow-release granular fertilizer. We also recommend a supplemental Summer feeding to maintain the plant's health.

ADDITIONAL ADVICE FOR PROPER CARE:

Scale may affect this grass, but it is not fatal and can be cured very easily. Just consult your garden center for proper advice.

Monkey Grass

Liriope muscari

This perennial herb of the Lily family matures in height to 12-18". With several varieties available, Monkey Grass grows in tufts of foliage that can be

either solid green, variegated green and white, or bright white. It displays pur-
ple to white spiked flowers. In mass plantings or when used as a border,
Monkey Grass creates a forgiving, soft texture to the landscape.

WHEN TO PLANT:
Since Monkey Grass is grown in containers, it can be planted anytime during the Spring through Fall seasons, as long as the soil is not frozen or too wet.

WHY YOU PLANT:
Monkey Grass is one of the easiest plants to grow, and grow successfully. If you can't grow Monkey Grass, you definitely don't have a green thumb! This grass is perfect for borders and is used effectively as a ground cover.

WHERE YOU PLANT:
Monkey Grass will thrive in just about any soil condition, but if planted in a bed that is filled with excellent soil, it will respond with dramatic results.

HOW YOU PLANT:
1) Dig a hole twice the width and as deep as the container.
2) Remove from container and position in prepared hole.
3) Add a liquid starter fertilizer.
4) Backfill with a medium soil mix.
5) Apply a weed preventer such as Treflan.
6) Mulch to a depth of 1-2".
7) Water very well.

WHEN YOU WATER:
Water generously, especially when plants are young and during prolonged droughts. A soil moisture meter will be of great assistance.

HOW/WHEN YOU PRUNE:
Unless your personal taste dictates it, Monkey Grass should not be pruned during the growing season. In late Winter, however, it must be trimmed to the ground. Just be sure you do this

before the emergence of new growth.

HOW/WHEN YOU FERTILIZE:
Fertilize in the Spring with a well-balanced, slow-release granular fertilizer. We also recommend a supplemental Summer feeding to maintain the plant's health.

WALT'S WISDOM

Is life a

problem to

be solved or

a gift to be

enjoyed?

ADDITIONAL ADVICE FOR PROPER CARE:
There are no major problems with Monkey Grass. If you notice Scale, you may want to consult your garden center for control advice, but this is not considered a major threat to the grass.

Pampas Grass
Cortaderia selloana

Pampas Grass is the monarch and the grandfather of Ornamental Grasses. It grows 8-10 feet tall with blades 1-1 1/2" wide. Foliage in Summer is light green, turning beige to light tan in the colder seasons. In the Fall and through the Winter, Pampas Grass develops its signature feature - 18-24" long, 6-10" wide plumes that are very striking. They remain throughout the Winter, providing visual appeal, especially in windy conditions when the tall plumes are continuously on the move.

WHEN TO PLANT:
Pampas Grass may be planted anytime the soil is not frozen or too wet, during the Spring through Fall seasons.

WHY YOU PLANT:
In addition to its dominant presence in the landscape, this large clump-forming grass is often a choice for its low-maintenance requirements and high tolerance of drought conditions.

WHERE YOU PLANT:

Plant in full sun in well-drained soil. Pampas Grass is quite adaptable to a range of soil conditions. Pampas Grass may be used effectively as a single specimen, or planted in groups, 6-8 feet apart.

HOW YOU PLANT:

1) Dig a hole twice the width and as deep as the container.
2) Remove from container and position in prepared hole.
3) Add a liquid starter fertilizer.
4) Backfill with a medium soil mix.
5) Apply a weed preventer such as Treflan.
6) Mulch to a depth of 1-2".
7) Water very well.

WHEN YOU WATER:

For new plantings, use a hand-held, open-ended hose, watering plants directly. Do this until the roots are established, generally one growing season, or when new growth is evident. Light, frequent watering is preferred over heavy watering. When in doubt, check the soil's wetness with a moisture meter before watering. A moisture meter is a "must" for gardening peace of mind.

HOW/WHEN YOU PRUNE:

Cut back entire plant in late Winter or early Spring before any new growth begins.

HOW/WHEN YOU FERTILIZE:

After pruning in the late Winter, apply a well-balanced, slow-release lawn fertilizer Also, a supplemental feeding is recommended during the Summer to promote healthy growth.

ADDITIONAL ADVICE FOR PROPER CARE:

Plant Pampas Grass, jump back, and enjoy its growth and its unmistakable Fall and Winter plumes.

ORNAMENTAL GRASSES

Sweet Flag, Variegated
Acorus calamus

Variegated Sweet Flag is unique among our choices of Ornamental Grasses. Its size fills the gap between the taller varieties, such as Pampas Grass and the smaller clumping selections, like Blue Clump Fescue. Variegated Sweet Flag displays grass-like green leaves, edged in white, that grow to 18" in height. It resembles miniature tufts of Iris. Given its size and visual features, Variegated Sweet Flag offers valuable options in the landscape.

WHEN TO PLANT:
Since it is container-grown, Variegated Sweet Flag can be planted anytime from Spring through Fall, as long as the soil is not frozen or too wet.

WHY YOU PLANT:
It offers the benefit of a useful size, while providing texture variations and season-long color to landscaped areas.

WHERE YOU PLANT:
Variegated Sweet Flag's 18" height makes it ideal for use around pools, as well as other distinct landscape features. Its variegated coloration is a bonus when planning an area that calls for a medium-height Ornamental Grass.

HOW YOU PLANT:
1) Dig a hole twice the width and as deep as the container.
2) Remove from container and position in prepared hole.
3) Add a liquid starter fertilizer.
4) Backfill with a medium soil mix.
5) Apply a weed preventer such as Treflan.
6) Mulch to a depth of 1-2".
7) Water very well.

WHEN YOU WATER:
Water generously and frequently until new plants are established. Once it is showing new growth, less frequent watering is

required. Make use of a moisture meter to help you determine proper watering habits.

HOW/WHEN YOU PRUNE:

No regular pruning is necessary, however, you will need to cut back old growth before new growth emerges in late Winter or early Spring.

HOW/WHEN YOU FERTILIZE:

Fertilize in the Spring with a well-balanced, slow-release granular fertilizer. We also recommend a supplemental Summer feeding to maintain the plant's health.

ADDITIONAL ADVICE FOR PROPER CARE:

Variegated Sweet Flag is generally pest and disease-free.

Zebra Grass

Miscanthus sinensis 'Zebrinus'

Zebra Grass is a clump-growing Ornamental Grass that grows to 6-7 feet in height and 4-5 feet in width. It features unusual horizontally striped yellow foliage, hence its name. In the Fall, beautiful flowering plumes appear, remaining throughout the Winter. This is a common characteristic of Ornamental Grasses that has made them increasingly popular.

WHEN TO PLANT:

Plant during the Spring through Fall season, as long as the soil is not frozen or too wet.

WHY YOU PLANT:

Zebra Grass is ideal when planted as a single specimen and it works quite well when planted in masses. If a mass grouping is desired, be sure to allow for growth by planting Zebra Grass 3-5 feet apart. Zebra Grass is effective near water features and adds color contrast to the landscape wherever it is planted.

WHERE YOU PLANT:
Zebra Grass is most vigorous when planted in full sun in moist soil conditions.

HOW YOU PLANT:
1) Dig a hole twice the width and as deep as the container.
2) Remove from container and position in prepared hole.
3) Add a liquid starter fertilizer.
4) Backfill with a medium soil mix.
5) Apply a weed preventer such as Treflan.
6) Mulch to a depth of 1-2".
7) Water very well.

The things we learn only make a difference when we put them into action.

WHEN YOU WATER:
For new plantings, use a hand-held, open-ended hose, watering plants directly. Do this until the plant's roots are established, generally one growing season, or when new growth is evident. Light, frequent watering is preferred over heavy watering. When in doubt, check the soil's wetness with a moisture meter before watering. A moisture meter is a "must" for gardening peace of mind.

HOW/WHEN YOU PRUNE:
In late Winter or early Spring, prior to the emergence of new growth, cut back foliage to 12-18" from ground level.

HOW/WHEN YOU FERTILIZE:
After pruning in the late Winter, apply a well-balanced, slow-release fertilizer. Also, a supplemental feeding is recommended during the Summer to promote healthy growth.

ADDITIONAL ADVICE FOR PROPER CARE:
While Zebra Grass is somewhat similar to Pampas Grass, it is not as forgiving when it comes to drought resistance. Zebra Grass requires ample moisture to perform satisfactorily.

Notes:

Bulbs

*S*OME FLOWERS ARE popular because they represent important events or the change of seasons. For example, one can't help but think of Easter and the arrival of Spring when Tulips and Crocus begin to bloom!

When it comes to a discussion of bulbs, there are many commonly used terms to identify this category of plants. Corm, rhizome, tuber, and even rootstock, are all used to describe bulbs. For our purposes here, we will use the term "bulbs" in the interest of clarity and to reduce confusion.

There are bulbs for all seasons in Tennessee. Perhaps the most notable is the Iris, the state flower. A simple and yet dramatic representative of the bulb family, Iris is a must for every Tennessee garden. Actually from a rhizome rootstock, Iris is a tried and true perennial flower that multiplies quickly and is almost maintenance free. It comes in hundreds of colors, varieties and blooming times.

CHAPTER FOUR

While the familiar Crocus and Daffodils are valuable garden varieties that grow and bloom easily in Tennessee, they will have finished their showy performance before Spring is even over. There are many choices of Summer and Fall or even Winter color available in the bulb world here in Tennessee. Try Caladiums and Hybrid Lilies for that not-so-sunny area and try Cannas and Dahlias for intense color in extreme heat.

The choices in bulb varieties have different care requirements as well. Some will be fine left in the garden for years without any disturbance, but others will need a little lifting and storing each Winter to get them through until their next showtime in the Spring or Summer.

Caladium

Caladium hortulanum

These beautiful foliage plants prove blooms are not everything! Caladiums come in many varieties of shape, color and size. This plant is not Winter-hardy and must be lifted each Fall. They are available in sun-loving and more common shade-loving types. Heights range from dwarf at 10" high to tall at 30" high.

WHEN TO PLANT:
Plant Caladium bulbs in the garden when the nighttime temperature is above 50 degrees. Also, garden center and nursery plants can be planted any time after the end of April.

WHY YOU PLANT:
Caladiums are the perfect plants for shady gardens. These plants, especially the white varieties, make a strong visual statement in a shady nook or dull green area of the garden.

WHERE YOU PLANT:
You may want to plant your Caladiums indoors initially, in well-drained containers. While you wait for the temperatures to rise outside, you can select the location where you will transplant. As a suggestion, Caladiums make great backdrops for shady borders. Consider these in your mixed flowering patio pots and even in window boxes.

HOW YOU PLANT:
Plant in loose metro-mix type soil in containers indoors in March and keep moist and warm. Transplant outdoors in late April (after last chance of frost). Bulbs can be planted directly into the garden in May, in a well-drained, shady spot. Make sure the ground is well-drained, and that you have added loose soil in with the existing soil when planting. Bury the bulbs 3-4" deep and water-in well.

WHEN YOU WATER:
Water potted bulbs two to three times a week in Spring and Summer. In the ground, bulbs need water once a week, but you will need to increase watering to two times a week during hot Summer months.

HOW/WHEN YOU PRUNE:
No pruning is necessary until frost kills all the foliage. At this time, the foliage can be cut back all the way to the ground. Also, by removing the insignificant bloom pods during the growing season, you will increase the much-desired foliage production.

HOW/WHEN YOU FERTILIZE:
Feed with a bulb booster fertilizer after planting by broadcasting it on top of the soil and watering-in well.

ADDITIONAL ADVICE FOR PROPER CARE:
Be sure to dust bulbs with dusting sulphur (a safe fungicide) before storing them for Winter dormancy. Also, make sure the bulbs are dry before placing in an old potato sack or brown bag to store.

Canna
Canna

A great Summer-blooming bulb that will grow in full sun and offers color in foliage and blooms. Blooms range from salmons, corals, pinks, to yellows, oranges and reds. Bi-colors have become available in the last decade. The heights range from 2-3 feet high and up to 6-7 feet tall. These plants are very sturdy during the heat of the Summer.

WHEN TO PLANT:

Spring is the best time to plant Canna bulbs. Some "in-bloom" plants are available from garden centers and nurseries and you may actually plant these during the Summer with proper care.

WHY YOU PLANT:

These plants are ideal for providing privacy screening because of their dense, thick foliage. Blooms can be enjoyed all Summer, and even into early Fall. Cannas are extremely tolerant of dry Summers. Some newer varieties have striking burgundy foliage for a great bold contrast in the perennial garden.

WHERE YOU PLANT:

Plant near a patio for screening or at the back of a flower bed for an effective backdrop. Planted in a grouping, or as a perimeter border, Cannas are a striking addition to the landscape.

HOW YOU PLANT:

Simply till the ground and bury the bulbs around 4-6" deep, adding some bulb booster or other slow-release granular food suitable for bulbs.

WHEN YOU WATER:

Water well after planting. Water once a week during the growing season and twice a week during extreme heat.

HOW/WHEN YOU PRUNE:

Prune any lower yellow leaves as needed and cut back spent bloom stalks. Once a heavy frost has come in the Fall, cut foliage all the way to the ground. Remove (with pruners or scissors) any spent bloom stalks to encourage more color.

HOW/WHEN YOU FERTILIZE:

Feed a basic bulb food by scratching in and around the clumps of the plants and water-in well. Repeat in mid-Summer, being careful to avoid extreme temperatures when fertilizing.

ADDITIONAL ADVICE FOR PROPER CARE:
Some gardeners in West and Middle Tennessee have had over-Wintering success by mulching heavily for insulation from the cold, then removing mulch in early Spring. Colder areas of the state, such as East Tennessee and the extreme northern border areas, have relied on the traditional method of lifting bulbs or roots after the first frost and storing them like Caladiums through the Winter.

Crocus
Crocus

The ultimate first breath of Spring can be found in almost any color of the rainbow. There are late Winter/ early Spring bloomers as well as Autumn-blooming Crocus. The heights range from 3-6".

WHEN TO PLANT:
Crocus should be planted between mid-October and December for the best performance the following Spring.

WHY YOU PLANT:
Crocus has the distinction of being one of the earliest signs of Spring and is often planted for this reason alone. It is admired because it provides the first glimpse of color after a dull and dreary Winter.

WHERE YOU PLANT:
Crocus works well in small rock gardens, at entrance areas, or wherever up-close views of the garden are available. Crocus needs to be planted in a well-drained soil for best results.

HOW YOU PLANT:

Follow individual Crocus planting instructions regarding depth for planting. Interestingly, the Crocus is actually a corm, not a bulb. Be sure to dig a deep and wide hole, then work in some bulb booster, a complete granular bulb food enriched with bone meal. Place bulbs the recommended distance apart and cover with soil. Planting groups of 15 to 25 bulbs in pockets, instead of individual holes, makes for easier gardening and a better show of color in the garden.

WHEN YOU WATER:

Bulbs should be watered well after planting and maybe once or twice during Winter months, if rainfall has been light.

HOW/WHEN YOU PRUNE:

Not much to do except enjoy the blooms and allow the foliage to naturally die back.

HOW/WHEN YOU FERTILIZE:

Feed when planting by working an all-purpose bulb food into the soil. Repeat just after blooming by placing bulb food on top of the ground around the bulbs and water-in well.

ADDITIONAL ADVICE FOR PROPER CARE:

No care is really needed after you plant, but be sure and let the foliage die back after blooming has ceased. This is important for the following year's bloom production.

Daffodil
Narcissus

Spring is not complete without the wonderful display of Daffodils in the Tennessee landscape. The choices can range from early-blooming February varieties to those that bloom as late as April. The colors range from a creamy white, as found in 'Mt. Hood' and 'Ice Follies,' to the double-blooming varieties like 'Tahiti' with a yellow and orange combination. Try 'Baby Moon' for a small rock garden and 'Peeping Tom' for blooms lasting three times longer than any of the other small yellow varieties.

WHEN TO PLANT:

Daffodils should be planted between mid-October and December for the best performance the following Spring.

WHY YOU PLANT:

Daffodils are the traditional signal that Spring has finally arrived. Daffodils have the honor of providing the first burst of color to the late-Winter landscape. The abundance of Daffodil varieties makes it easy to select a choice other than the familiar solid yellow color that springs up almost overnight after a few warm days. Daffodils are a sheer delight when used as an indoor centerpiece, especially while the weather is still cold and dreary. We all have fond memories of these early arrivals that Grandma called "buttercups".

WHERE YOU PLANT:

The fact that Daffodils require some sun is not a problem since they arrive before deciduous trees provide shade. Plant where these flowers can be viewed from indoors during early Spring. Also, plant Daffodils in and around early-Summer blooming perennials, and even pansies, so they can complement each other while they are both in bloom. Always select soil that is well-drained.

HOW YOU PLANT:

Follow individual Daffodil instructions regarding planting depth. Be sure to dig a planting hole that is deep and wide, and work in some bulb booster, which is a complete granular bulb food enriched with bone meal. Place bulbs the recommended distance apart and cover with soil. Planting groups of 15 to 25 bulbs in pockets instead of individual holes makes for easier gardening and produces a better display of color in the garden.

WHEN YOU WATER:
Bulbs should be watered well after planting and maybe once or twice during Winter months if rainfall has been limited.

HOW/WHEN YOU PRUNE:
Other than picking flowers for bouquets, Daffodils require no pruning. It is important to allow foliage to turn yellow and naturally die back. Resist the urge to mow the foliage, since it is during this process that the bulbs are storing food for the production of next year's blooms.

HOW/WHEN YOU FERTILIZE:
Feed when planting by working an all-purpose bulb food, such as bulb booster, into the soil. Repeat just after blooming by placing bulb booster on the soil around the bulbs.

ADDITIONAL ADVICE FOR PROPER CARE:
Every five years or so, Daffodils need to be lifted, divided and replanted. You may want to neatly tie up or braid foliage to keep it from flopping over nearby plants. It is a good idea to plant taller Daffodil varieties toward the back of the flower bed, so other plants will hide the unsightly foliage after Daffodil blooms have faded.

Dahlia
Dahlia

These almost fool-proof beauties are tremendously varied in color, shape and size. The heights can range from 8-10" to over 5 feet tall. Dahlia blooms have

been measured up to 1 foot in diameter and as small as a quarter. The blooms
can range from a single, daisy-like size to a huge dinner plate variety.

WHEN TO PLANT:
Dahlias should be planted in Springtime here in Tennessee.
The Dahlia actually comes from a tuber, which can be consid-
ered a bulb.

WHY YOU PLANT:
Dahlias are quite easy to grow and a number of varieties are
now suitable for window boxes and border plants. Also, Dahlias
are grown for cutting gardens to provide indoor bouquets and
for exhibition.

WHERE YOU PLANT:
One common characteristic of tubers is that they require full
sun, so keep this in mind when you decide where to plant
Dahlias. These plants have many applications. Tall varieties can
be planted for the background of a flower bed. Short varieties
are perfect for borders and even patio pots and window boxes.

HOW YOU PLANT:
Loosen soil prior to planting and add peat moss and a bulb
booster fertilizer to the planting hole. Place the tuber in the
hole, cover with soil, and water well. If you are planting Dahlias
in containers, make sure they have sufficient drainage and are
potted with a loose, quality soil.

WHEN YOU WATER:
Do not let potted Dahlias dry out between waterings. In the full
sun of mid-Summer, they will need watering two or three times
a week. Otherwise, one to two waterings a week will be sufficient. If planted in the ground, once a week watering is sufficient.

HOW/WHEN YOU PRUNE:

All spent blooms should be deadheaded by clipping off the stem all the way to the main stalk of the plant. Do not remove just the flower head, since leaving the stem is unsightly and detracts from a continual show of color. Once frost occurs, remove all foliage and lift bulbs for storage (see below).

HOW/WHEN YOU FERTILIZE:

Feeding with a granular slow-release fertilizer formulated specifically for bulbs (such as bulb booster) is recommended during planting. Repeat in June, scratching the top layer of soil around the Dahlias. Be sure to water well.

ADDITIONAL ADVICE FOR PROPER CARE:

When Fall comes, lift tubers carefully from the garden. Clean them and allow to air dry. Dust with sulphur or a fungicide before packing them upside-down in shoe boxes or baskets. Pack perlite, dry peat moss, or sand around them. Store in a cool, dry place until Spring. Some gardeners in the southern area of Tennessee actually leave them in the ground and heavily apply mulch for over-Wintering. Be sure to remove mulch early in the Spring to avoid the rotting of new Spring growth.

Iris, Bearded
Iris Hybrida

Tennessee's state flower comes in as many colors as the rainbow and is a favorite welcome during mid Spring. The foliage is quite striking almost year-round. There is even an Iris with variegated foliage for a real conversation piece in the garden. One showstopper we've rediscovered is the 'Eleanor Roosevelt.' This purple-blue beauty actually repeats her blooms not just in the

Spring, but again in the Fall for a second season of color! This is truly a must for every Tennessee garden.

WHEN TO PLANT:

Iris are practically indestructible and can be planted almost any-time the ground is workable! The perfect time to plant and/or divide Iris is in August or September.

WHY YOU PLANT:

Of course, being our state flower is reason enough to want to plant this lovely, old-fashioned beauty. The Iris is almost fool-proof as a perennial bloomer and will tolerate almost total neglect. The foliage also remains long after its blooms have faded and gone and creates a striking contrast and adds vertical height in any perennial garden.

WHERE YOU PLANT:

Iris love lots of direct, hot sun, but will still perform quite nicely when given only half a day's sun. The roots need to be in a soil that is able to drain to avoid root rot. I suggest planting near other perennial flowers that will help cover up or add interest once the blooms have done their thing!

HOW YOU PLANT:

Iris are quite easy to plant because they don't need a lot of soil preparation. Till or work up the soil and add a little organic humus or peat moss in the area. Make sure the roots are planted just under the surface of the soil and cover with no more than an inch or so of soil.

WHEN YOU WATER:

Newly planted Iris require some irrigation. Depending on the time of year you plant, weekly watering during the heat of the summer is plenty. Once established, no real watering schedule is needed. Mother Nature will be sufficient!

How/When you prune:

The foliage of Iris can be cut back sometime in late Summer by cutting all the way back to the shape of your "hand." We call it "fanning" back. The end result should be similar to a fan by cutting with sharp garden scissors or pruners. Be sure and tag at this time to remember variety and color.

How/When you fertilize:

When first planting Iris roots, place a good well-balanced bulb food that contains bone meal in the soil. About once in the Spring and again in late Summer you can side dress the plants with a slow-release granular flower food.

Additional advice for proper care:

Be careful not to plant too deep, and be sure to divide and separate at least every 3-5 years. Watch for small pen-point-size holes made by Iris borers and be prepared to spray foliage with an insecticide to avoid the borer damage. They enter foliage and eventually work their way in and out of the Iris root.

Lily
Lillium

These elegant flowers grace Summer flower beds unlike any other flower. These bulbs are different from the perennial Daylily. These hybrid Lily bulbs come in a variety of colors and have the freckled look of a 'Tiger Lily.' Some have solid colors with no distinct markings. The heights range from 10" to 3 feet.

When to plant:

Depending on the variety of choice, you will need to plant some Lilies in Fall, and others in Spring. Check label or package for proper instructions.

WHY YOU PLANT:

The primary reason gardeners plant Lilies is to enjoy them as cut flowers. Lilies make a unique statement and their fragrance is simply incredible when enjoyed indoors.

WHERE YOU PLANT:

Plant in an area that provides protection from the hot afternoon sun. Also, many varieties of hybrid Lilies are very suitable for pots and container gardening. These selections, like most bulbs, need a well-drained soil, whether planted in the garden or container.

HOW YOU PLANT:

Follow the packaging instructions of the individual bulbs regarding planting depth. As a rule of thumb, twice the diameter of the bulb is the required depth for planting. Lilies do best if planted on their side, instead of straight up. Dust with a fungicide or dusting sulphur while planting to avoid potential problems.

WHEN YOU WATER:

When growing Lilies in pots, be sure that you do not allow them to dry out. Water at least two times a week and even three times a week while in bloom. In the ground, Lilies need to be watered twice a week during the growing season.

HOW/WHEN YOU PRUNE:

When cutting for bouquets, leave at least half the bloom stalk intact. This is important for the future season's blooms. After the first light frost, you may lift the bulbs, prune the remaining stem and store the bulbs for Winter.

HOW/WHEN YOU FERTILIZE:

Feed when planting by working an all-purpose bulb food, such as bulb booster, into the soil. Repeat just after blooming by scratching bulb booster into the soil around the bulbs.

ADDITIONAL ADVICE FOR PROPER CARE:

When lifting bulbs for Winter storage, be sure to clean away any soil, then spray or dust with a fungicide. Place in a dark non-freezing storage area until Spring. Outdoors, perennial Lilies need mulching to get them through Winter. Also, all Lilies love "cool feet" during the growing season, so they would all benefit from a good mulching.

WALT'S WISDOM

"Life is but a

stage and we

are but actors

passing

through..."

Enjoy Life!

Snowdrop
Galanthus nivalis

This sweet little bulb has a greeting for Spring that can occur as early as late Winter. It grows only 4-6" tall and sports little white tear drop blooms that dangle off its stems.

WHEN TO PLANT:
Plant between mid-October and December, with November being the prime time.

WHY YOU PLANT:
Snowdrop is another early Spring bloomer that provides a welcome burst of color in the Spring garden and bestows a gentle fragrance to the garden.

WHERE YOU PLANT:
Plant near the patio or house, for up-close viewing. Snowdrops also work well in rock gardens or in the foreground of the flower garden. Be sure to select a spot that has good drainage.

HOW YOU PLANT:
Plant according to package directions for planting depth and

use a bulb booster fertilizer when planting. Repeat feeding after the bulbs bloom by scratching fertilizer into the soil around the base of the plants. Water well.

WHEN YOU WATER:
Water well when first planting. Water one to two times during Winter if limited snow or rain has fallen. Other than that, no additional watering is necessary.

HOW/WHEN YOU PRUNE:
No pruning is necessary. Leave foliage alone and allow it to die back naturally. Again, like most bulbs, this will assure more blooms the following year.

HOW/WHEN YOU FERTILIZE:
Feed Snowdrops with bulb booster when you plant. Sprinkle it in the planting hole before placing the bulbs, then water well after covering the bulbs with soil. Repeat feeding after bulbs bloom by broadcasting fertilizer on top of the soil. Water well.

ADDITIONAL ADVICE FOR PROPER CARE:
After three or four years, you may want to divide and separate your Snowdrops and share them with fellow gardening friends.

Tulip
Tulip

Probably the most popular of all Spring-blooming bulbs, the Tulip has difficulty in repeating its impressive show year after year. In Tennessee, our Winter temperatures fluctuate so much that it is hard to find a Tulip that will tolerate our conditions. Try to select the Darwin series for the most likely repeat performances. Tulips come in varieties that bloom from March to late May and the color selection is phenomenal. Varieties include peony-flowering, double-blooming, parrot, fringed, Triumph and more, to offer the gardener a full range of selections. The heights can vary from 4-6" to 36" tall. Some varieties are scented and there are even those with variegated foliage with crisp, creamy white and green stripes.

When to plant:
Tulips should be planted between mid-October and December for the best performance the following Spring.

Why you plant:
These beauties bless the garden with a gorgeous show of bold color. There is no equal for sheer color. Tulips are also wonderful for hand-picked bouquets and great for planting with other Spring blooming bulbs and perennials for a complete look in the Spring flower bed.

Where you plant:
Plant in a well-drained area where there is no chance of moisture retention during our wet Tennessee Springtimes. Plant close for viewing from indoor living spaces.

How you plant:
Follow individual instructions for Tulip planting depth. Be sure to dig a planting hole that is deep and wide, then work in some bulb booster, which is a complete granular bulb food enriched with bone meal. Place bulbs the recommended distance apart and cover. Planting groups of 15 to 25 bulbs together in pockets, instead of individual planting holes, makes for easier gardening and a more dramatic display of color in the garden.

When you water:
Bulbs should be watered well after planting and maybe once or twice during Winter months if limited rainfall has occurred.

How/When you prune:
Other than picking flowers for bouquets, no pruning is required.

It is important to allow foliage to turn yellow and naturally die back. During this process, the bulb is storing food for the production of next year's blooms. Unless you are planting 'Triumph' or 'Darwin', you probably should treat Tulips as annuals, removing and discarding them after blooming.

How/When you fertilize:
If planting 'Darwin' series, feed while planting by working into the soil an all-purpose bulb food, such as bulb booster. Repeat just after blooming by scratching bulb booster on top of the ground around the bulbs. If planting other varieties, feed when planting with bulb booster. There is no need to feed after blooming if you plan on discarding them.

Additional advice for proper care:
Sometimes hungry varmints find Tulips a real treat during the Winter months. You may want to spray bulbs as you are planting with an animal repellent designed especially for bulbs, or sprinkle cayenne pepper on top of bulbs before covering with soil.

Notes:

Annuals

*T*HE MOST MEMORABLE LANDSCAPED areas are those that benefit from the planned use of color. While color is available from a wide selection of garden plants, the Annuals evoke the most response. When the appropriate varieties are grown in just the right spot, Annuals have the effect of an artist's touch on canvas. Annuals can be used to enhance the color provided by neighboring plants and can even provide a vibrant contrast with subdued background plantings.

These days, perennials are growing in popularity, and rightfully so. They obediently return year after year and usually provide a bigger and better show than the year before. While this is certainly true, you will rarely find a striking garden that doesn't devote some strategic location or pocket to Annual color. Again, it is the color that grabs and holds your attention in the landscape.

From a practical point of view, Annuals provide the garden with consistent color between perennial blooming times.

CHAPTER FIVE

Also, many Annuals have the ability to reseed themselves, an added benefit to the gardener who is prepared to take advantage of this asset. This reseeding enables the gardener to relocate, or share the plant with a friend.

There is a rainbow of color choice with Annuals and varieties are available that will thrive in sun or shade. Plan on making an addition to your garden with Annuals, and you will certainly have reason to be proud of the results.

Begonia, Wax Leaf

Begonia semperflorens

This common annual has often been overused in mass plantings and subdivision entrances. This may be because of its extreme tolerance to Summer droughts and scorching temperatures. There are many varieties of Begonias, from bulbs, to perennials, to the one we are discussing, an annual. It's waxy leaves come in several shades of green, red and even a bronze. Bloom colors can be pink, coral, white, red and bi-colored. The blooms are now available in gorgeous singles and even doubles (they look like little rose buds). The plants will grow from 6-12" high depending on the variety selected and will spread up to one foot in width.

WHEN TO PLANT:

You may plant Begonias after the last killing frost of the year. Planting is usually safe by May. If you are planting from seed directly into the garden, be sure to wait at least until May. If starting indoors, you may begin Begonias in late Winter or early Spring.

WHY YOU PLANT:

The Wax Leaf Begonia has a wonderful tolerance to extreme neglect, heat and drought. Planting can take place any time during the Spring or Summer for an instant show, not only from the blooms but also from the foliage.

WHERE YOU PLANT:

Begonias are great for containers and poor soil conditions. They thrive in full sun, yet tolerate some shade. They are very effective in mass plantings, such as front entrances, commercial beds and even near mailboxes, and those "difficult-to-water" spots are also ideal for Begonias.

HOW YOU PLANT:

Work up the soil and add a little peat moss or organic humus into the bed. Then dig a hole a little larger than the root ball of the plant. Loosen the roots gently and place the plant into the hole. Cover the roots with soil and mulch lightly. Be sure to water-in well with a liquid root stimulator.

WHEN YOU WATER:

Be sure to water at least twice a week for 3-4 weeks after planting. After this, Begonias can grow with little additional watering.

HOW/WHEN YOU PRUNE:

No pruning is necessary. Once our first frost has arrived, the "melted" plants can be removed from the garden and added to your compost pile.

HOW/WHEN YOU FERTILIZE:

Fertilizing is not a must, however, like most annuals, Begonias will perform much better if watered weekly with a water soluable flower food. A slow-release granular fertilizer that is high in phosphorous can be scratched in around the plants every other month during the growing season. Be sure to water-in well after each application.

ADDITIONAL ADVICE FO PROPER CARE:

Be aware that the Wax Leaf Begonia is extremely sensitive to any light frost and must be covered with newspaper or a light cloth material for protection.

Browallia
Browallia speciosa

Shaped like small petunias, Browallia will grow to a height of 12-20" and produce a brilliant blue, violet, or white flower. These colored flowers contrast wonderfully with the rich green foliage.

WHEN TO PLANT:

Plant seeds indoors, 8-10 weeks before the last killing frost date, or transplant starter plants outdoors after the last killing frost.

WHY YOU PLANT:

This plant blooms profusely from Summer until frost. Note: If cut back, transplanted, and brought indoors, the Browallia will bloom again during the Winter, making it truly a plant for all seasons. If you are tired of Impatiens, this is a great alternative!

WHERE YOU PLANT:

Place in partial shade and moist soil. Browallia is used as a border and a ground cover for flower beds, and we have found they work well in a mixed container.

HOW YOU PLANT:

Plant by seed or transplants, spacing 9-12" apart. If you are planting from seed, germination takes from 12-21 days.

WHEN YOU WATER:

Water to maintain adequate moisture.

HOW/WHEN YOU PRUNE:

Browallia needs very little pruning or deadheading. It is a great "rebloomer" on it's own!

HOW/WHEN YOU FERTILIZE:

It is recommended to fertilize weekly with a liquid flower food, or a dry, granular flower food at six-week intervals-just make sure that the food you use is high in phosphorous.

ADDITIONAL ADVICE FOR PROPER CARE:
Watch for white fly infestation. It's a good idea to spray lightly with a fine horticultural oil to keep these pests down.

Cosmos
Cosmos

A beautiful plant that has a feathery foliage, Cosmos will add an unusual look to your garden. This rather tall plant, that is somewhat daisy-like, will bloom in either yellow, orange, red, pink, or white. Try and combine Cosmos with other annuals in your garden to give it a look that is unlike that of your neighbors. Try some of our favorites in the 'Bright Lights' series.

WHEN TO PLANT:
Sow seeds outdoors during the Spring after the danger of frost has passed, or you can sow Fall seeds for the next Spring.

WHY YOU PLANT:
The Cosmos' rapid and tall growth habits make it good for use as a background planting to the dwarf varieties of annuals. It has also been used as a "wild" flower when mixed with other perennials, and is a very good plant for cut flower bouquets.

WHERE YOU PLANT:
Place in full sun, sowing seeds in well-draining, average soil. Like wildflowers, the Cosmos grows best in dry—not fertile—soil.

HOW YOU PLANT:
Till the area to be seeded with no other special soil preparation. The seeds germinate in 5-7 days if planted in warm May soil.

WHEN YOU WATER:

After the Cosmos is established, very little watering maintenance is required.

HOW/WHEN YOU PRUNE:

Remove the spent flowers to promote continual blooming.
Cosmos will often self-sow.

HOW/WHEN YOU FERTILIZE:

Very little fertilization, if any, is required, but you may want to
use a high-phosphorous granular food in the Spring if your soil
is poor.

ADDITIONAL ADVICE FOR PROPER CARE:

Staking the taller varieties (5-7 feet) to keep them upright is
advisable.

Daisy, Swan River
Brachycome

*This sweet little flower creates a "happy look" when it is planted with other
garden friends. The tiny dime-sized blooms are blue-lavender in color with a
bright yellow center, and the flowers cover the entire plant. While this plant is
very delicate in appearance, it is very tolerant of our Tennessee Summers.*

WHEN TO PLANT:

Plant outside after the danger of frost has passed, or sow outdoors in early Spring.

WHY YOU PLANT:

The soft hues lend contrast to warmer-colored annuals, such as
Zinnias and Marigolds, and this plant is very tolerant to the

heat of our Tennessee Summers once it has been established.

WHERE YOU PLANT:
Place these in full sun in gardens, hanging baskets, containers, rock gardens, or raised beds.

HOW YOU PLANT:
Plant seed directly in ordinary garden soil, covering lightly. For earlier blooms, start indoors or use starter transplants. Germination takes about eight days, and successive planting of seeds provides a longer blooming period.

WHEN YOU WATER:
Water as needed. Swan River Daisies are somewhat drought-tolerant.

HOW/WHEN YOU PRUNE:
Pinch back plants to 2″ in order to promote full, bushy growth. Set plants 5-6″ apart. Flowering begins at about 13 weeks after planting and continues throughout the season.

HOW/WHEN YOU FERTILIZE:
Very little fertilization, if any, is needed.

ADDITIONAL ADVICE FOR PROPER CARE:
These daisies are fragile. Place short, bushy twigs among the plants to reduce bending and breakage from beating rain.

Impatiens
Impatiens

There is no better plant for the novice gardener to bring some colorful life to the patio. Find an area where there is some shade and you will bring that area to life! Impatiens come in a wide variety of colors and can be mixed very effectively. Be sure and plant some white with your selection—we have found that they show up very well at night.

WHEN TO PLANT:
Set out transplants in Spring after the danger of frost has passed. It is best to buy pre-started plants from a garden center or nursery. These plants will voluntarily reseed from pods, which when touched, pop open "impatiently," and spill seeds on the ground.

WHY YOU PLANT:
These are the most shade-tolerant of annual flowers, and the variety and tone of colors are unique to this species. Additionally, Impatiens provide color to the garden that does not stop until the first killing frost.

WHERE YOU PLANT:
Most varieties prefer partial to full shade areas. The New Guinea Hybrids will grow in full sun to partial shade areas. Place in slightly acidic, moist, well-draining soil.

HOW YOU PLANT:
Prior to planting, incorporate a starter fertilizer to the planting area. After setting out the transplants, use a liquid root stimulator to reduce shock. Then, lightly mulch to conserve moisture and stabilize soil temperature.

WHEN YOU WATER:
After setting out Impatiens, soak the soil thoroughly and maintain moist conditions throughout the growing season.

HOW/WHEN YOU PRUNE:
No pruning is needed.

How/When you fertilize:

A mid-Summer, supplemental feeding with a dry granular flower food should be considered for extra growth and color.

Additional advice for proper care:

Because of the damp, shady environment which suits Impatiens, slugs may be a problem. By avoiding night watering, you reduce the chance of slug infestation.

Lobelia, 'Crystal Palace'
Lobelia erinus 'Crystal Palace'

This may be the showiest plant available for its size! Available in both perennial and annual varieties, this plant caught our attention very early because of its shocking neon blue color and its ability to bloom in shady gardens. This plant can grow 10" wide, but will hardly ever grow more than 6" tall. Try planting in patio planters and mixed with other flowers in hanging baskets.

When to plant:

It is essential to start this slow-growing flower by transplants. Plant during the Spring after the danger of frost has passed.

Why you plant:

This annual is chosen because it is a dainty, fine-textured plant with outstanding blue flowers.

Where you plant:

Use as a border plant. We suggest placing this plant in half day sun, preferably morning sun. We also suggest planting this gorgeous little flower with pinks, whites and silvers! Try planting with your shade Impatiens to add a little extra zip to your landscape.

HOW YOU PLANT:

Prior to planting, incorporate a starter fertilizer into the planting area, and space transplants 6" apart in ordinary garden soil. After setting out the transplants, use a liquid root stimulator to reduce shock. Then, lightly mulch to conserve moisture and stabilize soil temperatures.

WHEN YOU WATER:

Provide plenty of water during dry periods.

HOW/WHEN YOU PRUNE:

As these plants develop, pinch back the very new growth once or twice during the season to promote fullness. When flowers begin to die back, cut back by lightly shearing the dead blooms to promote more blooms.

HOW/WHEN YOU FERTILIZE:

Lobelias enjoy a mid-Summer feeding with a basic flower food for extra growth and color.

ADDITIONAL ADVICE FOR PROPER CARE:

No particular problems are noted.

Marigold
Tagetes

Marigolds are one of the most popular Tennessee Annuals. They will quickly produce vibrant blossoms that are either red, orange, white, or yellow. These plants have even been known to ward off some insects if planted in the vegetable garden. While growing to a height of 36" and 36" wide, your Marigolds will offer color from the Spring through the Fall. Try some of the newer varieties such as 'Early Saffron Spice' and 'Dainty Marietta.'

WHEN TO PLANT:

Sow seeds outdoors or set out transplants in the Spring after all danger of frost has passed. Some gardeners have begun to sow a late crop in Summer for Fall color instead of Chrysanthemums.

WHY YOU PLANT:

Marigolds are easy to grow, and have a large selection of heights, bloom sizes, and colors. The flower cuttings are very long-lasting in fresh bouquets. Also, these colors will carry nicely into a Fall garden. These plants are excellent for poor soil in the hot Summer months.

WHERE YOU PLANT:

Place Marigolds in full sun in ordinary garden soils. Be careful not to plant in rich, high-nitrogen soil, as this will produce foliage at the expense of flowers. Marigolds are great in large, mass plantings where irrigation is a problem. Plant in mixed patio containers for contrasting color and textures.

HOW YOU PLANT:

The seeds are quite large and should be planted at a depth of one-fourth inch. They will germinate in 7-10 days with temperatures of 75 degrees and higher. For early flowers, use transplants or start seeds indoors 5-6 weeks prior to the planting date. Space tall varieties 12-24" apart and dwarf varieties 6" apart.

WHEN YOU WATER:

Water once a week in Spring and water in the Summer if we have dry spells. Otherwise, they should do well with little care.

HOW/WHEN YOU PRUNE:

Remove spent blooms to promote continuous flowering. When using as cut flowers, strip off most of the foliage to reduce the pungent odor.

Note: Stake taller varieties for support.

Avoid the over-stimulation of nitrogen fertilizers. Instead, use a bloom-starter fertilizer which is high in phosphorous, and use at least once after planting on top of the soil. Always water well after feeding.

ADDITIONAL ADVICE FOR PROPER CARE:
No serious diseases or insects are noted. In fact, Marigolds are used as a pest deterrent.

Pansy
Viola

These may be our favorite annuals! You may get confused by classifying Pansies as a perennial due to the fact that they can reappear in the Spring after a Fall planting, but the fact is that Pansies can only survive for 6-8 months before they need to be replaced. Another great benefit of Pansies is the wide variety of available colors. When choosing your pansies, consider 'Crystal Bowl', 'Bingo,' 'Azure' or 'Presto.' All of these are great bloomers that happen to be a little more heat-tolerant than others.

WHEN TO PLANT:
The best time to plant for the most "bang for your buck" is in early Fall. However, if you are inspired by all the early Spring color, you still may want to plant some in Spring also!

WHY YOU PLANT:
Pansies are what we like to call "God's little miracles!" Here in Tennessee, they are truly one of the only showy flowers that can actually have color from early Fall into Winter. They rest for a month or so and bounce back usually bigger and better in early Spring to early Summer, a little investment for a lot of color.

WHERE YOU PLANT:
Place in full sun to partial shade. Use in rock gardens, hanging baskets, containers, and mass groupings with Spring bulbs.

HOW YOU PLANT:
Plant transplants in moist, fertile soil. Mulch to keep soil cool and retain moisture.

WHEN YOU WATER:
Water as needed. Pansies may need watering after extended, dry, sub-freezing weather during Winter periods.

HOW/WHEN YOU PRUNE:
Deadhead and cut back leggy plants to prolong and increase blooming.

HOW/WHEN YOU FERTILIZE:
Fall plantings respond to early Spring, supplemental feeding of granular slow-release fertilizers that are high in phosphorous. It will help insure that your plants remain healthy.

ADDITIONAL ADVICE FOR PROPER CARE:
No real disease or insect problems should be expected, but you may want to sprinkle pine straw over them if temperatures fall into the teens. The pine straw also deters snails and slugs in Spring flower beds where moist conditions prevail.

Petunia
Petunia x hybrida

This is a sturdy annual for every garden. While Petunias will only grow 1-2 feet, they will spread 3 feet or more. Color choices include pink, purple, red, white and yellow. Be sure and look for some of the newer varieties that are veined and multi-colored. If you will be careful and consistent in your pruning, Petunias will be a great addition to your garden.

WHEN TO PLANT:

Set out transplants after the danger of frost has passed, usually by mid-April.

WHY YOU PLANT:

Use Petunias in perennial beds to maintain a showy look during any lapse in perennial flowering. Also, the new multiflora varieties need very little care from deadheading and pruning. These plants will insure good color from Spring until a hard frost in the Fall, and they are a great draw for butterflies, and even have a great aroma.

WHERE YOU PLANT:

Place Petunias in full sun areas. Use many Petunias in a mass planting to give a very full look to your garden.

HOW YOU PLANT:

Place transplants 7-10" apart after working up the soil and loosening the roots of the plants. Afterwards, water well with a liquid root stimulator.

WHEN YOU WATER:

After setting out, maintain soil moisture until new growth appears, indicating that the plants are established.

HOW/WHEN YOU PRUNE:

As these plants become leggy or scraggly, prune them to encourage new, fuller growth. Some varieties need deadheading in order to form new blooms. However, there are new types of multiflora Petunias, like the "Madness" series, which do not require deadheading. Consult your local garden center or nursery for more information.

WALT'S WISDOM

Gossip goes

in one ear

and out the

mouth.

HOW/WHEN YOU FERTILIZE:
Use a starter fertilizer at the time of planting, and side-dress monthly with flower food that is slow-release and high in phosphorous.

ADDITIONAL ADVICE FOR PROPER CARE:
Sometimes certain varieties will become very scraggly, but by cutting almost halfway back in late Summer, you can have a nice, full plant for the Fall. Petunias will tolerate a light frost or two before they die.

Poppy
Papaver

If you love to go out into the garden and cut flowers, this is the flower for you! The Poppy comes in both an annual and perennial variety, and comes in an abundance of colors and heights. The tissue-like petals make this flower seem fragile, but it needs to be planted in full sun.

WHEN TO PLANT:
Plant or sow seeds during the Fall or very early Spring. Fall is the preferable planting time for Poppies.

WHY YOU PLANT:
There is nothing more eye-catching than a mass planting of Poppies in full bloom. Remember the scene from "The Wizard of Oz?" (Those were Poppies). Whew! I wish my garden looked like that.

WHERE YOU PLANT:
Place Poppies in full sun in average soil conditions. Try planting them in the rear of your flower bed to give the bed a great looking backdrop.

How you plant:

Broadcast seed by mixing with some sand to obtain a proper distribution. Seeds will germinate in 7-14 days. For container plants, plant 6-12" apart after you have made sure the ground has been worked up very well.

When you water:

Poppies are quite drought tolerant, so watering can be very infrequent.

How/When you prune:

No special care is required to maintain a healthy appearance.

How/When you fertilize:

Poppies require little to no fertilization to grow and thrive, but if the ground is poor, add some time-release fertilizer high in phosphorous.

Additional advice for proper care:

Poppies are truly trouble free.

Salvia, Victoria Blue
Salvia farinacea 'Victoria'

Salvia is one of our favorite plants! Growing to a height of 20," it blooms with blue and silver/white flowers. Try planting them in mass groups where they will bloom and look good over an extended period of time. This plant is considered an annual but has been known to reappear for several years. If it is hot, Salvia will thrive.

When to plant:

The very best time to plant is in mid-Spring here in Tennessee. You can actually plant throughout our growing season as long as the plants are available.

WHY YOU PLANT:

Salvia is extremely easy to grow, particularly when purchased as starter plants. Blue Salvia will just keep blooming, and blooming, and blooming. It is great for cutting and drying for arrangements, wreaths and other crafts, and dries similar to a lavender bloom head. Also it will be a main feature or accent to a landscape from Spring through Fall.

WHERE YOU PLANT:

Place in full sun to partial shade and plant in average, well-prepared soil. Salvia prefers as much sun as possible for the best show of color.

HOW YOU PLANT:

Sow seeds, which will germinate in 12-15 days, in a moist planting medium. Space Salvia transplants up to 12" apart, and try to plant small container plants available from your local garden center.

WHEN YOU WATER:

Water to keep moist until the plants are established and blooming. After they begin blooming, they are quite carefree.

HOW/WHEN YOU PRUNE:

Salvia need some grooming during the flowering season to keep good, continuous color. Prune dead bloom heads off about every other week by following the flower stems back to the main plant and removing the stem.

HOW/WHEN YOU FERTILIZE:

Use a starter fertilizer at the time of planting, and side-dress with a flower food during mid-season.

ADDITIONAL ADVICE FOR PROPER CARE:

If these plants are not in enough full sun and in a small, crowded growing space, white fly may cause problems. The solution is to plant in a roomy, full-sun area.

Sunflower

Helianthus

If you want to grow a REALLY BIG FLOWER, plant some Sunflowers. Whew! These heads can grow up to 24" in width. Available in either single or double head varieties, they come in colors that vary from creamy white, to yellow and even maroon. And remember, by planting Sunflowers you are doing our bird friends a great favor.

WHEN TO PLANT:
Plant in Spring, 2-4 weeks after the last killing frost.

WHY YOU PLANT:
As the lion stands out in the animal kingdom, the Sunflowers stand out in your garden. They are awesome in appearance and quite productive in bearing birdseed. Sunflowers are also a fast-growing screen or backdrop to the garden. The shorter varieties are excellent for cut flower bouquets.

WHERE YOU PLANT:
Place in full sun and average garden soil. Planting options vary, from along fence rows or property boundaries to Perennial beds or vegetable gardens. Small varieties are even suitable for patio container gardening.

HOW YOU PLANT:
Plant these in a tilled bed, covering the seed one-half inch with soil, leaving them 18" apart. The seeds will geminate in about 10 days, depending on the soil temperature and moisture content.

WHEN YOU WATER:
Water until plants are established, and also during drought periods.

HOW/WHEN YOU PRUNE:

To save seeds for Winter (bird food), remove the heads after the seeds have matured, making sure the back of the bloom has lost its green color and has turned brown.

HOW/WHEN YOU FERTILIZE:

Side-dress once during the early growing season using a complete garden fertilizer. This will promote active growth and seed production.

ADDITIONAL ADVICE FOR PROPER CARE:

Because the taller varieties may grow quite large, they may require some staking. Also, the tall flower stems or stalks get a little leggy toward the base, so you may want to plant a shorter variety, or another flower at the base to hide them.

Torenia

Torenia fournieri

Torenia, or the Wishbone Flower as it is commonly called, has small flowers 1" across with petals that are blocked with contrasting color and a wishbone-shaped stamen in the center of the blosssom. The Torenia is a moderately fast-growing annual that grows to a 10" height.

WHEN TO PLANT:

Plant during the Spring after all danger of frost has passed.

WHY YOU PLANT:

The blue, lavender, violet, red, pink, and white colors in blocks make a cheery setting. The serrated, light green leaves provide a nice background for the flowers.

WHERE YOU PLANT:

Plant Torenia in partial shade areas where it is effectively used for bed edges and borders. Torenia may be transplanted into a container during the Fall and used as a Winter house plant.

HOW YOU PLANT:

At a temperature of 70 degrees, the uncovered seeds will germinate in 7-15 days. You may set out the transplants in moist, fertile soil after all danger of frost has passed.

WHEN YOU WATER:

Keep the Torenia watered throughout the Spring and Summer. It should be watered well each week.

HOW/WHEN YOU PRUNE:

Pinch back the Torenia to promote full, bushy growth.

HOW/WHEN YOU FERTILIZE:

Use a starter fertilizer at the time of planting, and side-dress with a flower food during mid-season to promote growth and color.

ADDITIONAL ADVICE FOR PROPER CARE:

No serious disease or insect problems are expected with this variety.

Zinnia
Zinnia elegans

Zinnias are an ever-popular annual. Easily grown, the plants are available in many heights, shapes, and colors. If you love to cut flowers, Zinnias will pro-vide a wonderful addition to your bouquets. You will not believe how long a Zinnia will last after it has been cut.

WHEN TO PLANT:

Sow the seeds after the soil has warmed, approximately 4 to
6 weeks after the last frost. You may transplant small plants,
when available through garden centers, in mid-Spring through
early Summer.

WHY YOU PLANT:

Zinnias bloom during the intense heat of the Summer months
and display a change of color during the late Summer. Zinnias
add strength to perennial beds and are great in cut flower
arrangements. There is a whole other group of low ground
cover-type Zinnias called Zinnia linearis (augustifolia) that are
certainly worth investigating. We've been so pleased with the
drought and disease resistant qualities. Another attribute is the
colors they are available in (bright oranges and creams) are such
a refreshing addition to the early Fall garden! Also incredible
when utilized in mixed patio pots, they spill over the sides and
add a real splash of color on the hottest of Summer days.

WHERE YOU PLANT:

Place Zinnias in full sun with average soil. Use them in annual
and perennial beds, as mass groupings, along fence rows, and as
flower borders. They may also be used to decorate a vegetable
garden.

HOW YOU PLANT:

Sow seeds in average garden soil when the temperature is 70
to 80 degrees. Cover the seed lightly, gently firm the soil over
the seed, then water thoroughly. The seed will germinate in
7-10 days.

WHEN YOU WATER:

Water well each week during Spring and Summer. Remember
when watering to avoid doing so in the evening and avoid getting the foliage real wet. Hopefully by following this advice you
will avoid the problems so many gardeners experience with

Powdery Mildew on the lower foliage of their Zinnias. This is
rarely a problem with the above-mentioned Zinnia linearis.

HOW/WHEN YOU PRUNE:
Thin the young seedlings 6-12″ apart and no pruning will be
necessary, other than removing spent bloom heads which can
be saved for next year's plants.

HOW/WHEN YOU FERTILIZE:
Fertilize at the time of planting with a starter fertilizer and side-
dress with a flower food in mid-season.

ADDITIONAL ADVICE FOR PROPER CARE:
Powdery Mildew is often a problem with this variety. To keep
the foliage dry, avoid watering prior to nightfall. Consult your
local garden center or nursery for resistant varieties of Zinnia if
Powdery Mildew becomes a nuisance.

Notes:

Notes:

Roses

$\mathscr{T}$HE ROSE IS BY FAR THE "Queen of the Flowers." Roses are, and probably always will be, the most popular flower in the world. The reasons are vast and yet quite obvious—for sheer beauty and fragrance, this timeless blossom has no equal. Rosarians, meaning those who grow and tend this beloved flower, are a dedicated and special group of gardeners who are willing to commit the extra care which these flowers demand.

The Rose is certainly the world's favorite token to symbolize love, and through the centuries there have been thousands of hybridized varieties developed to express emotion and romance. This flower, in all its abundant varieties, still corners the market on how to say "I love you" without a word spoken.

Throughout the years, the Hybrid Tea Rose has remained the most popular variety. In recent years, however, the smaller Floribundas (hedge or bush) and Miniatures have really become popular for their carefree growth and low-maintenance requirements.

C H A P T E R   S I X

If treated with proper feeding and a timely maintenance program, roses in Tennessee will bear their wonderful blooms for up to eight months of the year. "Things are rosy," and "everything is coming up roses" when things are hopeful, good, and prosperous. Gardeners will be hard-pressed to find a more inspirational flower than the Rose for striking impact in the home landscape.

Roses, Climbing
Rosa

Nothing is more desirable than a gorgeous climbing rose flowing over a white picket fence. In fact, in the past several years, avid gardeners and novices alike are tempted to install trellises, arbors, pergolas and even small gazebos as excuses to grow climbing roses. Climbers come in just about any color, any size, and any fullness you could imagine. Some are heavily scented for a full, fragrant smell, and others have only the slightest hint of aromatic appeal. Traditionally, the large-flowered Climbers are the most popular because of their longer flowering time. With the Climbing Rose, there is a single group known as 'Ramblers.' These roses bloom only once in late Spring to early Summer, but their full-bloom impact is well worth the wait. Ramblers have a growth potential of up to 20 feet. For beauty and spread potential, you may just want to consider giving a home to a "Ramblin' Rose."

WHEN TO PLANT:
Just about any time plants are available to you is a good time to plant (if followed by proper care and maintenance). However, the very best time is either Fall or early Spring.

WHY YOU PLANT:
The reasons for planting Climbing Roses are almost endless. Nothing can compare to the instant "curb appeal" a Climbing red Rose creates when framing a white arbor, picket fence or trellis. The fragrance produced by these beauties is wonderful as it wafts across the landscape, and many varieties are spectacular when cut and arranged in fresh bouquets.

WHERE YOU PLANT:
Plant Climbers in at least five hours of good, intense sun and in well-drained soil. In general, Roses like a rich, slightly acidic soil. Obviously, Climbers need some type of support, whether it's from brick walls, arbors, trellises, or archways. A Climbing

Rose will turn the look of your house into that of a home.

HOW YOU PLANT:

Dig up or till the soil and blend in plenty of organic humus, peat moss and composted cow manure into the existing soil. Once the soil and amendments are all blended, remove enough to create a hole large enough to accommodate the Rose's roots. If you are planting a boxed or container Rose, be very careful when removing the box or pot. Try to keep the ball intact and place gently into the hole. If you are planting a grafted rose, you will need to make sure the bud union (the swollen bulge at the base of the plant) is just above the soil level. This is where the desirable hybrid Rose is grafted onto wild Rose root stock. Carefully backfill the hole and firmly pack the soil until level with the existing ground. Water-in well with a liquid root stimu-lator and then mulch with pine mulch or pine straw.

When planting bareroot Roses, be sure you handle with care! The roots need to be spread out and placed on a small mound you have built up in the bottom of the planting hole. This will ensure good root-to-soil contact and reduce the chance for development of air pockets around the roots.

WHEN YOU WATER:

Although Roses must be in well-drained soil, they love lots of water during the growing season. They will certainly survive with once-a-week watering, or even less after getting estab-lished the first year. The more often you water, the better off the Rose will be. When watering, keep the foliage dry. Water in the morning and keep in mind that Roses would much rather have one good soaking rather than three or four sprinklings per week. As a rule, Roses prefer 1-2" of water per week and need moisture to penetrate 18" deep. When in doubt, use a moisture meter to check the efficiency of your watering. Some Rosarians use drip irrigation, soaker hoses and even bubbler attachments on their hoses to aid in their watering.

How/When you prune:

Ideally, the first 2-3 years of a new Climber's life should be without any pruning activity other than removal of wood that is clearly dead. After this, prune in Winter or in early Spring (preferable). Ramblers bloom all at once and can be pruned right after this singular blooming. You will need to cut and remove the older, grey canes as well as the new spindly canes. As with most Rose bushes, try to always retain at least 3-5 healthy new canes. Also when pruning, you should consider sealing your cuts to prevent Rose Borer infestation. Seal each cut with a tree wound dressing compound or you can even use regular household white glue. Some Rosarians have been known to color the glue with black or green food coloring to avoid the distraction of the white spots!

How/When you fertilize:

There are numerous Rose foods designed to create beautiful blooms and lush, green foliage...and probably just as many opinions on how to do it. The one thing all Rosarians agree on is that Roses love to be fed! Some folks are very successful using all organics, such as composted manures, cottonseed meal, bone meal, green sand and compost. Others are equally successful with commercially packaged formulated Rose food. There are even foods that contain systemic insecticides which some Rosarians swear by. The best recommendation we can make is to have your local garden center help determine what your plant's specific needs are. Have a soil test taken and bring the results with you on your visit. Then, experiment to see what works for you and your Roses.

Additional advice for proper care:

Climber's canes tend to need more substantial support than the

Ramblers. The stiff canes benefit from some carefully placed vine support products found at your garden center. While at the garden center, be sure to get advice on suggested spray schedules for Roses in your area. Spray with a dormant oil spray at least once in Spring, prior to blooming, to help prevent problems.

Roses, Grandiflora
Rosa

A cross between the Hybrid Tea and Floribunda varieties, Grandifloras are quite large and must have plenty of room to grow, as the name suggests. They aren't as popular in Tennessee gardens, because they take quite a bit more work to maintain their large size which sometimes reaches 6 feet and taller. Because of the height of the Grandiflora, it is difficult to enjoy the blooms unless you are looking down from above, as from a second story or raised deck. But for those of you who like the idea of a "bigger is better" Rose, this is one to consider in your garden.

WHEN TO PLANT:
All Roses do best when planted in their dormant stage, but once the Rose breaks dormancy, you can still successfully plant them throughout the growing season.

WHY YOU PLANT:
Roses are one of the few plants that can provide constant color and fragrance in the garden from Spring through Fall. Their beauty can be enjoyed outdoors, and their flowers can be cut and savored indoors.

WHERE YOU PLANT:
Roses must have at least five hours of intense sunshine to thrive, and they prefer full sun all day long. Roses also require good, organic-enriched soil with excellent drainage.

HOW YOU PLANT:

Dig up or till the soil and blend in plenty of organic humus, peat moss and composted cow manure into the existing soil. Once the soil and amendments are all blended, remove enough to create a hole large enough to accommodate the Rose's roots. If you are planting a boxed or container Rose, be very careful when removing the box or pot. Try to keep the ball intact and place gently into the hole. If you are planting a grafted Rose, you will need to make sure the bud union (the swollen bulge at the base of the plant) is just above the soil level. This is where the desirable hybrid Rose is grafted onto wild Rose root stock. Carefully backfill the hole and firmly pack the soil until level with the existing ground. Water-in well with a liquid root stimulator and then mulch with pine mulch or pine straw.

When planting bareroot Roses, be sure you handle with care! The roots need to be spread out and placed on a small mound you have built up in the bottom of the planting hole. This will ensure good root-to-soil contact and reduce the chance for development of air pockets around the roots.

WHEN YOU WATER:

Although Roses must be in well-drained soil, they love lots of water during the growing season. They will certainly survive with once-a-week watering, or even less after getting established the first year. The more often you water, the better off the Rose will be. When watering, keep the foliage dry. Water in the morning and keep in mind that Roses would much rather have one good soaking rather than three or four sprinklings per week. As a rule, Roses prefer 1-2" of water per week and need moisture to penetrate 18" deep. When in doubt, use a moisture meter to check the efficiency of your watering. Some Rosarians use drip irrigation, soaker hoses and even bubbler attachments on their hoses to aid in their watering.

How/When you prune:

Roses love to be trimmed often, using quality pruning shears. Prune in late Fall to early Winter, leaving enough cane so you can prune off Winter damage in the Spring. Also when pruning, you should consider sealing your cuts to prevent Rose Borer infestation. Seal each cut with a tree wound dressing compound or you can even use regular household white glue. Some Rosarians have been known to color the glue with black or green food coloring to avoid the distraction of the white spots!

How/When you fertilize:

There are numerous Rose foods designed to create beautiful blooms and lush, green foliage...and probably just as many opinions on how to do it. The one thing all Rosarians agree on is that Roses love to be fed! Some folks are very successful using all organics, such as composted manures, cottonseed meal, bone meal, green sand and compost. Others are equally successful with commercially packaged formulated Rose food. There are even foods that contain systemic insecticides which some Rosarians swear by. The best recommendation we can make is to have your local garden center help determine what your plant's specific needs are. Have a soil test taken and bring the results with you on your visit. Then, experiment to see what works for you and your Roses.

Additional advice for proper care:

Be sure to consider insecticide and fungicide sprays in your Grandiflora maintenance program. Keeping the plants clean of damaged leaves and keeping them healthy by feeding can be the first steps to successful Rose gardening. Consult your local garden center for the proper Rose care products for Grandiflora in your area.

Roses, Ground Cover

Rosa

This group of Roses has become quite popular only in the last decade. Imagine an entire landscape peppered with the beauty and fragrance which only the Rose can offer. They are a constant source of color in the garden from Spring until late Fall, and there is a vast selection of colors to choose from. There are even some newer cultivars with semi-evergreen foliage which make ground cover Roses a consideration in a Tennessee garden.

WHEN TO PLANT:

All Roses do best when planted in a dormant stage, but once the rose breaks dormancy, you can be successful in planting them throughout the growing season.

WHY YOU PLANT:

Roses are one of the few plants that can provide constant color and fragrance in the garden from Spring through Fall. Their beauty can be enjoyed outdoors, and their flowers can be cut and savored indoors. The ground cover rose can even be planted on steep banks.

WHERE YOU PLANT:

Roses must be in at least five hours of intense sunshine to thrive, and they prefer full sun all day. Roses also require good, organic-enriched soil with excellent drainage. The ground cover Rose is excellent for planting in masses, or in large "pockets" of color. You may even utilize these Roses in large planters and in window boxes.

HOW YOU PLANT:

Dig up or till the soil and blend in plenty of organic humus, peat moss and composted cow manure into the existing soil. Once the soil and amendments are all blended, remove enough to create a hole large enough to accommodate the Rose's roots.

If you are planting a boxed or container Rose, be very careful when removing the box or pot. Try to keep the ball intact and place gently into the hole. If you are planting a grafted Rose, you will need to make sure the bud union (the swollen bulge at the base of the plant) is just above the soil level. This is where the desirable hybrid Rose is grafted onto wild Rose root stock. Carefully backfill the hole and firmly pack the soil until level with the existing ground. Water-in well with a liquid root stimulator and then mulch with pine mulch or pine straw.

When planting bareroot Roses, be sure you handle with care! The roots need to be spread out and placed on a small mound you have built up in the bottom of the planting hole. This will ensure good root-to-soil contact and reduce the chance for development of air pockets around the roots.

WHEN YOU WATER:

Although Roses must be in well-drained soil, they love lots of water during the growing season. They will certainly survive with once-a-week watering, or even less after getting established the first year. The more often you water, the better off the Rose will be. When watering, keep the foliage dry. Water in the morning and keep in mind that Roses would much rather have one good soaking rather than three or four sprinklings per week. As a rule, Roses prefer 1-2" of water per week and need moisture to penetrate 18" deep. When in doubt, use a moisture meter to check the efficiency of your watering. Some Rosarians use drip irrigation, soaker hoses and even bubbler attachments on their hoses to aid in their watering.

HOW/WHEN YOU PRUNE:

Roses love to be trimmed often, using quality pruning shears. Prune in late Fall to early Winter, leaving enough cane so you can prune off Winter damage in the Spring. Ground cover

Roses are not picky about their pruning requirements. One good trimming of at least one-third of the growth in early Spring would be sufficient. Also when pruning, you should consider sealing your cuts to prevent Rose Borer infestation. Seal each cut with a tree wound dressing compound or you can even use regular household white glue. Some Rosarians have been known to color the glue with black or green food coloring to avoid the distraction of the white spots!

HOW/WHEN YOU FERTILIZE:

There are numerous Rose foods designed to create beautiful blooms and lush, green foliage...and probably just as many opinions on how to do it. The one thing all Rosarians agree on is that Roses love to be fed! Some folks are very successful using all organics, such as composted manures, cottonseed meal, bone meal, green sand and compost. Others are equally successful with commercially-packaged formulated Rose food. There are even foods that contain systemic insecticides which some Rosarians swear by. The best recommendation we can make is to have your local garden center help determine what your plant's specific needs are. Have a soil test taken and bring the results with you on your visit. Then, experiment to see what works for you and your Roses.

ADDITIONAL ADVICE FOR PROPER CARE:

Be sure to consider insecticide and fungicide sprays as part of your maintenance program. Keeping the plants clean of damaged leaves and keeping them healthy can be the first steps to successful Roses.

Roses, Hybrid Tea
Rosa

Of all the selections to choose from in the "World of Roses," the Hybrid Tea is by far the most popular. This is the one you give to the girlfriend or wife to get out of the doghouse. It is the long stems and beautiful blooms which make this the Rose of choice. The colors are truly endless and the fragrances can range from sweet and fruity to bold and spicy.

WHEN TO PLANT:
All Roses do best when planted in their dormant stage, but once the rose breaks dormancy, you can be successful in planting them throughout the growing season.

WHY YOU PLANT:
Roses are one of the few plants that can provide constant color and fragrance in the garden from Spring through Fall. Their beauty can be enjoyed outdoors, and their flowers can be cut and savored indoors as well. Hybrid Tea Roses are the eternal expression of love for that special someone.

WHERE YOU PLANT:
Roses must be in at least five hours of intense sunshine to thrive, and they prefer full sun all day. Roses also require good, organic-enriched soil with excellent drainage. Hybrid Teas need the most maintenance of all Roses, so be sure when planting them to provide enough room to comfortably move around them for spraying and fertilizing. Most people will devote one particular garden just to Hybrid Tea Roses.

HOW YOU PLANT:
Dig up or till the soil and blend in plenty of organic humus, peat moss and composted cow manure into the existing soil. Once the soil and amendments are all blended, remove enough

to create a hole large enough to accommodate the Rose's roots. If you are planting a boxed or container Rose, be very careful when removing the box or pot. Try to keep the ball intact and place gently into the hole. If you are planting a grafted Rose, you will need to make sure the bud union (the swollen bulge at the base of the plant) is just above the soil level. This is where the desirable hybrid Rose is grafted onto wild Rose root stock. Carefully backfill the hole and firmly pack the soil until level with the existing ground. Water-in well with a liquid root stimulator and then mulch with pine mulch or pine straw.

When planting bareroot Roses, be sure you handle with care! The roots need to be spread out and placed on a small mound you have built up in the bottom of the planting hole. This will ensure good root-to-soil contact and reduce the chance for development of air pockets around the roots.

WHEN YOU WATER:

Although Roses must be in well-drained soil, they love lots of water during the growing season. They will certainly survive with once-a-week watering, or even less after getting established the first year. The more often you water, the better off the Rose will be. When watering, keep the foliage dry. Water in the morning and keep in mind that Roses would much rather have one good soaking rather than three or four sprinklings per week. As a rule, Roses prefer 1-2″ of water per week and need moisture to penetrate 18″ deep. When in doubt, use a moisture meter to check the efficiency of your watering. Some Rosarians use drip irrigation, soaker hoses and even bubbler attachments on their hoses to aid in their watering.

HOW/WHEN YOU PRUNE:

Roses love to be trimmed often, using quality pruning shears. Prune in late Fall to early Winter, leaving enough cane so you can prune off Winter damage in the Spring. When cutting to create bouquets, be sure to cut at an angle right above a leaf node and before the first set of five or more leaves. Put them in water as soon as possible. Also when pruning, you should consider sealing your cuts to prevent Rose Borer infestation. Seal each cut with a tree wound dressing compound or you can even use regular household white glue. Some Rosarians have been known to color the glue with black or green food coloring to avoid the distraction of the white spots!

HOW/WHEN YOU FERTILIZE:

There are numerous Rose foods designed to create beautiful blooms and lush, green foliage...and probably just as many opinions on how to do it. The one thing all Rosarians agree on is that Roses love to be fed! Some folks are very successful using all organics, such as composted manures, cottonseed meal, bone meal, green sand and compost. Others are equally successful with commercially packaged formulated Rose food. There are even foods that contain systemic insecticides which some Rosarians swear by. The best recommendation we can make is to have your local garden center help determine what your plant's specific needs are. Have a soil test taken and bring the results with you on your visit. Then, experiment to see what works for you and your Roses.

ADDITIONAL ADVICE FOR PROPER CARE:

Be sure to consider an insecticide and fungicide spray and feeding program for your Hybrid Teas. Keeping the plants clean of damaged leaves and keeping them healthy by feeding can be the first steps to successful Rose gardening. A program approach is the key to successfully growing Hybrid Teas, so consult your local garden center for the proper program and products.

Roses, Miniature
Rosa

These little jewels are Tennessee's best-kept secret in the Rose world. Because they are not grafted and grow on their own root stock, they will handle our unpredictable Winters like the little troopers they are, peeking their small heads out as the Spring arrives. These miniatures are great to plant as a border in a perennial or shrub bed. They are available in a vast selection of colors and cultivars. Like an intricate tapestry, these tiny gems will lend a visually captivating element to any garden area.

WHEN TO PLANT:

All Roses do best when planted in their dormant stage, but once the rose breaks dormancy, you can be successful in planting them throughout the growing season.

WHY YOU PLANT:

Roses are one of the few plants that can provide constant color and fragrance in the garden from Spring through Fall. Their beauty can be enjoyed outdoors, and their flowers can be cut and savored indoors as well.

WHERE YOU PLANT:

Roses must be in at least five hours of intense sunshine to thrive, and they prefer full sun all day. Roses also require good organic-enriched soil with excellent drainage. The Miniatures may be planted in hanging baskets, patio containers and even as a mass border for your flower and shrub beds.

HOW YOU PLANT:

Dig or till up the soil and blend plenty of organic humus, peat moss and composted cow manure into the existing soil. Once the soil and amendments are blended, remove enough to create a hole large enough to accommodate the Rose's roots. If you are planting a boxed or container Rose, be very careful when removing the box or pot. Try to keep the "ball" intact and place gently into the hole. If you are planting a grafted Rose, you will need to make sure the bud union (the swollen bulge at the base of the plant) is just above the soil level. This is where the desirable hybrid Rose is grafted onto a wild Rose root stock. Carefully backfill the hole and firmly pack the soil until level with the existing ground. You may water in well with a liquid root stimulator and then mulch with pine mulch or pine straw. When planting in a container, be sure it has good drainage and a very rich, but porous soil. You should move the container to shelter during severe Winters.

When planting bareroot Roses, be sure you handle with care! The roots need to be spread out and placed on a small mound you have built up in the bottom of the planting hole. This will ensure good root-to-soil contact and reduce the chance for development of air pockets around the roots.

WHEN YOU WATER:
Although Roses must be in well-drained soil, they love lots of water during the growing season. They will certainly survive with once-a-week watering, or even less after getting established the first year. The more often you water, the better off the Rose will be. When watering, keep the foliage dry. Water in the morning and keep in mind that Roses would much rather have one good soaking rather than three or four sprinklings per week. As a rule, Roses prefer 1-2" of water per week and need moisture to penetrate 18" deep. When in doubt, use a moisture meter to check the efficiency of your watering. Some Rosarians use drip irrigation, soaker hoses and even bubbler attachments on their hoses to aid in their watering.

HOW/WHEN YOU PRUNE:
Prune your Miniatures back one-half in late Fall. In mid-April,

you should cut canes back to active new growth, and remove any Winter-damaged canes to maintain an appealing and healthy appearance. Also when pruning, you should consider sealing your cuts to prevent Rose Borer infestation. Seal each cut with a tree wound dressing compound or you can even use regular household white glue. Some Rosarians have been known to color the glue with black or green food coloring to avoid the distraction of the white spots!

How/When you fertilize:

There are numerous Rose foods designed to create beautiful blooms and lush, green foliage...and probably just as many opinions on how to do it. The one thing all Rosarians agree on is that Roses love to be fed! Some folks are very successful using all organics, such as composted manures, cottonseed meal, bone meal, green sand and compost. Others are equally successful with commercially packaged formulated Rose food. There are even foods that contain systemic insecticides which some Rosarians swear by. The best recommendation we can make is to have your local garden center help determine what your plant's specific needs are. Have a soil test taken and bring the results with you on your visit. Then, experiment to see what works for you and your Roses.

Additional advice for proper care:

Be sure to keep a look out for White Powdery Mildew and Blackspot. If either occurs, spray with a fungicide and remove all infected foliage in and around the plants. You may also want to consider a spray program prescribed by your local garden center to ensure the health of these petite beauties. After pruning in late Fall, consider a light mulching of pine straw over the entire plant for Winter protection. Remove in early Spring.

Roses, Old Garden
Rosa

This group of Roses is certainly making a comeback in popularity all over the country. In Tennessee gardens, Old Garden Roses are sought after because of their hardiness, disease resistance and heavy fragrance, unlike many of the newer Hybrid Teas. The Old Garden Rose category consists of Roses that were introduced prior to 1867, making them the true matriarchs of any Rose garden. From single blooms to the Cabbage Rose 'Centifolia,' the colors are vast and the heights range from 3-9 feet.

WHEN TO PLANT:

The best time for planting is either Fall or early Spring. These popular varieties are sometimes not as easy to locate as other types of Roses, therefore, purchase them early when the selection is best.

WHY YOU PLANT:

Old Garden Roses are planted because their old-fashioned look is reminiscent of grandmother's garden. Also, the renewed interest in them is quite understandable because of the gorgeous, fragrant blooms these Roses offer. They are quite rugged during our hot, dry Summers and they have few problems with insects and diseases. Old Garden Roses should not be limited to just the formal Rose garden. They can be worked into the permanent landscape, a perennial backdrop, or even in a large urn or patio container.

WHERE YOU PLANT:

Roses must be in at least five hours of intense sunshine to thrive, and they prefer full sun all day. Roses also require good organic-enriched soil with excellent drainage. Old Garden Roses are ideal for the formal Rose garden, but they also may be planted in the general landscape, or even in containers.

HOW YOU PLANT:

Dig or till up the soil and blend plenty of organic humus, peat moss and composted cow manure into the existing soil. Once the soil and amendments are all blended, remove enough to create a hole large enough to accommodate the Rose's roots. If you are planting a boxed or container Rose, be very careful when removing the box or pot. Try to keep the "ball" intact and place gently into the hole. If you are planting a grafted Rose, you will need to make sure the bud union (the swollen bulge at the base of the plant) is just above the soil level. This is where the desirable hybrid Rose is grafted onto a wild Rose root stock. Carefully backfill the hole and firmly pack the soil until level with the existing ground. You may water in well with a liquid root stimulator and then mulch with pine mulch or pine straw. When planting in a container, be sure it has good drainage and a very rich, but porous soil. You should move the container to shelter during severe Winters.

When planting bareroot Roses, be sure you handle with care! The roots need to be spread out and placed on a small mound you have built up in the bottom of the planting hole. This will ensure good root-to-soil contact and reduce the chance for development of air pockets around the roots.

WHEN YOU WATER:

Although Roses must be in well-drained soil, they love lots of water during the growing season. They will certainly survive with once-a-week watering, or even less after getting established the first year. The more often you water, the better off the Rose will be. When watering, keep the foliage dry. Water in the morning and keep in mind that Roses would much rather have one good soaking rather than three or four sprinklings per week. As a rule, Roses prefer 1-2" of water per week and need moisture to penetrate 18" deep. When in doubt, use a moisture meter to check the efficiency of your watering. Some Rosarians use drip irrigation, soaker hoses and even bubbler attachments on their hoses to aid in their watering.

HOW/WHEN YOU PRUNE:

Roses love to be trimmed often, using quality pruning shears. Prune in late Fall to early Winter leaving enough cane so you can prune off Winter damage in the Spring. Also when pruning, you should consider sealing your cuts to prevent Rose Borer infestation. Seal each cut with a tree wound dressing compound or you can even use regular household white glue. Some Rosarians have been known to color the glue with black or green food coloring to avoid the distraction of the white spots!

HOW/WHEN YOU FERTILIZE:

There are numerous Rose foods designed to create beautiful blooms and lush, green foliage...and probably just as many opinions on how to do it. The one thing all Rosarians agree on is that Roses love to be fed! Some folks are very successful using all organics, such as composted manures, cottonseed meal, bone meal, green sand and compost. Others are equally successful with commercially packaged formulated Rose food. There are even foods that contain systemic insecticides which some Rosarians swear by. The best recommendation we can make is to have your local garden center help determine what your plant's specific needs are. Have a soil test taken and bring the results with you on your visit. Then, experiment to see what works for you and your Roses.

ADDITIONAL ADVICE FOR PROPER CARE:

Special care isn't really needed when growing these Old Roses. You can spray with dormant oil during the Winter and repeat in Spring.

Roses, Polyantha
Rosa

Polyantha Roses were introduced in the late 19th Century. These low growing Roses are now available in single, semi-double and double blooms, and colors range from yellow, orange, red and white to all shades of coral, salmon and pink. Polyanthas are a cross between the Asian Multiflora and Hybrid Teas, and are known for the hundreds of blooms they offer. Here in Tennessee, they begin blooming in Spring and hardly take a break until late Fall. Most varieties grow to a height and a spread of 2-3 feet, but some will reach up to 5 feet tall. The 'Fairy' is an old favorite that was introduced in the 1930s. It produces large clusters of 1 1/2" fragrant, double pink blooms. The bush is very compact, has deep, glossy green foliage, and features disease-resistance like other Polyanthas.

WHEN TO PLANT:

Fall or early Spring is the ideal time to plant. However, most garden centers will have selections throughout the growing season. Your Polyantha can be a success no matter when it is planted if proper care is taken after planting.

WHY YOU PLANT:

Polyantha Roses have a wonderful ability to bloom from Spring all the way into late Fall. Some varieties are fragrant and have an abundance of blooms, made even more appealing by the fact that they are disease-resistant and require little maintenance as compared to the Hybrid Teas.

WHERE YOU PLANT:

Make sure you select a spot with good drainage and full sun, but don't limit your choice only to the formal rose garden. Allow your Polyantha to share a space in your perennial or flower bed, or give them a try in large patio pots and containers. Steep slopes and banks may also be covered effectively with the Polyantha.

HOW YOU PLANT:

Dig or till up the soil and blend plenty of organic humus, peat moss and composted cow manure into the existing soil. Once the soil and amendments are all blended, remove enough to create a hole large enough to accommodate the Rose's roots. If you are planting a boxed or container Rose, be very careful when removing the box or pot. Try to keep the "ball" intact and place gently into the hole. If you are planting a grafted Rose, you will need to make sure the bud union (the swollen bulge at the base of the plant) is just above the soil level. This is where the desirable hybrid Rose is grafted onto a wild Rose root stock. Carefully backfill the hole and firmly pack the soil until level with the existing ground. You may water in well with a liquid root stimulator and then mulch with pine mulch or pine straw. When planting in a container, be sure it has good drainage and a very rich, but porous soil. You should move the container to shelter during severe Winters.

When planting bareroot Roses, be sure you handle with care! The roots need to be spread out and placed on a small mound you have built up in the bottom of the planting hole. This will ensure good root-to-soil contact and reduce the chance for development of air pockets around the roots.

WHEN YOU WATER:

Although Roses must be in well-drained soil, they love lots of water during the growing season. They will certainly survive with once-a-week watering, or even less after getting established the first year. The more often you water, the better off the Rose will be. When watering, keep the foliage dry. Water in the morning and keep in mind that Roses would much rather have one good soaking rather than three or four sprinklings per week. As a rule, Roses prefer 1-2" of water per week and need moisture to penetrate 18" deep. When in doubt, use a moisture meter to check the efficiency of your watering. Some Rosarians use drip irrigation, soaker hoses and even bubbler attachments on their hoses to aid in their watering.

How/When you prune:

Not much pruning is really necessary with Polyanthas, as part of their charm is their carefree natural growth habit. A good pruning in Winter or early Spring is recommended, when you prune back halfway and remove any dead wood from inside the bush. Also when pruning, you should consider sealing your cuts to prevent Rose Borer infestation. Seal each cut with a tree wound dressing compound or you can even use regular household white glue. Some Rosarians have been known to color the glue with black or green food coloring to avoid the distraction of the white spots!

How/When you fertilize:

There are numerous Rose foods designed to create beautiful blooms and lush, green foliage...and probably just as many opinions on how to do it. The one thing all Rosarians agree on is that Roses love to be fed! Some folks are very successful using all organics, such as composted manures, cottonseed meal, bone meal, green sand and compost. Others are equally successful with commercially packaged formulated Rose food. There are even foods that contain systemic insecticides which some Rosarians swear by. The best recommendation we can make is to have your local garden center help determine what your plant's specific needs are. Have a soil test taken and bring the results with you on your visit. Then, experiment to see what works for you and your Roses.

Additional advice for proper care:

Very little care is needed. Once the large clusters of blooms have "done their thing," you may prune and remove these clusters to make room for more. Spray with dormant oil in Spring after new growth has emerged, but prior to first blooms to help prevent insect problems.

Roses, Shrub and Hedge

Rosa

This is the perfect selection for the beginning Rosarian. Great success may be achieved by planting a hedge or shrub Rose, giving the "budding" Rose gardener a great boost of confidence that may not be achieved as easily with the more difficult Hybrid Tea varieties. 'Bonica' is a pale, but showy, clear pink and is a prolific bloomer, growing to 4-5 feet in height and width. A tamer version would be the 'Simplicity' hedge rose, which is available in bright pink, white and red. The 'Meidiland' is a series which comes in an array of colors and remains quite compact in height, and spreads full and dense (approximately 2 feet in height and 2-3 feet in width). Regardless of the choice, each of these is a comparatively "forgiving" beauty as compared to their more demanding sister varieties.

WHEN TO PLANT:

All Roses do best when planted during their dormant stage, but once the Rose breaks dormancy, you can be successful in planting them throughout the growing season.

WHY YOU PLANT:

Roses are one of the few plants that can provide constant color and fragrance in the garden from Spring through Fall. Their beauty can be enjoyed outdoors, and their flowers can be cut and savored indoors as well. These Roses are sure to provide confidence for the gardener while they provide beauty in the garden.

WHERE YOU PLANT:

Roses must be in at least five hours of intense sunshine to thrive, and they prefer full sun all day. Roses also require good, organic-enriched soil with excellent drainage. The Hedge Rose can be planted to perform just as its name implies, creating a beautiful hedge.

How you plant:

Dig or till up the soil and blend plenty of organic humus, peat moss and composted cow manure into the existing soil. Once the soil and amendments are all blended, remove enough to create a hole large enough to accommodate the Rose's roots. If you are planting a boxed or container Rose, be very careful when removing the box or pot. Try to keep the "ball" intact and place gently into the hole. If you are planting a grafted Rose, you will need to make sure the bud union (the swollen bulge at the base of the plant) is just above the soil level. This is where the desirable hybrid Rose is grafted onto a wild Rose root stock. Carefully backfill the hole and firmly pack the soil until level with the existing ground. You may water in well with a liquid root stimulator and then mulch with pine mulch or pine straw. When planting in a container, be sure it has good drainage and a very rich, but porous soil. You should move the container to shelter during severe Winters.

When planting bareroot Roses, be sure you handle with care! The roots need to be spread out and placed on a small mound you have built up in the bottom of the planting hole. This will ensure good root-to-soil contact and reduce the chance for development of air pockets around the roots.

When you water:

Although Roses must be in well-drained soil, they love lots of water during the growing season. They will certainly survive with once-a-week watering, or even less after getting established the first year. The more often you water, the better off the Rose will be. When watering, keep the foliage dry. Water in the morning and keep in mind that Roses would much rather have one good soaking rather than three or four sprinklings per week. As a rule, Roses prefer 1-2" of water per week and need moisture to penetrate 18" deep. When in doubt, use a moisture meter to check the efficiency of your watering. Some Rosarians use drip irrigation, soaker hoses and even bubbler attachments on their hoses to aid in their watering.

How/When you prune:

Roses love to be trimmed often, and you should always use quality pruning shears. Prune in late Fall to early Winter, and leave enough to be able to prune off Winter damage in the Spring. Shrub roses need to be pruned back at least by one-half to the ground each year, and one-third of the older canes removed every 2-3 years. Also when pruning, you should consider sealing your cuts to prevent Rose Borer infestation. Seal each cut with a tree wound dressing compound or you can even use regular household white glue. Some Rosarians have been known to color the glue with black or green food coloring to avoid the distraction of the white spots!

How/When you fertilize:

There are numerous Rose foods designed to create beautiful blooms and lush, green foliage...and probably just as many opinions on how to do it. The one thing all Rosarians agree on is that Roses love to be fed! Some folks are very successful using all organics, such as composted manures, cottonseed meal, bone meal, green sand and compost. Others are equally successful with commercially packaged formulated Rose food. There are even foods that contain systemic insecticides which some Rosarians swear by. The best recommendation we can make is to have your local garden center help determine what your plant's specific needs are. Have a soil test taken and bring the results with you on your visit. Then, experiment to see what works for you and your Roses.

Additional advice for proper care:

Hedge and Shrub Roses take the least amount of care in the "family of roses." Watch for White Powdery Mildew and Blackspot. If either occurs, spray with a fungicide and remove all infected foliage in and around the plants. You may also want to consider a spray program prescribed by your local garden center.

Herbs

MANY A BOOK HAS BEEN WRITTEN exclusively on the subject of Herbs. These wonderful little gifts from God have so many benefits, you could probably dedicate a volume to each of them individually.

Besides using Herbs to lend flavor to favorite recipes, there is also a world of medicinal applications of Herbs benefiting the human body, though this usage is the source of considerable debate.

In Tennessee, we are blessed with the ability to grow a vast selection of advantageous Herbs. Some are treated as perennials and the seed for others is sown annually, with abundant harvests throughout the growing seasons.

Herbs are what you might call the "team players", the unsung heroes of your garden. They aren't really too particular about the quality of the soil where they are planted, and they don't need a great amount of food. These plants add a natural ornamental dimension to any garden, give zest to that recipe needing a little something, and maybe even cure what ails you.

Another use for Herbs is right at your back door. Why not add some Herbs to your patio pots and even window boxes? We've added some of the fragrant low-growing thymes and even rosemary to our mixed flowering container gardens for a great contrast of color and fragrance.

Hanging baskets are another opportunity to enjoy Herbs with easy access and mobility. You may have even considered cultivating your own little indoor windowsill Herb garden through our bleak Tennessee winters.

Whether planting Herbs for their medicinal, culinary or ornamental value, they make a worthy addition to your Tennessee garden. If you are new to Herbs, give them a try—they are easy to grow and eager to please.

Basil

Ocimum basilicum

This particular Herb is an annual and is mostly grown for its culinary purposes. It is wonderful in Italian dishes, pesto, soups, sauces, and more. There are many new varieties such as lemon, cinnamon, chocolate, lettuce leaf, purple, and the list goes on. All are simple to grow and are rapid performers.

There has been a real interest in Basil for ornamental use in perennial and flower gardens. 'Purple Ruffles' has a wonderful deep, rich purple color and as its name implies, very frilly foliage. This Basil variety is wonderful in a garden for its striking contrast of color. Another Basil, utilized as a border plant, is 'Spicy Globe.' From afar, its small, compact growth habit almost looks like a Korean or miniature Boxwood. It has been used to completely border small Herb gardens and even used in Knot gardens.

WHEN TO PLANT:

Most Basils do just fine when seeds are sown directly in the ground after the last chance of a killing frost. In Tennessee, this is usually between April 15th and April 20th. To get a real head start, you may begin sowing seeds indoors in February or March.

WHY YOU PLANT:

Basil is a very popular culinary Herb utilized in gardens throughout the South, enjoyed from April through late Summer. It has wonderful versatility from a gorgeous presence in the garden to a tasty hint in favorite Italian dishes.

WHERE YOU PLANT:

The best location for Basil is definitely in the sun. Basil can be planted in containers with other companion plants or by itself. Basil can also be used directly in a vegetable or Herb garden and in rows or "pockets." Smaller dwarf varieties can be planted around the border of an Herb garden or utilized very strikingly in a Knot garden.

HOW YOU PLANT:

Till or work up the soil and sow the seed according to the seed packet directions. If transplanting small plants, carefully loosen the roots before planting directly in the soil. Utilize a good soil amendment, then water-in well with root stimulator fertilizer.

WHEN YOU WATER:

Basils are "heavy drinkers." They really need a good amount of water during the beginning of their heavy growing season. This will be at least two times a week, and more if they are in containers. During the heat of the Summer, water them at least once a week if they are in the garden, or twice a week if they are in containers. Do not allow them to become dry.

HOW/WHEN YOU PRUNE:

Pruning or harvesting the plant is a must! The flowers should be constantly pinched off and removed. Allowing the plant to bloom slows up production of foliage, the most common reason for growing this plant. Whenever you need to harvest leaves for the kitchen, snip the desired amount with scissors, and the plant will naturally fork or branch out with new growth at that point. This will actually increase the plant's overall production. Be sure to harvest the entire plant before our first killing frost. Basil is a tender plant and is not at all cold-tolerant.

HOW/WHEN YOU FERTILIZE:

Like most Herbs, Basil is not a heavy feeder. If you have poor soil quality, you may want to consider an organic food such as fish emulsion or liquid kelp.

ADDITIONAL ADVICE FOR PROPER CARE:

Be sure to allow plenty of room in your garden for this vigorous grower. Some varieties will grow to 3-4 feet tall with a spread of 2-3 feet. Do not transplant new plants into the garden too soon, since Basil is very sensitive to cold temperatures.

Chives

Allium schoenoprasum

This versatile perennial Herb is a must in any flower, Herb or window sill garden. This plant will add great vertical contrast and drama wherever it is planted. The flower is quite noticeable compared to most Herb flowers. The blooms are a showy, fluffy globe-shaped pink ball on a slender stem. The blooms can be enjoyed in arrangements or in the garden. This plant is quite easy to grow and will grace your garden for years to come.

WHEN TO PLANT:
The prime time to plant Chives is in the early Fall or Spring. You can plant any time the ground is not frozen.

WHY YOU PLANT:
The most common use for Chives is for scattering on top of a steaming baked potato. This plant is also incredibly maintenance free and quite showy, with striking dramatic lines. The blooms can be dried and enjoyed in arrangements for home or office.

WHERE YOU PLANT:
This great little Herb is wonderful in a patio or windowsill container. Be sure to give it at least a half-day of sunlight, and well-drained soil if planted in the ground. If you want to use it fresh in the kitchen, plant it close by for easy picking!

HOW YOU PLANT:
Plant directly in the ground by digging a hole at least the size of the plant's root ball. Work up the soil and add a little soil conditioner, such as organic humus. Return the blended soil to the hole. Choose a clay pot for container planting. Use a rich but porous soil, similar to Pro-Mix or Metro-Mix, and be sure the pot has good drainage.

WHEN YOU WATER:

Allow the plant to dry out slightly between waterings. If this is its first year, water at least once a week during Spring and Fall, and two times a week during the hot Summer. Those planted in a container need to be watered a little more often.

HOW/WHEN YOU PRUNE:

You may cut or snip the onion-like foliage anytime you need some Chives in the kitchen. After a hard freeze, remove dead growth, lightly mulch and mark the location with a label.

HOW/WHEN YOU FERTILIZE:

Chives do not need much extra fertilizer if they are planted in decent soil. If you choose to feed, utilize a mild organic food like blood meal or cottonseed meal, and limit to two feedings during the growing season.

ADDITIONAL ADVICE FOR PROPER CARE:

Be sure to select a spot that has good drainage and gets a half-day of sun, preferably during the intense afternoon period.

Coriander/Cilantro

Coriandrum sativum

This particular Herb has become popular in the last few years. Many Southwestern dishes make frequent use of Coriander, also known as Cilantro. The seeds of Coriander are utilized in pickling and hot spiced drinks. This plant is easy to grow and it can be planted from seed or small transplants from the garden center or nursery. Coriander is an annual and, like most Herbs, prefers lots of bright, direct sun.

WHEN TO PLANT:

Sow seeds for this variety indoors in February or March, and transplant outdoors in mid-April. However, most avid gardeners simply wait until April or May and sow seeds directly into the garden.

WHY YOU PLANT:
Coriander has really increased in popularity in recent years. This Herb has been utilized in Mediterranean, Latin American, Spanish and even Oriental cooking. It is grown for its foliage and seeds, and most say a little will go a long way!

WHERE YOU PLANT:
Coriander prefers a very bright, sunny location, whether in the ground or in a container on the deck or patio. Soil quality is not crucial, however, a loose soil makes it easier on both the gardener and the plants' roots. Make sure the soil has decent drainage.

HOW YOU PLANT:
Sow Coriander seed in rows directly in the garden following directions on the seed packet. Some gardeners, especially those with small spaces, will plant two or three transplants purchased from a grower or garden center.

WHEN YOU WATER:
Water well just after planting. Coriander prefers weekly watering or twice weekly in extreme heat.

HOW/WHEN YOU PRUNE:
Harvest Coriander as often as you need it. If drying and storing it for later use, harvest the entire plant just before Fall. Simply pull up and hang to dry. Also, the seeds can be gathered and stored.

WALT'S WISDOM

Test your good manners by tolerating bad manners.

HOW/WHEN YOU FERTILIZE:

Coriander is not a heavy feeder. If you choose to, broadcast an organic fertilizer in Spring, and repeat this later in the Summer or in early Fall.

ADDITIONAL ADVICE FOR PROPER CARE:

Like most Herbs, Coriander is almost maintenance free. The plants will almost take care of themselves. If you are growing the plant for foliage, you should trim potential blooms to prevent seed production. Obviously, if seeds are what you are after, let it bloom!

Dill

Anethum graveolens

This Herb is extremely easy to grow and its appearance takes on the same carefree look. Almost fern-like, the airy foliage is actually quite sturdy. The plant can grow 1-3 feet tall and has a bloom that looks like yellow Queen Anne's Lace.

WHEN TO PLANT:

Sow the seeds as early as April and continue every 2-3 weeks to ensure a steady harvest through Fall.

WHY YOU PLANT:

This great Herb is used extensively in pickling. Fresh Dill is used as a garnish in soups, salads, breads, meats, etc.

WHERE YOU PLANT:

Dill, as most Herbs, does best in full sun. Preferably, Dill is planted in vegetable garden rows, but it also has been spotted in clumps or pockets in the perennial border.

HOW YOU PLANT:
Simply till up the soil and rake or scatter seed, then lightly cover with a layer of loose soil. Always follow instructions on the seed packet.

WHEN YOU WATER:
Water well twice weekly and once plants are at least 4-6" high, water once a week.

HOW/WHEN YOU PRUNE:
Harvest as needed by cutting at the base of the plant. Hang, dry, then collect the Dill seeds, if desired. This can be done after blooms have faded.

HOW/WHEN YOU FERTILIZE:
No fertilization is really necessary. If you have very poor soil, work in peat moss or organic humus during the tilling process, before sowing seeds.

ADDITIONAL ADVICE FOR PROPER CARE:
If you have a small garden space, you may choose some of the smaller compact "bouquet" varieties.

Mint
Mentha

This is a great perennial for a Tennessee garden. Everyone can be a successful gardener with this aromatic, but sometimes massive plant. Mint is truly maintenance free if planted in a wet area. There are many varieties and new ones are being developed every couple of years. Mints do love damp areas, but can survive in dry spots, too. They will also adapt to almost any light condition.

WHEN TO PLANT:

Early Spring or Fall is the ideal time to plant this popular, fragrant Herb. If you get clumps, or a start from a friend, you can transplant them at any time of the year, as long as the soil is not frozen.

WHY YOU PLANT:

Mints are great to have at arm's reach to put in your iced tea or Mint Julep, for sipping under the big Magnolia your granddaddy planted so long ago. Also, Mint helps discourage certain garden pests, and can even be placed in cabinets or drawers to discourage insects.

WHERE YOU PLANT:

Mint is great for covering a large, hard-to-maintain area. Mint can really tolerate the extremes of soils; from a "bog-type" area, all the way to a dry clay soil. Be careful, though. Some varieties will become invasive and can even take over an Herb or flower garden. If dealing with limited space, you may want to consider planting Mint in a hanging basket or container. Choose a spot that gets some direct sun, even though Mints will tolerate shade.

HOW YOU PLANT:

There is not much preparation in planting Mint. The soil should be tilled, or "turned over." Plant in a hole that is at least the size of the root ball, or a little larger. Add some organic humus or peat moss.

WHEN YOU WATER:

Keep Mint moist when first established in the garden. If not planted in a "bog-type" area, Mint will need water two to three times a week. Mint can survive with less watering, but it will not thrive. Once established, very little care is needed.

HOW/WHEN YOU PRUNE:

Trim as needed for teas and culinary uses throughout the growing season. Just snip the stems with small pruners or scissors, making a cut just above a leaf node. After a hard freeze, go ahead and cut back, or simply remove all the foliage from the past season and mulch lightly.

How/When you fertilize:
Mints are not heavy feeders. If you choose to encourage growth from this naturally aggressive grower, you can use an organic food such as fish emulsion, blood meal or liquid kelp.

Additional advice for proper care:
Most people are amazed how rapidly Mints grow. The most popular and aggressive varieties are 'M. piperita' (peppermint) and 'M. spicata' (spearmint). A little on the less aggressive side are 'M. pulegium' (pennyroyal) and the tiny, more temperamental 'M. requienii' (corsican).

Parsley
Petroselinum crispum

This bright green Herb comes in several varieties that can grow from 10-18" high. Its popular use is as the garnish we all find on our dinner plates. The Italian variety, however, has gained interest from chefs. Parsley is considered a biennial Herb and is quite easy to grow. Its growth habit is a nice, compact bushy look.

When to plant:
Parsley seed can be sown outdoors in late April or started indoors in late Winter. Small starter plants from garden centers can be transplanted almost any time during the growing season, with proper care.

WHY YOU PLANT:

Parsley is a great plant that softens the look of the herb garden, and like most Herbs, it is quite care free. The culinary uses are not as vast as other Herbs. However, it is useful in the garden to attract caterpillars which, in turn, will become enjoyable butterflies.

WHERE YOU PLANT:

Plant Parsley in lots of sun and in soil that is well-drained. You could even try mixing it with other flowers in patio pots for a unique combination.

HOW YOU PLANT:

Simply follow directions on seed packets when sowing, or plant starter plants directly into loose soil. Loosen up the root ball carefully and place it in a hole a little larger than the ball. Cover with soil and water-in well.

WHEN YOU WATER:

If growing Parsley in containers, allow soil to slightly dry out between waterings. If planted in the Herb garden or flower bed, water well once a week during the growing season.

HOW/WHEN YOU PRUNE:

No pruning is necessary other than harvesting fresh sprigs for cooking. Simply snip with scissors.

HOW/WHEN YOU FERTILIZE:

No fertilizer is needed. Parsley will adapt to almost any soil condition. A light application of liquid kelp or fish emulsion could be applied once in late Spring.

ADDITIONAL ADVICE FOR PROPER CARE:

Remember, if you want future butterflies in your garden, allow the caterpillars to feed on your parsley. Just plant extra for them. If you do not want them, just remove the caterpillars.

Rosemary
Rosmarinus officinalis

Rosemary can boast being used by many Tennessee gardeners. The 'Arp' variety is the one most likely to survive our unpredictable Winters. Overall, this plant would be considered a half-hardy, or tender perennial. It is well worth a spot in your Herb or flower garden, whether it makes it through the Winter or not. Rosemary has intense aromatic foliage - not many Herbs are as profusely fragrant. The plant can be used dried or fresh in cooking. Also, it is wonderful for homemade skin and hair care products. Potpourris are made from Rosemary foliage and its petite blue blooms. The plant will grow from 2-3 feet tall if over-Wintered indoors in a container. Also, it is a real sun-lover. Like most Herbs, Rosemary has an endless list of uses, other than just being ornamental.

WALT'S WISDOM

Our duty is not to see through someone, but to see someone through.

WHEN TO PLANT:
Rosemary does best if placed outdoors between March and May. It could be transplanted at almost any time if proper care is taken afterwards.

WHY YOU PLANT:
This plant is used almost exclusively for culinary purposes. However, many people highly recommend Rosemary for medicinal purposes as well.
The plant is of value to herbalists and for manufacturing fragrances. Also, it can also be used strictly as an ornamental.

WHERE YOU PLANT:
Rosemary thrives in extremely well-drained, loose soil. If planting in containers, use terra cotta pots and porous, rich soil. Select a spot with at least a half day to a full day of sun.

How you plant:

Be sure to plant Rosemary a little above the soil level, leaving one-fourth of the root exposed. Mound a mixture of organic humus and/or peat moss up around the base of the plant, covering the roots. In Middle and East Tennessee, you should place the planting pot in the ground, then remove it in the Fall to Winterize indoors.

When you water:

If Rosemary is planted in the ground, water well at least two times a week during the growing season. When established, water only once a week. Container plants need to be watered frequently (three times a week) in the Summer, and less often (once a week) in early Spring and late Fall.

How/When you prune:

You shouldn't have to worry about extensive pruning if you are harvesting Rosemary to preserve it. Use a small pair of pruners or garden scissors and trim stems. Where you make your cuts for harvesting is up to you.

How/When you fertilize:

Like most Herbs, Rosemary is not a heavy feeder, and one organic food application should be sufficient during the growing season. Try fish emulsion, liquid kelp, cottonseed or bone meal.

Additional advice for proper care:

Keeping your plant indoors through the Winter may prove a challenge. Rosemary loves as much direct light as possible but the dry heat indoors can be a problem. Good ventilation and humidity are helpful. During the growing season, move your plant outdoors and enjoy!

Sage
Salvia officinalis

New Sage varieties have come along recently to lend a little more excitement to the herb garden. There are variegated Sages with creamy yellow swirls and even a tri-color Sage with hues of pink, green and creamy white. Sage can grow 18-20" high and spread to almost the same width.

WHEN TO PLANT:
There are starter plants available almost year round in the garden centers that can be transplanted successfully. The best time to plant is Fall or early Spring. If sowing seeds, plant directly in the soil after April.

WHY YOU PLANT:
Sage is a tough perennial Herb that adds interest to any perennial or Herb garden. These plants are drought tolerant and do not get too invasive like other Herbs. Obviously, Sage is a valuable culinary Herb.

WHERE YOU PLANT:
All Sage varieties love to be planted in well-drained, full-sun gardens.

HOW YOU PLANT:
Sage is easy to transplant. Simply loosen the soil and dig a hole a little larger than the plant's root ball. Loosen the ball and place in the hole. Keep the root ball a little above the existing soil level. Then cover with loose soil and water well. It will eventually settle to ground level.

WHEN YOU WATER:
For the first year, water well once a week during the Summer months. Once established, little water is needed.

How/When you prune:
No pruning is necessary, other than harvesting Sage when needed.

How/When you fertilize:
Sage is not a heavy feeder. If you have poor soil, you may blend in organic humus or peat moss when planting.

Additional advice for proper care:
Not much special care is needed for Sage. The most important care factors are proper drainage and lots of sun.

Thyme
Thymus vulgaris

Thyme can be an asset in a Tennessee garden for so many reasons. In small gardens, it may become aggressive and overpowering. However, it is a full-sun, hardy semi-evergreen perennial ground cover. The successful Tennessee varieties are: Lemon Thyme, 'Doone's Valley,' 'Mother of Thyme' and several others. All have small clusters of blooms throughout the growing season. Some are showier in size and bloom color. The plant can spread 2-3 feet in diameter while growing no more than 4-6" tall.

When to plant:
Plant any "Thyme" when the ground is workable (not frozen). The very best "Thyme" is in early Spring or early Fall. However, the best nursery and garden center selections are available in April and May.

Why you plant:
Thyme has many ornamental, culinary, and fragrance benefits. Also, it is an incredibly tough ground cover. It will keep weeds smothered out with its mat-like growth habit.

WHERE YOU PLANT:

Plant in open areas that need coverage. Thyme is excellent when planted around walkways and stepping stones. Fragrance is immediately released when you touch it or brush against it. Make sure the plant is in full sun and in well-drained soil.

HOW YOU PLANT:

After selecting a good spot, dig a hole at least the size of the root ball. Add a small amount of amended soil and mix well before placing the plant in the hole. Plant slightly above ground and mound soil around it if drainage is a concern. Thyme does not like "wet feet."

WHEN YOU WATER:

Be sure to water well after planting. Thyme can handle dry spells, but benefits from watering once a week during the growing season.

HOW/WHEN YOU PRUNE:

Very little pruning is needed. If you are utilizing it in cooking, simply trim the new growth with scissors when desired. Prune approximately one-third to one-half off in Fall or early Spring. This should be done once yearly or at least every other year.

HOW/WHEN YOU FERTILIZE:

Thyme is not particular about feeding schedules. If planted in decent quality soil and full sun, it will spread wonderfully. If fed, certain varieties can be invasive.

ADDITIONAL ADVICE FOR PROPER CARE:

If planted around walkways and stepping stones, choose a variety with heavy fragrance, such as lemon Thyme. These plants are very hardy and practically maintenance free, with an incredibly aromatic payoff!

Notes:

Water & Bog Plants

*I*N THE PAST DECADE, WATER GARDENING has made a major comeback. One reason is that water gardens remind us of an earlier time. Some of us remember ponds and water gardens from childhood. They were magical places we fondly recall, full of the kinds of things that appeal to a child's imagination. Today, many families have learned they can recreate these memories right in the backyard, helping their children to begin their own special memories.

With so many different products available today, we can enjoy water gardening on the smallest scale, or create large, multi-level backyard ponds. Water gardening is three dimensional. We enjoy watching the fish swimming in the pond, enjoy the unique plant varieties that thrive in water and bog environments, and everyone agrees there is nothing more soothing and relaxing than the simple, serene sound of trickling water rolling off the edge of the rock ledges into your pond. The audio aspect of gardening can be fully appreciated with the addition of a backyard water garden.

C H A P T E R E I G H T

Tennesseans have an array of choices in water garden plants. From Winter-hardy blooming Water Lilies, to the exotic Lotus that needs over-Wintering care, many choices are available.

There are dozens of plants that can grace a small pond. Bog plants will perennially return to bloom at the water's edge in any region of our state. Then there are the free-spirited floating plants, such as Water Hyacinths. These harmless, inexpensive plants can actually take over a small pond in less than one growing season.

This type of gardening offers an entirely new landscaping option that many gardeners will find fascinating. Also, it can be started on a small scale, then expanded. Water gardening is definitely unique and can be gratifying for the entire family.

Cattails
Typha latifolia

Most every water garden or boggy area has a spot just waiting for Cattails. These great accents will grow from a dwarf variety of 2-3 feet all the way to 8 feet tall. These plants bloom in Summer with a moderately showy spike of beige flowers, and then later in Summer, the blooms are followed by a dark brown seed head, better known as the "Cattail." This plant is Winter-hardy in Tennessee and also can become a slight bit invasive. Be sure to stay with the dwarf varieties for the small garden pond.

WHEN TO PLANT:
Plant any time the Cattails are available to you and the ground is workable. Spring or Fall is your optimum time.

WHY YOU PLANT:
Vertical lines are a must in the flower and water garden. Nothing is more suitable to grace the edge of a water pond than a striking vertical feature.

WHERE YOU PLANT:
Cattails can be very helpful in an area that is too wet to grow other plants and they will fill in nicely. While Cattails will tolerate some shade, full sun is required to achieve blooms and then later, the "Cattails." Cattails must have plenty of moisture, so they do best in and around ponds or bogs.

HOW YOU PLANT:
Dig the hole somewhat larger than the clump, or root ball, and add some peat moss to the existing soil. Return the soil/peat mixture while you position the Cattails in the planting hole. You may choose to utilize Cattails as a single plant. If so, leave the plant in a pot and sink it in the pond a few inches below pot level. To avoid soil mixture floating away, add heavy pea gravel

on top of the soil before lowering into the pond.

WHEN YOU WATER:
If not planted in the pond, this plant will thrive with watering two to three times a week. Cattails will survive with little attention. However, they will not thrive without adequate water.

HOW/WHEN YOU PRUNE:
Very little pruning is necessary. Many water gardeners enjoy leaving dried foliage in place until early Spring. This does provide visual interest and the added benefit of the sound created by rustling of foliage in the wind during the Fall and Winter months.

HOW/WHEN YOU FERTILIZE:
Cattails do not require much feeding. Broadcast an organic fertilizer such as blood meal, bone meal, cottonseed meal or even liquid kelp around plant bases. Apply in Spring and follow up in Summer. Be careful of extreme temperatures when applying fertilizer.

ADDITIONAL ADVICE FOR PROPER CARE:
If harvesting stalks of Cattails for home decorating, be aware of the saying "timing is everything." You must cut them just as the color begins to darken on the tails. Then bring them in and hang in a dry, warm, dark location. If picked too late, Cattails can create a mess in the house.

Iris, Japanese and Siberian
Iris

This group of plants is related to our state flower. However, these are real lovers of mud! They perform best when planted at the water's edge or actually submerged in the pond, treating them like bog plants. The vertical lines are a real delight, plus the colors can range from purples to yellows, and even to a clear white. These Iris are hardy during the Winter and will give you lots of pleasure in and around the pond.

WHEN TO PLANT:
The best times to plant are Spring and Fall. You may actually transplant any time you wish, as long as the ground isn't frozen.

WHY YOU PLANT:
Japanese and Siberian Iris are often selected as focal points in and around the flower or water garden. The tall, striking vertical lines add visual interest, and when in bloom, they are very rewarding. This plant also is a delight to share because of its rapid growth habit.

WHERE YOU PLANT:
Lots of full sun is welcome to these Iris. However, you may get blooms with only a half day of sun.

The wetter the area, the better for these Iris. Those that thrive are planted just on the bank or edge of the pond. You may choose to actually submerge the plant in the pond, treating it like a bog plant.

HOW YOU PLANT:
Dig a hole as large as the clump or root ball and add some peat moss to the existing soil. Be sure to blend together. If you choose to utilize it as a single large plant, leave it in a pot and sink it in the pond a few inches below pot level. To avoid soil mixture floating away, add heavy pea gravel on top of soil before lowering into the pond.

WHEN YOU WATER:
If not planted in your pond, this plant will thrive with watering

two to three times a week. These Iris will survive with little attention. However, they will not thrive without adequate water.

HOW/WHEN YOU PRUNE:
Pruning should be done only at the end of the growing season. Once a hard frost has occurred, you may remove the submerged plant and cut it back to a height of two inches above the top of the water. Then set it back into the water for the Winter. If it is growing on the pond's edge, you can either cut it back in Winter or early Spring in the same manner.

HOW/WHEN YOU FERTILIZE:
Japanese and Siberian Iris do not require much feeding. Broadcast an organic fertilizer such as blood meal, bone meal, cottonseed meal or even liquid kelp around the bases of the plants. Apply in Spring and follow up in Summer. Be careful of extreme temperatures when applying fertilizer.

ADDITIONAL ADVICE FOR PROPER CARE:
You will need to be aware of the aggressive growth habit of these particular Iris, which requires that they be divided every 3-4 years. Also, the colors are exquisite, so you may choose to grow several varieties. Tennessee gardeners have found a favorite Siberian variety you may want to try called 'Caesar's Brother.'

Lotus
Nelumbo nucifera

This is the most incredible plant available to Tennessee water gardens! That's a strong statement to make, but this plant makes more than a large statement. These Lotus varieties can offer an impressive foliage size. The blue-green plate-like leaves can range in size from a dinner plate to 4 feet in diameter. Average foliage size in our region would be around 20-24" in

diameter, depending on the Lotus variety and the size of your pond. These plants have incredible blooms, and the center is almost unreal in appearance. The Lotus pod is filled with seeds, and prior to going to seed, the bloom is a beautiful pink flesh-tone on the "Sacred Lily" (Nelumbo nucifera).

WHEN TO PLANT:
Early to mid-Spring is preferred, or late Summer is acceptable.

WHY YOU PLANT:
Some would say that for a complete collection of "must" pond plants, the Lotus would rival the Water Lily for interest and beauty. This plant is breathtaking and definitely a conversation piece in the pond.

WHERE YOU PLANT:
Plant in ponds with plenty of room. If you were going to devote your pond to the Lotus, you would need a pond at least 18" deep and 4 feet wide. If other plants are desired, you would need an even larger pond. Also, Lotus needs at least 4-5 hours of sun per day.

HOW YOU PLANT:
Do not try to plant directly on the pond floor here in Tennessee. You need to pot Lotus in a large container, from 18-20" in diameter and at least 10" tall. The potting soil should be top dressed with small pea gravel, then submerge the container below the water level.

WHEN YOU WATER:
Obviously, you should not allow the plant to dry out. The plant's container should always stay below your pond's water level.

HOW/WHEN YOU PRUNE:
Not much pruning is needed, other than some trimming of dead or spent blooms and grooming yellow or dead leaves. This can be done throughout the season as needed.

HOW/WHEN YOU FERTILIZE:

Lotus love to be fed monthly during the growing season. You can use Water Lily pond tablets and follow instructions on the label for Lotus.

ADDITIONAL ADVICE FOR PROPER CARE:

Be aware of aphids on the tall stem of the bloom. Organic control is advisable because of wildlife in and around the pond. Some gardeners have released aphid-eating ladybugs to handle the problem, while others use a garden hose to spray them off the stems.

Pickerel Weed

Pontaderia cordata

This deciduous perennial is a great selection available to the Tennessee water gardener. Pickerel Weed grows to about 24-36" high and has the potential to spread at least that wide. Pickerel Weed comes in lavender-blues and white flowers. This is a sun lover, but will tolerate some filtered sun situations.

WHEN TO PLANT:

Pickerel Weed could be planted around or submerged in a bog or pond almost any time. As is the rule with most plants, Spring and Fall are ideal.

WHY YOU PLANT:

This is an interesting choice which offers flowers and striking foliage to add variety to the edge of the pond, and this plant is quite hardy.

WHERE YOU PLANT:

Pickerel Weed plants do love sun, which insures pretty and abundant blooms. Also, they like to be planted in a very wet bog or simply on your plant shelf in the pond. Keep the top of the pot covered by the water level.

HOW YOU PLANT:

Dig a hole as large as the clump or root ball and add some peat moss to the existing soil. Return mixture to the hole as you are planting the Pickerel Weed. If you choose to utilize it as a single large plant, leave it in the pot and sink it in the pond a few inches below water level. To avoid soil mixture floating away, add heavy pea gravel on top of the soil before lowering into the pond.

WHEN YOU WATER:

If not planted in your pond, this plant will thrive with watering two to three times a week. Pickerel Weed will survive with little attention. However, it will not thrive without adequate water.

HOW/WHEN YOU PRUNE:

Pickerel Weed appreciates any cleaning and grooming of yellow foliage and spent blooms. However, this certainly is not a must. The plant can be completely cut back once a year during early Winter or early Spring. Simply remove all growth just above the base of the pot.

HOW/WHEN YOU FERTILIZE:

Pickerel Weed does not require much feeding. Broadcast an organic fertilizer, such as blood meal, bone meal, cottonseed meal, or even liquid kelp around the bases of the plants. Apply in Spring and follow up in Summer. Be careful of extreme temperatures when fertilizing.

ADDITIONAL ADVICE FOR PROPER CARE:
Deadheading of spent blooms can help to encourage more blossoms. Be advised that Pickerel Weed can be very aggressive and does not mind being dug up and separated.

Water Hyacinth
Eichhornia crassipes

This inexpensive floating plant is not Winter-hardy in Tennessee, but it can literally take over an entire small backyard garden pond. In fact, there are strict laws in Southern coastal states against growing Water Hyacinth in heavily travelled canals. The Water Hyacinth has a wonderful orchid-shaped lavender bloom that sits up off the water on a stem and blooms in clusters. The plants will bloom off and on throughout the Spring, Summer, and even the Fall. This variety of water plant should be treated like a fast-multiplying annual and replaced each Spring.

WHEN TO PLANT:
Water Hyacinths can be planted any time during the growing season and can easily be relocated to your pond at any time. The ideal seasons for "planting" are Spring and early Summer.

WHY YOU PLANT:
There are a number of reasons to utilize this little plant in your pond. First is the fact that it is an inexpensive way to achieve the look of rather expensive Water Lilies. Not only do Water Hyacinths provide showy blooms, but they also create shade for the fish. The free-floating root system of the Water Hyacinth has several benefits as well. The roots provide an ideal place for fish to lay their larvae, and some fish enjoy Water Hyacinth as a source of food. Many water gardeners grow Water Hyacinth for its water oxygenating and filtration benefits, which contribute

significantly to the pond's cleanliness and clarity.

WHERE YOU PLANT:
The Water Hyacinth must be allowed to float in water where it lives throughout its life span. However, it does not require potting. The plants do require full sun for at least half the day to reproduce and bloom profusely.

HOW YOU PLANT:
Literally, you just allow Water Hyacinths to float freely on the surface of the water, from Spring until Fall.

WHEN YOU WATER:
Obviously, Water Hyacinths need their roots totally immersed in water, and do best with a water level of 10" or more.

HOW/WHEN YOU PRUNE:
Very little actual pruning is needed. The plants multiply almost overnight at the height of their growing season. Because of the rapid growth rate, you will want to do some "thinning out" from time to time, and share with friends. The time to do your thinning is when pond surface area becomes limited.

HOW/WHEN YOU FERTILIZE:
Seldom do you need to feed Water Hyacinths. If you do need to feed because of lack of bloom, NEVER use a water-soluble fertilizer directly in the pond. (This simply feeds the unwanted "green enemy," algae). The procedure for feeding these plants is to prepare a diluted fertilizer (high in phosphorous) solution in a large bucket or tub of water, then remove the plants from the pond and place them in the bucket for a day or so. You then return the plants to the pond and repeat every week or so, until you begin to get blooms.

ADDITIONAL ADVICE FOR PROPER CARE:
This plant is truly care free when you follow these recommendations. You should be aware of the rapid growth and may want

to start out in the Spring with just a few small clumps. With the first hard frost, they will turn brown and crispy. At this point, you may remove them and add to your compost pile. If you have a greenhouse, you may try to over-Winter a few plants, then return them to the pond in the Spring. Be sure to place them in a bucket of water situated where it will get lots of light during the Winter.

Water Lily
Nymphaea

This is considered the favorite of all water garden flowers. There are gorgeous night-blooming varieties and fragrant tropicals. Water Lilies can be over-Wintered in Tennessee water gardens. Of course, the tropical variety must be purchased each year like other annuals, or over-Wintered in a heated green-house. Water Lilies have assorted shapes and colors in both their foliage and their blooms.

WHEN TO PLANT:
The Water Lily can be "planted" anytime it's available. Nurseries, garden centers and mail order sources are the best options for locating a good choice of varieties. These plants are best selected when actually in bloom. Water Lilies should remain in their original pot while blooming.

WHY YOU PLANT:
These plants have an incredible effect on a pond. Their blooms are such an exciting part of water gardening, you will want to be aware of the blooming times offered by the different vari-eties. You must take into consideration your lifestyle and what part of the day you will be home to enjoy the blooms. Also, the blooms on some Water Lilies are quite fragrant. When they are

not blooming, Water Lilies have the traditional-looking "lily pad" foliage which is very helpful to the wildlife of your pond. Water Lilies provide shade for the fish and a place for the bull frogs to sit.

WHERE YOU PLANT:
Water Lilies need at least four hours of good, bright, full sun each day. Any less light and they will produce foliage; but very few, if any, blooms. These plants need to be positioned so you can enjoy them from several vantage points, both from inside and outside your home.

HOW YOU PLANT:
Most water gardeners do not actually plant their Water Lilies on the pond floor. Submerging your potted Water Lilies at least 18" below the water level is recommended for Tennessee ponds. As a rule of thumb, the submerged depth of your Water Lily will equal the average overall spread, or diameter. For example, if a Lily is 24" below the water level, it will spread 24" wide.

WHEN YOU WATER:
Well, this is a no-brainer! Just remember all ponds like to be full. Do not allow the water level to drop below the top of the pot containing your Water Lily.

HOW/WHEN YOU PRUNE:
Some pruning is required throughout the growing season. There are nice long-handled pruners specially designed for removing spent blooms and yellowed foliage. This should be done every two weeks, or as needed. After the first hard-killing frost, you should remove the plant from the water and cut back all prior season's growth before placing the pot back into the pond for the Winter.

HOW/WHEN YOU FERTILIZE:
Lilies are heavy feeders. Water Lilies have specific fertilizer requirements for their specific needs. They love to be removed from the water once a month, just long enough to insert Water

Lily fertilizer tablets deep into the pot. Follow instructions and repeat each month from April through August.

ADDITIONAL ADVICE FOR PROPER CARE:
Be sure to determine the amount of room you want to devote to Water Lilies in your pond. Also, remember some smaller varieties can be grown in "drainless" pots on your patio. Consult your local garden center or water garden society for these selections.

Notes:

WATER & BOG PLANTS

Perennials

$\mathcal{P}$ERENNIALS ARE THOSE PLANTS which return year after year to grace the landscapes of Tennessee with a full palette of colors. These gems will shine even under the extreme conditions of brutally hot, dry Summers, and their hardiness is further displayed by standing up to the constant temperature fluctuations of those roller coaster Tennessee Winters.

The ever-growing popularity of the Perennial is something to behold. By choosing varieties for blooming times and growth habits, your garden becomes a canvas which will display artful color throughout the year.

Most assuredly, no Tennessee garden would have the finishing touch without our state flower, the Iris. This is a wonderful selection that comes back "perennially."

Perennial gardening has become so popular in the last decade, and understandably so. These wonderful little plants can be dug, divided and shared with fellow gardeners. Some folks have actually "handed down" Peony roots from generation to generation!

What a beautiful way to be remembered by your future great-grandchildren.

Anemone, Japanese

Anemone x hybrida

This great Fall-blooming Perennial is actually in the buttercup family. The Japanese Anemone can grow from 2-5 feet tall and spread almost as far. The foliage is an attractive green that actually resembles a maple leaf. The plant's shape begins full at the base and as the plant grows, the growth is more sparse. The upper 1-2 feet are bare stems that support beautiful poppy-like blooms in mid to late Fall. Colors range from white to pinks.

WHEN TO PLANT:

You may plant Japanese Anemone any time the ground is not frozen. However, the best time is early Spring or early Fall.

WHY YOU PLANT:

These plants are wonderful for great Fall color in semi-shady spots. Their tall, slender stems are good for cutting and arranging in bouquets.

WHERE YOU PLANT:

Plant in a shady garden or in an area that gets shelter from the hot afternoon sun. The Japanese Anemone works well at the back of your Perennial flower bed.

HOW YOU PLANT:

Japanese Anemone is quite easy to transplant from starter plants or clumps, or from the larger "in-bloom" nursery-grown container plants. If planting a container or clump, dig a hole about twice the size of the root and add peat moss or organic humus and blend with the existing soil. Place the plant in the hole, being sure to loosen the roots, then backfill to lightly cover the top of the roots. Mulch lightly.

WHEN YOU WATER:

Water well with a liquid root stimulator after planting. Water once a week during Spring and Summer, and water more often during drought.

HOW/WHEN YOU PRUNE:

Trim back dead flower heads by snipping off their stems at the base of the plant. Also, you may remove all dead foliage in late Winter or early Spring.

HOW/WHEN YOU FERTILIZE:

Japanese Anemone are not particular eaters. In fact, if they are in decent soil, they will be happy if you only scratch in a little super-phosphate around the dripline of the plant in early Spring, after pulling away the light Winter layer of mulch. Also, if you are feeding your other flowers with a water-soluble food, your Japanese Anemone would appreciate this as well.

ADDITIONAL ADVICE FOR PROPER CARE:

Spray in the Spring with a quality dormant oil when new growth is 1-2 feet tall. This will help prevent mites and other insects.

Aster
Aster michaelmas

With Aster, there are many varieties to choose from, including low clump forms, spreaders (to 6 feet) and upright growers. The Aster has a daisy-like flower which has a near universal appeal. Each bloom has a central disk, usually yellow, surrounded by one or more rows of ray-like petals. Its leaves are narrow and lance-shaped. The Aster blooms during the Summer and lasts into the Fall. With Aster, height and shape variations are vast. 'Monch' is light and airy and grows to 36" in height. By comparison, the short and bushy 'Professor A. Kippenburg' grows to a height of 15".

WHEN TO PLANT:
Plant in Spring or Fall as soil conditions permit.

WHY YOU PLANT:
Most Asters and members in the Daisy family add a balance
of color in the garden with their cool, soft hues. The 4 foot
'Harrington Pink' is a long-flowering cultivar.

WHERE YOU PLANT:
Give Asters a place in the sun with average to good
soil conditions. Well-draining soil is a must since
wet soil during the Winter can cause root rot.

HOW YOU PLANT:
Dig a hole that is twice the size of the root ball,
then add a little organic humus or sphagnum peat
moss. Mix into the existing soil, then gently loosen
the root ball. Keep the top of the root ball just
above the existing soil level. Do not plant too deep.

WHEN YOU WATER:
Water well with a root stimulator immediately after
planting. If planted in the Fall or early Spring, continue to water every week. If planted during the
rapid growing season, frequent watering (two times
a week) is advisable. Once the plant is well-established, water twice monthly.

HOW/WHEN YOU PRUNE:
Asters should be trimmed during the growing season to encourage compact growth. Divide and replant Asters when its vigor
diminishes and the clump's center becomes bare and woody.

HOW/WHEN YOU FERTILIZE:
If you are blessed with good, rich, loose soil, simply plant and
let it grow. However, like most plants, it would benefit from
supplementary feeding with a well-balanced, slow-release granu-

lar food scratched in around the dripline in early Spring.

ADDITIONAL ADVICE FOR PROPER CARE:
Powdery Mildew can be minimized by keeping the plants well-watered, but avoid soggy conditions.

Astilbe
Astilbe

A great choice for a shade garden, Astilbe features some dwarf varieties ranging from 8" to taller, showy specimens of 3 feet with a spread of 2-3 feet. The foliage has the look of a lacy fern. When not in bloom, these plants are very attractive and useful in a combination planting. The choice of bloom color ranges from pink, lavender and creamy white to peach and red. Its plume-like feathery blooms are extremely showy.

WHEN TO PLANT:
Astilbe can be planted almost any time during the year, but mid-Spring or Fall is best.

WHY YOU PLANT:
These plants add color to a shady spot and their blooms are known to attract butterflies. Though not known for their fragrance, they certainly make up for it with the choice of bloom colors available. Their foliage looks almost identical to a beautiful fern, so they will even bring rewards when not in bloom.

WHERE YOU PLANT:
Nestled near or against a rock or boulder is very effective. Also, the taller varieties work well near the back of a shady flowerbed. Plant in semi-shade or full shade and in a moist, but well-drained area.

HOW YOU PLANT:

Astilbe is easy to transplant from starter plants or clumps, or from the larger "in-bloom" nursery-grown container plants. Begin by digging the planting hole approximately twice the size of the root ball. Add peat moss or organic humus and blend it with the soil you have removed. Then add some of the blended soils back into the hole and place the plant into the hole. As you place the plant, gently loosen the roots, then backfill to the point where the top of the root ball is even with the existing soil level. Mulch lightly and water-in thoroughly.

WHEN YOU WATER:

Water well with liquid root stimulator after planting. During the first year's growth, water at least two times a week. After that, once a week through the peak growing season, and more often during drought.

HOW/WHEN YOU PRUNE:

Little pruning is needed. However, cutting back the spent bloom stalks helps to stimulate new growth. After a heavy freeze, cut back just above the ground, label and mulch lightly. If you choose, you may wait until Spring to cut last year's growth.

HOW/WHEN YOU FERTILIZE:

Feeding with a high phosphorus fertilizer will encourage blooms. Use a water-soluble food every week during Spring and Summer as you are feeding your flowers. Feed once in Spring and repeat in Summer with a dry, slow-release granular fertilizer. Work it in at the dripline and water well.

ADDITIONAL ADVICE FOR PROPER CARE:

Prune any yellow foliage that may occur at the base of the plant during the heat of Summer. Also, mulch with pine straw to discourage snails and slugs from damaging the foliage.

Beard Tongue

Penstemon

This is a bushy plant consisting of upright, glossy stems with narrow, pointed leaves. Bright, clear blue, pink, purple, red, or white tubular flowers are borne up and down a spike, resembling small Foxglove or Salvia blooms.

WHEN TO PLANT:
Plant during the Spring or Fall, as soil conditions permit.

WHY YOU PLANT:
This plant is not a long-lived Perennial, but it is very visible during the growing season, making its periodic replacement worthwhile. In warmer climates (West Tennessee), Penstemon is a good choice in place of the cooler-climate Foxglove.

WHERE YOU PLANT:
Place in full sun to partial shade areas. Use in average, well-draining soil. Excessively moist soil can be fatal to this variety.

HOW YOU PLANT:
Dig a hole that is twice the size of the root ball, then add a little organic humus or sphagnum peat moss. Mix into the existing soil, then gently loosen the root ball. Keep the top of the root ball just above the existing soil level. Do not plant too deep.

WHEN YOU WATER:
The Penstemon requires moderate watering, but avoid wet, soggy conditions.

HOW/WHEN YOU PRUNE:
Cut back plants after a burst of flowering has finished. It will flower again on the new growth. This species will produce for 3-4 years, and replacement plants are easy to start.

How/When you fertilize:

If you are blessed with good, rich, loose soil, simply plant and let it grow. However, like most plants, it would benefit from supplementary feeding with a well-balanced, slow-release granular food scratched in around the dripline in early Spring.

Additional advice for proper care:

No serious diseases or insects noted. Avoid soggy soil conditions.

Blue False Indigo
Baptisia australis

This upright Perennial's bloom bears a likeness to the popular old-fashioned Sweet Pea flower. The color is showy with a violet-blue Summer splash. The leaves are a cool, bright green and are divided into oval leaflets. The plant will tolerate full sun, and spread 2 feet in width and height. It prefers a moist spot, but tolerates some dry times.

When to plant:

Baptisia is best when planted in early to mid-Spring and Fall.

Why you plant:

This plant is wonderful for its great vertical lines of interest in the Perennial border. Also, the foliage has a light green appearance and soft texture, with blooms that can be used effectively in cut flower arrangements. This plant is able to adjust to drought conditions once it is established.

Where you plant:

Plant Baptisia in a sunny location. The violet-blue flowers are very compatible with fuschias, pinks and whites. Also select a spot where these plants can have some physical support—a taller companion plant, a fence, or a wall for support.

How you plant:
Baptisia is easy to transplant from starter plants or clumps or from larger "in-bloom" container-grown plants. Begin by digging the planting hole approximately twice the size of the root ball. Add peat moss or organic humus and blend it with the soil you have removed. Then add some of the blended soils back into the hole and place the plant into the hole. As you place the plant, gently loosen the roots, then backfill to the point where the top of the root ball is even with the existing soil level. Mulch lightly and water-in thoroughly.

When you water:
Water with liquid root stimulator after planting. During the first year's growth, water at least two times a week, and increase as necessary during the Summer months. After the first year, you may decrease watering to 2-3 times per month, as needed.

How/When you prune:
Cutting back spent bloom spikes will increase new blooms, but is not a must. You may cut it all the way to the ground, label and mulch after the first hard freeze.

How/When you fertilize:
Baptisia loves dry slow-release fertilizer, once in Spring and again in Summer or Fall. Work it in well around the dripline and water. In addition, you may add water-soluble food every week or so as you feed your flowers.

Additional advice for proper care:
Once established, little care is required. Just pick some blooms and enjoy them indoors, or use the seed pods for Winter decorations.

P
E
R
E
N
N
I
A
L
S

Butterfly Weed

Asclepias tuberosa

The Butterfly Weed is a native plant here in Tennessee and is a tried-and-true hardy sun Perennial. It will carry a tired garden through hot times with the bright orange clusters of tiny showy blooms. The plant has a height and spread of 1 1/3-3 feet. The foliage is a thick, deep green color, and because the plant is in the Milkweed family, its leaves secrete a milky substance when broken. Butterflies and hummingbirds love this plant when in bloom.

WHEN TO PLANT:

Fall or early Spring is the best time to plant the Butterfly Weed.

WHY YOU PLANT:

This plant is extremely tolerant of poor soil and accepts neglect like water. Also, when in bloom, this flower attracts swarms of butterflies (hence the name) and hummingbirds, too.

WHERE YOU PLANT:

Plant toward the back of your Perennial and flower beds, in areas that are normally poor sites for flowers that require better conditions. Butterfly Weed needs at least five hours of bright sun daily.

HOW YOU PLANT:

Butterfly Weed is easy to transplant from starter plants or clumps or from larger "in-bloom" container-grown plants. You may sow seed in late Summer (just like Mother Nature) by tilling up or raking the ground and scattering seed and sprinkling with a light layer of loose soil or wheat straw. If planting a container or clump, dig a hole about twice the size of the root, add peat moss or organic humus and blend with the existing soil. Place plant in hole, loosen roots, then backfill barely covering the top surface of the roots. Mulch lightly.

WHEN YOU WATER:
Water well with root stimulator when planting, then once a week during the Summer. Once established, no watering is necessary.

HOW/WHEN YOU PRUNE:
Cut back in early Winter and remove the previous season's growth and label your plant. Or you may leave it alone and cut it back in early Spring. Feel free to cut the stems for use in bouquets.

HOW/WHEN YOU FERTILIZE:
No fertilizer is necessary. This plant almost thrives on neglect.

ADDITIONAL ADVICE FOR PROPER CARE:
Allow Butterfly Weed to develop its milkweed-like fruit, or cut later and dry for use in Fall flower arrangements.

Columbine
Aquilegia

This graceful, charming plant has grey-green, maidenhair fern-like foliage. Its stems support flowers that seem poised for flight. Each blossom consists of five inner petals that form a cup, and five long, pointed petals which form a saucer for the cup. It also has five sprays that project backwards, giving it the ready-for-flight look. The color combinations are endless!

WHEN TO PLANT:
Plant in Spring or Fall, as soil conditions allow.

WHY YOU PLANT:
Columbine is a traditional plant featuring combinations of blue, purple, red, pink, yellow, cream, and white blooms. It flowers during Spring and early Summer. This plant will bloom in shade!

WHERE YOU PLANT:
Place in sun or partial shade areas.

HOW YOU PLANT:
Loosen the roots of plants grown in pots... thoroughly! Prepare a wide, shallow hole 3/4 as deep and twice as wide as the root ball. Make a mix of 1/3 soil, 1/3 coarse sand, and 1/3 peat moss, organic humus, or commercial planting mix. Pack firmly around sides of root ball. Add 1-3" of mulch on top, staying clear of the crown of the plant. Then water well with a root stimulator fertilizer. Note: Avoid planting when soil is frozen 1" deep or when soil is wet enough to form a mudball in your fist.

WHEN YOU WATER:
For newly planted Columbine, use a hand-held, open-ended hose, watering plants directly for one minute each day. Do this until the shrub's roots are established, generally one growing season, or when new growth is evident. The Columbine will respond well to continual watering in most Tennessee areas, with the exception of the mountain area in East Tennessee.

HOW/WHEN YOU PRUNE:
This plant has a life expectancy of 3-4 years. The Columbine can be divided during the Spring, so it is advisable to purchase new plants to be used for replacements. Also, seed heads can be left to mature and young plants started as replacements.

HOW/WHEN YOU FERTILIZE:
If you are blessed with good, rich, loose soil, simply plant and let it grow. However, like most plants, it would benefit from supplementary feeding with a well-balanced, slow-release granular food scratched in around the dripline in early Spring.

ADDITIONAL ADVICE FOR PROPER CARE:
No serious diseases or pests are noted.

Coneflower, Purple
Echinacea purpurea

This particular gorgeous pink daisy-like flower can be found in every photo you will ever see of a country flower garden or even an English or Victorian garden. Tennessee gardeners have definitely come to appreciate the bold cheery look this flower lends to the backdrop of a flower border. This plant grows to be about 3-5 feet tall and loves full sun. The Coneflower is also available in white and yellow, with both blooming all Summer and into Fall.

WHEN TO PLANT:
Early Spring and Fall is the best time to plant Purple Coneflower. Anytime you can work the soil and maintain good moisture conditions, you may transplant starter or mature plants. If planting from seed, do so in late Summer or early Fall (like Mother Nature), or wait until Spring. Do not expect blooms the first year if starting from seed.

WHY YOU PLANT:
This plant adds a striking contrast to any flower garden. It is a wonderful flower to have for cut-flower arrangements. Butterflies are greatly attracted to the huge flowers, and the plant will bloom—if deadheaded—continuously from mid-Summer to Fall.

WHERE YOU PLANT:
Purple Coneflower is a very carefree grower and needs lots of room to grow and spread. Both you and the flower will benefit from a spot at the back of your flowerbed and in at least one-half to full sun. It prefers to be in a well-drained soil. Also, remember to plant where it will be accessible when cutting flowers and for viewing from indoors during the Summer.

HOW YOU PLANT:
Not much work is required when planting the Purple Cone-flower. Be sure to add some form of soil conditioner and blend

(side tab) PERENNIALS

well. Dig a hole at least one and one-half times the size of the root ball and plant at ground level, adding blended soil mixtures in and around the roots. If planting from seed, wait until Fall or Spring and work up the soil, then sow the seed. Cover the seed lightly.

WHEN YOU WATER:
Always water well with a liquid root stimulator just after planting. As a rule, the Purple Coneflower is extremely tolerant of dry and poor quality soils. During its first year, water it at least once a week, and two times a week during extreme heat. Once established, you should only have to water it 2-3 times a month for years of enjoyment.

Walt's Wisdom

Spread ground up egg shells around your Hosta to deter slugs.

HOW/WHEN YOU PRUNE:
This prolific performer loves to be cut and enjoyed indoors. Once a bloom is spent, it should be deadheaded. Simply follow the stem until reaching a potential bloom bud, or "swelled" spot, on the flower's stem. Then, make the cut just above that bud. At the end of the season, the entire plant can be cut back to the ground.

HOW/WHEN YOU FERTILIZE:
These plants do not require fertilization to bloom, but you should consider feeding your Purple Coneflower twice a season. Feed with a slow-release granular fertilizer high in phosphorous, once in early Spring and again toward the middle to end of Summer. You may also supplement with a water-soluble food every week or so.

ADDITIONAL ADVICE FOR PROPER CARE:
Purple Coneflower is a great asset to any flower garden, and very few pests present a problem. A good dormant oil spray would be useful to eliminate over-Wintering pests, such as Spider Mites.

Daisy, Shasta

Chrysanthemum x superbum

One of the most common and popular looks in the Perennial garden, this plant has the basic look of the "she loves me, she loves me not..." daisy. The Shasta Daisy is in the Chrysanthemum family and also comes in many varieties. Our pick for a sturdy, good performer in your Tennessee garden would be 'Becky.' The plant grows to about 24-30" in height and spread. The Shastas bloom in mid-Summer and have beautiful, deep green foliage. A must for the Perennial garden.

WHEN TO PLANT:

The best planting time for Shasta Daisy is late Fall or early Spring, however, with proper care they can be successfully transplanted any time of year.

WHY YOU PLANT:

These daisies are easy to grow and will cheer up any flower garden. They will tolerate some neglect, and you can make use of individual petals or whole bouquets of this flower.

WHERE YOU PLANT:

Plant in an area that receives at least a half-day of hot afternoon sun. The entire Chrysanthemum family really enjoys a good amount of sun. Also, plant daisies in a location that is accessible for gathering with ease.

HOW YOU PLANT:

The Shasta Daisy is easy to transplant from starter plants or clumps or from larger "in-bloom" container-grown plants. Begin by digging the planting hole approximately twice the size of the root ball. Add peat moss or organic humus and blend it with the soil you have removed. Then add some of the blended soils back into the hole and place the plant into the hole. As you place the plant, gently loosen the roots, then backfill to the point where the top of the root ball is even with the existing soil level. Mulch lightly and water-in thoroughly.

WHEN YOU WATER:
Just after planting, as with most plants, Shasta Daisies would greatly benefit from watering with a liquid root stimulator. Newly-planted specimens should be watered at least two times a week during the growing season, and will then be virtually maintenance free. During extreme drought times you may need to water once every week or so as needed.

HOW/WHEN YOU PRUNE:
No pruning is necessary. You may choose to remove all the previous season's growth in late Fall to early Winter and then label the location. Some gardeners leave the growth all Winter and cut it back in early Spring. Deadhead blooms as needed throughout the Summer.

HOW/WHEN YOU FERTILIZE:
Shasta Daisies are not particular eaters. In fact, if they are in decent soil, they will be happy if you only scratch in a little super-phosphate around the dripline of the plant in early Spring, after pulling away the Winter layer of mulch. Also, if you are feeding your other flowers with a water-soluble food, your daisies would appreciate it as well.

ADDITIONAL ADVICE FOR PROPER CARE:
Every couple of years during late Summer or early Fall, divide the daisies and share the abundance with friends. A thorough application of dormant oil in mid-Spring is also advisable to prevent any insect infestations.

Daylily
Hemerocallis

Most folks here in Tennessee are familiar with the almost "wild" Daylily. They range in color from the common orange, to cream, purple, lavender, pink, yellow and bicolors. There are many new Daylilies out now, with vast selection in color, heights and blooming times. With a little planning you can stagger blooms from May all the way into October. Try to select varieties listed as repeat bloomers. There is no other Perennial more adaptable than the Daylily. These "neglectable" treasures are a must for any flower garden.

WHEN TO PLANT:

Almost year-round planting and transplanting can be successful in Tennessee, although the prime time is Summer to Fall.

WHY YOU PLANT:

This is one of the tried-and-true "maintenance-free," Summer-to-Fall blooming Perennials available to Tennessee gardeners. Daylilies are now used as massive ground cover, such as those found along highways throughout the state. This should certainly validate the low-maintenance aspect.

WHERE YOU PLANT:

In order to bloom abundantly, Daylilies need to be exposed to full sun. There are varieties that will tolerate some shade, but they don't perform as well. Daylilies will also adapt to almost any soil conditions, and may be planted on a very steep slope to help control erosion.

HOW YOU PLANT:

The preparation of your soil is not as important as with most other Perennials. When planting, loosen the soil and break up large clods with a shovel. Add peat moss or organic humus and water-soluble food. Don't plant Daylilies too deep, and be sure to loosen up the root ball before placing in the hole.

When you water:

After planting, be sure to water at least twice a week during the growing season. Once your Daylilies have gone through an entire growing season, once a week should prove ample. Twice a month should be sufficient for older, more established plants.

How/When you prune:

Daylilies are great about repeating blooms, whether you remove the faded blooms or not. However, once the "bloom stalk" has completely finished all potential blooms, you may follow it gently to the base of the plant and snap, or cut and remove it to maintain a more attractive look. Once the extreme cold weather sets in, you may remove all of the past season's growth and mulch lightly.

How/When you fertilize:

The Daylily loves a good dose of granular slow-release fertilizer with a high phosphorous content. This may be applied in early Spring, as new growth appears, and repeated in late Summer. Once a month during the growing season, you may use a water-soluble plant food in addition to granular.

Additional advice for proper care:

When selecting Daylilies, try several blooming heights and colors and be sure to allow plenty of room for spreading out. Some varieties can grow to a height of 4 feet, and some are as small and compact as the 'Stella d'Oro,' which only grows to be about 18" across and 20" high. Also, select a nice group of colors by choosing several varieties.

Dianthus

Dianthus

This is one of the favorite English garden looks for Tennessee. Dianthus varieties are endless, including 'Miss Lingard,' a mildew-resistant tall variety that blooms white in the Summer, and 'Bath's Pink,' a low-growing ground cover with an incredibly spicy fragrance and great blue-silver foliage year-round.

WHEN TO PLANT:
Early Spring or late Fall is a great time to plant, but Dianthus' most suitable planting time is while in dormancy. However, this plant is so hardy, it could be planted almost any time under proper planting procedures.

WHY YOU PLANT:
Dianthus have many wonderful features, both visual and fragrant. The fragrances vary from sweet to very spicy, and the variety of heights and blooming times allow for staggered blooming times. Many varieties have a high tolerance to drought and heat.

WHERE YOU PLANT:
All Dianthus prefer at least a half-day of direct sun and all love well-drained soil. Several of the shorter Dianthus are perfect for steep, hard to maintain slopes and banks. With their matted, dense growth habits, they seem to keep weeds from popping through.

HOW YOU PLANT:
When planting, be sure to work up the ground well, breaking up any clods of soil and blending with some organic humus, peat moss or soil conditioner. Also, be sure to make a hole up to twice the depth and width of the plant's root ball diameter. Loosen the ball, place the blended mix in the hole, then the plant, and fill in around the sides and cover with more blended soil. Plant so that the surface of the root ball is at ground level, and water well with a diluted solution of root stimulator.

WHEN YOU WATER:
Once established, after a year or so, you may only have to water this variety in drought situations. During the growing season, Dianthus should be watered well once a week.

HOW/WHEN YOU PRUNE:

Little pruning or deadheading is necessary—ground cover varieties need very little attention in this area—other than twice during the blooming season. You may want to shear off all the dead blooms from the plant, being careful not to take off any potential new buds or foliage tips. The taller, old-fashioned varieties may be selectively deadheaded after the clusters of blooms have faded by cutting the stem where you can see potential for more blooms. By late Fall to early Winter you may remove all the dead foliage to 2-3" above the ground, mulch lightly, and tag with a stake or marker.

HOW/WHEN YOU FERTILIZE:

Dianthus are not heavy feeders. A dry, slow-release organic fertilizer will be beneficial for abundant growth and blooms. Apply in early Spring and late Fall.

ADDITIONAL ADVICE FOR PROPER CARE:

Because Dianthus are great in mass plantings, after a couple of years of vigorous growth you may want to dig up and separate them. This is a perfect plant to share with friends or even trade for other varieties. Dianthus only seem to have problems when planted in wet, shady spots.

WALT'S WISDOM

A nation is as strong as the character of its people.

Fern

Fern

Choices are what you get when you begin looking at Ferns. These plants grow as low as a few inches off the ground to over 4 feet high. The selection in textures and colors is vast. Some ferns will tolerate full shade and others will tolerate some sun. All prefer moist, damp conditions.

WHEN TO PLANT:
Early to mid-Spring or Fall is the best time to plant Ferns. During the plant's dormant season is also a good time.

WHY YOU PLANT:
Ferns have a very calming effect and create a tropical, almost retreat-like feel. This plant works well with contrasting plants and helps soften the overall look.

WHERE YOU PLANT:
Plant Ferns in mixed containers, in a shady nook, or in a garden. Next to a water garden is also an effective look to soften a rock border.

HOW YOU PLANT:
Be careful not to break the delicate frond stems. Work up the ground well and add composted leaves, sphagnum peat moss, organic humus and any organic additives such as blood meal, cottonseed meal or even bone meal. Be sure to not plant too deep, and water well with liquid root stimulator after planting.

WHEN YOU WATER:
Water at least 3-4 times a week during the first growing season. After the first year's growing season, water one or two times a week.

HOW/WHEN YOU PRUNE:
Some varieties retain their foliage through the milder Tennessee Winters, but other varieties need pruning or cutting back after our first hard frost. You may wait until early Spring to cut back.

HOW/WHEN YOU FERTILIZE:
Natural leaf compost applied in Winter months can fertilize effectively and naturally. In poor soil conditions, you may supplement with a dry, slow-release balanced fertilizer scratched in 6-8" away from the base of the plant, once in Spring and once again in late Summer.

ADDITIONAL ADVICE FOR PROPER CARE:
Mulch with pine straw during the growing season to discourage snails and slugs. Also, try to water during morning hours to allow the soil to dry by evening, which will help keep them away.

Lenton Rose
Helleborus orientalis

Great for Winter interest in the Perennial garden, Lenton Rose is available in a white and pink-blooming flower. The plant maintains a dark green, glossy foliage all year long. The plants will grow from 12-18" high with a similar spread. The plant is a must for any garden that lacks Winter interest.

WHEN TO PLANT:
Fall or early to mid-Spring would be ideal for planting the Lenton Rose.

WHY YOU PLANT:
This plant will add much to any Perennial or flower bed in Winter. Its glossy foliage shows forth when everything else is drab and dead during the colder months. Helleborus is available in several colors of blooms.

WHERE YOU PLANT:
Helleborus should be planted where it can be appreciated from indoors during Winter. Also, consider that it needs some Summertime mid-day shade.

HOW YOU PLANT:
Helleborus is easy to transplant from starter plants or clumps or from larger "in-bloom" container-grown plants. Begin by digging the planting hole approximately twice the size of the root ball.

Add peat moss or organic humus and blend it with the soil you have removed. Then add some of the blended soils back into the hole and place the plant into the hole. As you place the plant, gently loosen the roots, then backfill to the point where the top of the root ball is even with the existing soil level. Mulch lightly and water-in thoroughly.

WHEN YOU WATER:
This plant needs to be watered well once a week during its first year's growth. Once established, you should only need to supplement watering during the heat of the Summer.

HOW/WHEN YOU PRUNE:
Early to mid-Spring, remove any old, Winter-damaged foliage. Other than this, very little maintenance is necessary.

HOW/WHEN YOU FERTILIZE:
Helleborus is basically self-sufficient. Feed twice a year (Spring and Fall) with a dry, slow-release all-purpose fertilizer.

ADDITIONAL ADVICE FOR PROPER CARE:
Help your Helleborus by spraying during November with a dormant oil spray or Wilt-Pruf (an anti-desiccant). This will help Helleborus through the Winter temperatures.

Loosestrife
Lythrum

This plant causes mixed emotions. In the Deep South some varieties of Lythrum have been known to be so invasive as to harm other native plants in marshlands. However, varieties such as 'Happy' (short bushy 12-15" high), to 'Robert' (3 feet in height) and 'Morden's Pink' (4 feet in height), are sterile varieties much more suitable for Tennessee gardens. They all adorn beautiful, full spikes covered with hundreds of pink blooms that are wonderful for attracting butterflies. Also, this plant simply thrives in boggy damp areas, yet can actually adjust to a dry spot. Sun is crucial for blooms, however, this plant can survive with a half-day of sun.

WHEN TO PLANT:

Early Spring or Fall is the optimum time to plant Lythrum. This plant can be successfully planted any time of year if the ground isn't frozen. However, if it is transplanted from container to garden in Summer, you should water it frequently.

WHY YOU PLANT:

This particular plant attracts more butterflies than most others in the flower garden. Its graceful, tall, "plume-type" blooms bend and sway in the slightest breeze. It has a great effect in a Perennial bed, especially the length of bloom time - they bring color all Summer long. Selection of color ranges from clear, soft pink shades to brave, bold magentas and shades of fuschia. These plants adore being placed in extra wet areas, and also tolerate dry areas, making them very adaptable.

WHERE YOU PLANT:

Lythrums may be planted in full, hot sun in hard, dry soil, or they may be planted on the edge of a pond, or standing on the shelf of a garden pond in mid-day sun.

HOW YOU PLANT:

Be sure to loosen the Lythrum's massive root ball. Utilize a pruning knife to cut into a packed root ball by penetrating the roots by one-half inch to one inch. Sink into a hole that has been dug and backflled with at least one-half original soil mixed with approximately one-half sphagnum peat moss. After placing the plant in the hole (twice the size of the ball), you can backfill with the soil and peat moss blend and make the top of the ball level with existing soil.

WHEN YOU WATER:

Water with a liquid root stimulator just after planting. During first season growth, water at least 2-3 times per week, and do not let it dry out during extreme heat. Once well established, if planted in a moist area, this plant should be almost invincible. If planted in poor soil, water once a week.

HOW/WHEN YOU PRUNE:

Pruning or cutting back may be done in late Fall or Winter, leaving 2-3" stumps above the ground. Deadheading during the blooming season will encourage longer color.

HOW/WHEN YOU FERTILIZE:

Feed like most Perennials: once in early Spring and again in mid to late Summer. (Avoid extreme heat when feeding. If the temperature is between 85 to 90 degrees, put off feeding until later). Use a good quality, high phosphorous, granular slow-release fertilizer. Work into the soil around the outer perimeter of the plant.

ADDITIONAL ADVICE FOR PROPER CARE:

Deadhead your Lythrum every other week. This plant needs a light covering of mulch through the Winter, such as pine straw or whatever might be available in late Fall/early Winter. However, the covering will need to be pulled away in early Spring to scratch in food. Do not reapply mulch until you see new Spring growth. Final removal of the past year's growth can be accomplished in late Fall or early Spring. Lythrum is a little late in making a Spring appearance, so don't panic. It will make it through the unpredictable Tennessee Winters.

Mums

Chrysanthemum x morifolium

Most folks here in Tennessee can't think about Fall without thinking about Mums. These beauties are very popular for sprucing up your tired Summer/ Fall landscape. Also, many gardeners have started collections because of the vast selection. These plants range in height from 1-3 feet and can spread even wider. They offer colors from white, lavender and purple to red, orange and yellow. There are cushion, pompon, daisy, buttons and literally over a dozen varieties in shapes of blooms.

WHEN TO PLANT:
Early Spring is a good time to start small plants. Fall allows selection based on true color, and planting conditions are good then, too.

WHY YOU PLANT:

These plants reflect the Fall mood in the garden, and in indoor bouquets. The flowers last in water for several weeks, the colors available are vast, and the plant is extremely easy to grow.

WHERE YOU PLANT:
Chrysanthemums enjoy a lot of sun and need a well-drained soil. Select a spot that does not stay damp during Winter months.

HOW YOU PLANT:
Mums are easy to transplant from starter plants or clumps or from larger "in-bloom" container-grown plants. Begin by digging the planting hole approximately twice the size of the root ball. Add peat moss or organic humus and blend it with the soil you have removed. Then add some of the blended soils back into the hole and place the plant into the hole. As you place the plant, gently loosen the roots, then back-fill to the point where the top of the root ball is even with the existing soil level. Mulch lightly and water-in thoroughly.

WHEN YOU WATER:
Just after planting, as with most plants, Mums will greatly bene-fit from watering with a liquid root stimulator. Newly-planted specimens should be watered at least two times a week during

the growing season, making them almost maintenance-free. During extreme drought, you may need to water once every week or so as necessary.

HOW/WHEN YOU PRUNE:

Chrysanthemums love to be pruned. Once your plant returns in the Spring, you should begin removing the very top part of the new growth. This procedure needs to begin once the shoots are about 6" tall. Remove the top 1" of new growth on each shoot, and repeat this every two weeks up through July. If you would like to stagger the blooms, pinch your first group the middle of July and do your final pinch on the last group the first of August. This will allow a longer display of color. However, some gardeners would rather have one big splash of color and then do their final pinch on all plants at the same time.

HOW/WHEN YOU FERTILIZE:

Mums are not particular feeders. In fact, if they are in decent soil, they will be happy if you only scratch in a little super-phosphate around the dripline of the plant in early Spring, after pulling away the light Winter layer of mulch. Also, if you are feeding your other flowers with a water-soluble food, your Mums would appreciate it as well.

ADDITIONAL ADVICE FOR PROPER CARE:

Sometimes aphids can be pests, but they will not kill the plant. However, you may combat them by spraying with a horticultural oil or releasing live (aphid-eating) ladybugs.

Peony
Paeonia

Gorgeous fragrance and blooms in mid-Spring will grace the Tennessee landscape when Peonies are present. This plant can many times outlast the gardener and even the garden. Peonies bloom in colors of whites, cream, pinks and reds. There are even yellow singles and unusual Tree Peonies that will survive here. Peonies need little care to perform if they are planted in the right spot. Their heights range from 2-4 feet and their spread is approximately the same. Flowering can extend 4-6 weeks by choosing a collection of early, mid and late-season blooming varieties.

WHEN TO PLANT:
Peony may be planted in Fall or late Winter to early Spring.

WHY YOU PLANT:
Fragrance and dramatic color in the flower garden are this plant's high points. Cutting the blooms for indoor bouquets is very popular.

WHERE YOU PLANT:
Most important for growing success is at least one half-day (preferably full) of sun and extremely well-drained soil.

HOW YOU PLANT:
Till the desired spot well, working in organic matter in advance of your planting time by a month or so. Place roots with "eyes"—growth buds—at the top and barely cover. Then mulch lightly with pine straw or shredded mulch, and water well with a liquid root stimulator.

WHEN YOU WATER:
Peonies hate "wet feet." Water once a week as needed until May, then you may need to water more often. A moisture meter would be helpful to determine whether or not watering is needed.

HOW/WHEN YOU PRUNE:
Cut blooms as needed for enjoying indoors. No other pruning is needed until Fall. Although the foliage looks a little rough in Summer, leave it alone until Fall to ensure nice, large, repeat blooms the next year.

How/When you fertilize:

Feed prior to planting with a bulb-booster fertilizer worked into the soil. Repeat this process after blooming, broadcasting around the dripline and watering well.

Additional advice for proper care:

Do not plant Peonies too deep. If the flower buds turn brown and fail to open, your plants may have a disease called Botrytis Blight. You will need to cut off and destroy infected plants and spray with a fungicide. Then, repeat again in the following Spring before buds show color. Also, ants present on the stems are usually after one of two things. First, the healthier the bloom, the higher the sugar content, so the ant is simply feeding its sweet tooth. Second, the ants could be an indicator of an aphid infestation. The ant is going after the "honeydew" from the aphids. Release some aphid-eating ladybugs, or spray off with a hose. To avoid the inevitable heavy damaging rains that come right as Peonies are blooming, try placing a support system, or grid, at the base of the plant at the beginning of Spring. Raise the grid as the plant grows. This method works quite well.

Plantain Lily
Hosta

What a wonderful, sturdy plant to add to your shade garden. Varieties range from a small 8-10" to plants that can create a spread of 5 feet and almost the same in height. These plants are suitable for a wide range of growing situations, from container gardening to backyard water gardening. Most Hostas prefer partial to full shade and well-drained but moist soil. There is an array of bloom and foliage colors available for any garden.

WHEN TO PLANT:
Hostas can be planted any time the ground is not frozen, but early to mid-Spring and Fall are best.

WHY YOU PLANT:
The Hosta family has several varieties offering fragrance for the garden. One favorite for the scented garden would be 'Honeybells.' Another reason for planting is the color and texture you can add to a rather shady, or boring, spot. Blue, yellow, green, cream... the choices are almost endless in foliage color.

WHERE YOU PLANT:
Plant these in any shady spot where you want to add color. This plant can be the perfect solution to grace the base of shade trees, and a border of taller Hosta toward the back of a shaded garden can create a wonderful background.

HOW YOU PLANT:
When planting, work up the ground well if the spot is at the base of a large shade tree. Always add some extra organic humus, peat moss or basic soil conditioner. Dig a hole at least a little larger—if not twice the size—of the root ball, then loosen the ball and place in the hole at the same level.

WHEN YOU WATER:
Water well after planting with liquid root stimulator and then water two times a week during the first year's growing period, and more frequently during the heat of Summer. After the first year's growth, you should only have to water 2-3 times a month.

HOW/WHEN YOU PRUNE:
Pruning can take place after the first hard frost turns the foliage wilted and yellow. Remove all foliage, lightly mulch, and label. During the blooming season, you can remove spent flower stalks by clipping them off.

How/When you fertilize:

Hostas will benefit from fertilizing twice a year, if not more. You can work in a dry, slow-release, all-purpose fertilizer near the dripline in the Spring and late Summer. During the growing season, you may also feed with a water-soluble food as you feed other flowers. Adding blood meal when planting is also advisable.

Additional advice for proper care:

Snails and slugs can be a real problem during the Spring. These sneaky creatures come out at night and love a cool, damp place. Try mulching with pine straw and watering early in the morning to prevent moisture at night.

Rudbeckia Goldstrum
Rudbeckia fulgida

This plant is a great one for the look of Grandmother's garden. A single plant can have impact in the Perennial garden and grace the planting bed with dozens of big "black-eyed Susan"-looking blooms! The plant grows to 3 feet high and 3 feet wide. The attractive green, teardrop-shaped foliage is fuzzy to the touch. The plant's growth habit tends to be bushy at the base and then a little spindly as it gets taller. The blooms sit high atop the tall, stiff stems, making it very suitable for indoor cut arrangements.

When to plant:

Early Spring and Fall are the best times to plant. Container specimens are available nearly all year in garden centers. Therefore, with proper watering, you may plant any time the ground is not frozen.

Why you plant:

Used for its long blooming period from Summer through Fall,

Rudbeckia has an incredible impact on the late Summer and Fall garden. Butterflies are attracted to the blooms, which make wonderful fresh cut bouquets. This plant is a great choice for drought-tolerant conditions.

WHERE YOU PLANT:
Place in full sun and average soil. Rudbeckia works well planted toward the back of your perennial and flower beds. Also, it is great in large patio pots mixed with other flowers and greenery.

HOW YOU PLANT:
Dig a hole that is twice the size of the root ball, then add a little organic humus or sphagnum peat moss. Mix into the existing soil, then gently loosen the root ball. Keep the top of the root ball just above the existing soil level. Do not plant too deep.

WHEN YOU WATER:
During Rudbeckia's first year, the plant will benefit from weekly waterings throughout the growing season. After that, the plant can survive on its own.

HOW/WHEN YOU PRUNE:
Rudbeckia needs only one pruning in either late Fall or early Spring, removing the last year's growth. The removal of spent blooms will encourage new blooms and lengthen the color into Fall.

HOW/WHEN YOU FERTILIZE:
If you are blessed with good, rich, loose soil, simply plant it and let it grow. However, like most plants, it would benefit from supplementary feeding with a well-balanced, slow-release granular food gently scratched in around the dripline in early Spring.

ADDITIONAL ADVICE FOR PROPER CARE:
Sometimes when crowded in a garden, Rudbeckia will develop Whiteflies and even Mites. Be sure to provide plenty of room and allow good air flow. A good spraying of dormant oil on the undersides and all over the foliage in mid-Spring is recommended.

Speedwell
Veronica

This particular flower gets a lot of attention in the Tennessee Perennial garden because of the crisp blue flower clusters that cover spikes that are evident from a distance in the garden. What a statement the medium-sized Veronica 'Sunny Border Blue' makes when nestled in any setting where color is welcome. These plants bloom mid-Summer and even into Fall. There are varieties ranging from ground covers up to 4 feet tall. Veronicas are found in pinks, blues and whites.

WHEN TO PLANT:
Any time you can find this plant at your local garden center, get it and plant it. The perfect time is either early Spring or Fall.

WHY YOU PLANT:
There are not many Perennials, or even annuals, that offer such an "electric" blue color in the garden as does this variety. Veronica offers a long blooming time compared to most other Perennials. These tough little plants can also adapt from medium to full, hot sun and will tolerate extreme drought situations.

WHERE YOU PLANT:
A good location is anywhere in your garden that gets medium to full sun. Choose a spot with good drainage, preferably next to a plant with contrasting shades of color and shapes of blooms. For example, the spiky, tall blooms on Veronica really work well in contrast with a daisy-shaped bloom.

HOW YOU PLANT:
Veronicas transplant wonderfully when planting individual plants instead of using seed. The larger varieties, such as 'Sunny Border Blue,' are known to have thick root balls. After digging a nice large hole and adding soil amendments, loosen up the root ball and place the plant in the hole, covering lightly with mulch.

WHEN YOU WATER:

During the first growing season water well—at least two times a week. After Veronica has made it through one full growing season, you should be able to get by with minimal watering.

HOW/WHEN YOU PRUNE:

To keep brilliant blue spikes blooming all Summer, you will need to deadhead. This takes a few minutes every other week during blooming. Just follow the faded bloom spike all the way to the base of the stem, cut and remove. Do not remove the potential small buds which may be coming out.

HOW/WHEN YOU FERTILIZE:

To insure the spectacular blue flower, feed with a slow-release, high phosphate fertilizer applied in early Spring, side dressed around the plant after removing Winter mulch. During late Summer, reapply with a well-balanced, all-purpose granular food. During the growing season, supplement weekly with a water-soluble food as you are feeding your annuals.

ADDITIONAL ADVICE FOR PROPER CARE:

Always remember to remove any yellow, stressed-out foliage evident toward the base. This does not occur unless there is an extraordinarily dry Summer. Deadheading is not a must, but it will ensure a long blooming season.

Stone Crop
Sedum

This sturdy family of plants is a must for any Tennessee rock garden or flower bed. It comes in a great variety of colors, heights and blooming times. The biggest asset of Sedums is that they require little attention.

WHEN TO PLANT:

Plant Sedum any time, as long as the ground is not frozen. The best time to transplant into your garden is early to mid-Spring.

WHY YOU PLANT:

This choice Tennessee Perennial withstands extreme drought and poor soil conditions. A true rock garden would not be complete without Creeping Sedum between rocks. Sedum varieties, such as 'Autumn Joy,' are wonderful to have in a late Summer to Fall garden. Sedums are the essence of carefree gardening.

WHERE YOU PLANT:

Though Sedums are almost foolproof, there are two places they will not survive—one is a dark, shady spot and the other, a damp, wet area. Sedums love full sun and well-drained soil to thrive. Rock gardens and Perennial flower beds can accommodate lots of Sedums.

HOW YOU PLANT:

Simply work up the existing site and dig the hole at least the size of the root ball and preferably another 6-8″ below and around. Then, backfill with the existing soil mixed with a little organic humus or compost. Add Sedum, leaving about one-fourth to one-eighth of the root ball above ground, then cover with the soil mixture.

WHEN YOU WATER:

Always water well with a liquid root stimulator immediately after planting. Once established, Sedums need little water, other than rainfall. However, during the first year, you will need to water well once a week.

HOW/WHEN YOU PRUNE:

Little pruning is needed for most ground cover Sedums. Cut back the taller Sedums just above ground level. Some folks enjoy leaving the dried bloom stalks in the garden until Spring to add an element of interest.

How/When you fertilize:

Normally, Sedums are utilized in poor, hard-to-grow soil conditions. In these areas, a little nutritional supplement would be advisable, such as dried blood, bone meal or a balanced organic food.

Additional advice for proper care:

Make sure your Sedum has good drainage, along with full sun. If you are growing a low ground cover Sedum, be aware of the ability to divide and share with gardening friends after a couple of years of growth.

Sundrops, Evening Primrose
Oenothera

This plant displays yellow, pink, or white blossoms with four broad, silky petals forming a bowl-shaped flower. Some species will flower in the daytime, but most will open as daytime wanes, closing the following morning.

When to plant:

Plant during the Spring in areas where Winters are cold—Middle and East Tennessee. It can be planted during the Fall in milder Winter areas—West Tennessee.

Why you plant:

The Primrose is used for its bright, appealing flowers. It provides a bounty of blossoms over a short period of time with little care required.

Where you plant:

Place in full sun and well-draining soil. Its low-growing habit allows it to be placed in front or it may be used as a border of the Perennial garden.

HOW YOU PLANT:

Dig a hole that is twice the size of the root ball, then add a little organic humus or sphagnum peat moss. Mix into the existing soil, then gently loosen the root ball. Keep the top of the root ball just above the existing soil level. Do not plant too deep.

WHEN YOU WATER:

Water well with root stimulator immediately after planting. If planted in the Fall or early Spring, continue to water every week. If planted during the rapid growing season, frequent watering (two times a week) is advisable. Once the plants are well-established, water twice a month.

HOW/WHEN YOU PRUNE:

To rejuvenate the Primrose, divide during Autumn in mild regions and early Spring in colder climates. New plants can be started from Spring cuttings.

HOW/WHEN YOU FERTILIZE:

If you are blessed with good, rich, loose soil, simply plant it and let it grow. However, like most plants, it would benefit from supplementary feeding with a well-balanced, slow-release granular food gently scratched in around the dripline in early Spring.

ADDITIONAL ADVICE FOR PROPER CARE:

No serious diseases or insects noted.

Tickseed
Coreopsis

Every flower garden in Tennessee needs a splash of Coreopsis because of its great Summer color. Most varieties range from a pale clear yellow to a brilliant golden orange. Coreopsis, if planted in sun, will perform profusely year after year and allow the gardener to divide it and share often.

WHEN TO PLANT:

Although Mother Nature plants in late Summer as the seed falls to the soil, the best time is Fall or early Spring. You may be more successful with plants (instead of seed) to get blooms the first season.

WHY YOU PLANT:

The hardiness and cheery color of the Coreopsis are what make it so desirable. There are many varied heights and textures of foliage available. The tall varieties, such as 'Sunray' (which is a double bloom), are ideal for cut flower arrangements. The shorter varieties, such as 'Moonbeam' and 'Zagreb,' are great for front borders or mass plantings.

WALT'S WISDOM

Only a fool tests the depth of water with both feet.

WHERE YOU PLANT:

Coreopsis need at least a half-day of full sun to really thrive. Certain varieties of Coreopsis need to be planted up against sturdy companion plants that can provide support. The taller varieties tend to flop over after rains and heavy winds, if not supported. Beware of companion plants that will bloom before and after Coreopsis' bloom time.

HOW YOU PLANT:

Coreopsis is easy to transplant from starter plants or clumps or from larger "in-bloom" container-grown plants. Begin by digging the planting hole approximately twice the size of the root ball. Add peat moss or organic humus. Blend it with the soil you have removed. Then add some of the blended soils back into the hole and place the plant into the hole. As you place the plant, gently loosen the roots, then backfill to the point where the top of the root ball is even with the existing soil level. Mulch lightly and water-in thoroughly.

WHEN YOU WATER:

Just after planting, Coreopsis would greatly benefit from watering with a liquid root stimulator. Newly planted specimens should be watered at least two times a week during the growing season. During drought, you may need to water once every week or so as needed.

HOW/WHEN YOU PRUNE:

Most Coreopsis need to be deadheaded to get the most length possible from its blooming time. However, here in Tennessee, most gardeners allow Coreopsis to do its thing, and never cut back the plant until it is finished blooming. The shorter varieties may be carefully but lightly top-sheared to remove the dead blooms, encouraging another surge of late blooms. The taller varieties tend to flop over and become unsightly if left untended after blooming. Cut back about halfway to keep from ruining the plants around it. During late Fall to early Winter, you may remove the past season's growth, although this is not necessary.

HOW/WHEN YOU FERTILIZE:

Coreopsis are not particular feeders. In fact, if they are in decent soil, they would be happy for you to scratch in a little super phosphate around the dripline during early Spring after you have pulled away the Winter layer of mulch. Also, while feeding your other flowers with a water-soluble food, your Coreopsis would appreciate it as well.

ADDITIONAL ADVICE FOR PROPER CARE:

Success is what you will have as long as you plant your Coreopsis in the sun.

Wormwood/Southernwood
Artemisia

This plant has been used in mixed container gardens, mass plantings, and huge Perennial beds. Artemisias are mostly appreciated for their gorgeous silver-blue to silver-grey foliage. The variation in textures is as vast as the heights they grow. Artemisias range from 10" to 4 feet high. Foliage can be harvested from several varieties and utilized in craft projects, such as herbal wreaths and dried floral arrangements.

WHEN TO PLANT:
You may plant container-grown Artemisia any time as long as proper care is taken. However, optimum time for planting is Fall and early Spring.

WHY YOU PLANT:
This is a plant that has a phenomenal effect in any flower bed or Perennial border. The plant is not known for its blooms, but for its contrasting effect on the garden. The striking silver-grey color plays a wonderful role in breaking up masses of blooms. This plant looks breathtaking when planted among blues and hot pinks, and will blend well with any color in the garden.

WHERE YOU PLANT:
Artemisias come in many varying heights, so you need to choose the proper variety according to your garden's needs. Plant in full sun and a very well-drained soil. Also, most of the larger varieties can be invasive. 'Powis Castle' will stay somewhat contained, unlike 'Silver King' and 'Silver Queen.'

HOW YOU PLANT:
After you have selected a spot with full sun, dig a hole up to twice the size of the root ball and add a little organic humus or sphagnum peat moss. Mix the existing soil, then gently loosen

the root ball, making sure to keep the top of the root ball just above the existing soil level. Do not plant too deep.

WHEN YOU WATER:

Water well with root stimulator immediately after planting. If planted in the Fall or early Spring, continue to water every week. If planted during the rapid growing season, frequent watering (two times a week) is advisable. Once the plants are well-established, water twice a month. Artemisias hate "wet feet" - in other words, you must allow them to become dry between waterings.

HOW/WHEN YOU PRUNE:

This is one of the few Perennials that likes to be left alone. It is best to allow Mother Nature to run her course; and as Spring arrives and new growth appears, you may begin selectively pruning away all Winter growth. Some varieties, such as 'Silver King' and 'Silver Queen,' can be harvested through the growing season for use in dried arrangements or wreaths.

HOW/WHEN YOU FERTILIZE:

Artemisias are not heavy feeders. If you are blessed with good, rich, loose soil, simply plant it and let it grow. However, like most plants, it would benefit from supplementary feeding with a well-balanced, slow-release granular food gently scratched in around the dripline in early Spring.

ADDITIONAL ADVICE FOR PROPER CARE:

Selecting your growing site is crucial. Drainage is most important to consider when growing Artemisias. Next is the need for full sun, then make sure you are aware of the potential spread and height of the variety you select. The most popular large Artemisia in Tennessee would have to be 'Powis Castle.' It is truly breathtaking with its soft, delicate, silver cloud-like appearance. 'Silver Mound' is the most popular compact variety, which can be found bordering and accenting the foreground of many a flower garden.

Yarrow, Fern Leaf
Achillea

What a great plant for a carefree gardener! This particular Perennial tolerates a little shade, but does best with some hot sun. It comes in many colors, from pale pink to red, and even a peach and creamy white. There is even a variety 'Pastel Shades,' that has several colors on one plant. The plants have fine textured foliage that is fern-like, as the name implies. They will grow about 3-4 feet high and can spread up to 3 feet wide. The flowers grow in showy, flat-topped clusters.

WHEN TO PLANT:
Yarrow may be planted any time the ground is workable, but the best time is Fall or early Spring.

WHY YOU PLANT:
The Fern Leaf Yarrow blooms almost all Summer. Its foliage is quite attractive, and even when not in bloom, it can create a wonderful contrast against other bolder, or variegated foliage. The blooms are great for cutting long lasting bouquets.

WHERE YOU PLANT:
This plant loves full sun, yet will tolerate some shade. It needs plenty of room in the garden due to its inevitable spreading habit. (This would not be a good choice for small-space gardening.)

HOW YOU PLANT:
Yarrow is easy to transplant from starter plants or clumps or from larger "in-bloom" container-grown plants. You may sow seed in late Summer (just like Mother Nature) by tilling up or raking the ground and scattering seed and sprinkling with a light layer of loose soil or wheat straw. If planting a container or clump, dig a hole about twice the size of the root, add peat moss or organic humus and blend with the existing soil. Place

plant in hole, loosen roots, then backfill barely covering the top surface of the roots. Mulch lightly.

WHEN YOU WATER:

Just after planting, Yarrow will benefit from watering with a liquid root stimulator. Newly-planted specimens should be watered at least two times a week during the growing season, making them virtually maintenance free. During extreme drought, you may need to water weekly.

HOW/WHEN YOU PRUNE:

Prune in late Summer, taking the spent blooms and stems down to the "ferny-clumps" of the main plant. This will ensure a neat Fall look with potential for Fall color. Also, cut back totally in late Winter.

HOW/WHEN YOU FERTILIZE:

Yarrow are not particular feeders. In fact, if they are in decent soil, they would simply be happy if you scratch in a little super phosphate around the dripline in early Spring after you have pulled away the light Winter layer of mulch. Also, if you are feeding your other flowers with a water soluble food, Yarrow would appreciate this as well.

ADDITIONAL ADVICE FOR PROPER CARE:

Dig and divide in early Spring and share with fellow gardeners.

Getting back on

track usually

means getting out

of the rut.

The

Gardener

who plans

reaps

the

Greatest

Reward

COOL
SPRINGS
PRESS

Ajuga
Ajuga reptans

Deadnettle
Lamium

Euonymus
Fortunei coloratus

English Ivy
Hedera helix

Creeping Juniper
Juniperus horizontalis

Pachysandra
Pachysandra terminalis

Snow on the Mountain
Aegopodium podagraria variegatum

Vinca-Periwinkle
Vinca minor

Blue Oat Grass
Helictotrichon sempervirens

Blue Clump Fescue
Festuca glauca

Fountain Grass
Pennisetum alopecuroides

Japanese Blood Grass
Imperata cylindrica rubra

Maiden Grass
Miscanthus sinensis gracillimus

Mondo Grass
Ophiopogon japonicus

Monkey Grass
Liriope muscari

Pampas Grass
Cortaderia selloana

Variegated Sweet Flag
Acorus calamus

Zebra Grass
Miscanthus sinensis 'Zebrinus'

Caladium
Caladium hortulanum

Canna
Canna

Crocus
Crocus

Daffodil
Narcissus

Dahlia
Dahlia

Bearded Iris
Iris Hybrida

Lily
Lillium

Snowdrop
Galanthus nivalis

Tulip
Tulip

Wax Leaf Begonia
Begonia semperflorens

Browallia
Browallia speciosa

Cosmos
Cosmos

Swan River Daisy
Brachycome

Impatiens
Impatiens

'Crystal Palace' Lobelia
Lobelia erinus 'Crystal Palace'

Marigold
Tagetes

Pansy
Viola

Petunia
Petunia x Hybrida

ROSES

Poppy
Papaver

Victoria Blue Salvia
Salvia farinacea 'Victoria'

Sunflower
Helianthus

Torenia
Torenia fournieri

Zinnia
Zinnia elegans

Climbing Roses
Rosa

Grandiflora Roses
Rosa

Ground Cover Roses
Rosa

Hybrid Tea Roses
Rosa

Miniature Roses
Rosa

Old Garden Roses
Rosa

Polyantha Roses
Rosa

Shrub and Hedge Roses
Rosa

Basil
Ocimum basilicum

Chives
Allium schoenoprasum

Coriander/Cilantro
Coriandrum sativum

Dill
Anethum graveolens

Mint
Mentha

Parsley
Petroselinum crispum

Rosemary
Rosmarinum officinalis

Sage
Salvia offinalis

Thyme
Thymus vulgaris

Cattails
Typha latifolia

Japanese and Siberian Iris
Iris

Lotus
Nelumbo nucifera

Pickerel Weed
Pontaderia cordata

Water Hyacinth
Eichbornia crassipes

Water Lily
Nymphaea

Japanese Anemone
Anemone x hybrida

Aster
Aster michaelmas

Astilbe
Astilbe

Beard Tongue
Penstemon

Blue False Indigo
Baptisia australis

Butterfly Weed
Asclepias tuberosa

Columbine
Aquilegia

Purple Coneflower
Echinacea purpurea

Shasta Daisy
Chrysanthemum

Daylily
Hemerocallis

Dianthus
Dianthus

Fern
Fern

Lenton Rose
Helleborus orientalis

Loosestrife
Lythrum

Mums
Chrysanthemum

Peony
Paeonia

Plantain Lily
Hosta

Rudbeckia Goldstrum
Rudbeckia

Speedwell
Veronica

Stone Crop
Sedum

SHRUBS

Evening Primrose Sundrops
Oenothera

Tickseed
Coreopsis

Wormwood/Southernwood
Artemisia

Fern Leaf Yarrow
Achillea

Abelia
Abelia x grandiflora

Althea (Rose of Sharon)
Hibiscus syriacus

Andromeda
Pieris japonica

Aucuba
Aucuba japonica

Exbury Azalea
Hybrids

Girard Azalea
Hybrids

Glenn Dale Azalea
Hybrids

Gumpo Azalea
Satsuki

Indica Azalea
Hybrids

Kurume Azalea
Hybrids

Robin Hill Azalea
Satsuki Hybrids

Crimson Pygmy Barberry
Berberis thunbergii (var. atropurpurea)

Golden Barberry
Berberis

Common Boxwood
Buxus sempervirens

Korean (Littleleaf) Boxwood
Buxus microphylla

Butterfly Bush
Buddleia

Camellia
Camellia japonica

Japanese Cedar
Cryptomeria japonica

Chastetree
Vitex agnus-castus

Cotoneaster
Cotoneaster dammeri

SHRUBS

Crape Myrtle
Lagerstroemia

Deutzia
Deutzia gracilis

Bloodtwig Dogwood
Cornus sanguinea

Redtwig Dogwood
Cornus sericea

Yellowtwig Dogwood
Cornus lutea

Firethorn
Pyracantha coccinea

Forsythia
Forsythia x intermedia

Gold Thread or Mops
Chamaecyparis obtusa

American Holly
Ilex opaca

Chinese Holly
Ilex cornuta

Foster Holly
Ilex x attenuata 'Fosteri'

Japanese Holly
Ilex crenata

Winter Berry Holly
Ilex verticillata

Yaupon Holly
Ilex vomitoria

Big Leaf Hydrangea
Hydrangea macrophylla

Oak Leaf Hydrangea
Hydrangea quercifolia

Smooth Leaf Hydrangea
Hydrangea arborescens

Inkberry
Ilex glabra

Winter Jasmine
Jasminum nudiflorum

English Laurel (Cherrylaurel)
Prunus laurocerasus

Common Lilac
Syringa vulgaris

Persian Lilac
Syringa x persica

Mock Orange
Philadelphus coronarius

Nandina
Nandina domestica

Oregon Grape
Mahonia bealei

Red-Tip Photina
Photina x fraseri

Japanese Privet
Ligustrum japonicum

Flowering Quince
Chaenomeles speciosa

Rhododendron
Rhododendron

'P.J.M.' Rhododendron
Rhododendron

Japanese Spirea
Spirea x bumalda

Shasta Viburnum
Viburnum

Weigela
Weigela florida

Common Witchhazel
Hamamelis virginiana

Intermedia Witchhazel
Hamamelis intermedia

Vernal Witchhazel
Hamamelis vernalis

Yucca (Adam's Needle)
Yucca filamentosa

Clematis
Clematis

Cypress Vine
Ipomoea quamoclit

Honeysuckle
Lonicera sempervirens

Hyacinth Bean Vine
Lablab purpureus (Dolichos Lablab)

Climbing Hydrangea
Hydrangea anomala subsp. petiolaris

Carolina Jessamine
Gelsemium sempervirens

Moonvine
Ipomoea alba

Morning Glory
Ipomoea

Sweet Pea
Lathyrus odoratus

Trumpet Vine
Campsis radicans

Japanese Wisteria
Wisteria floribunda

American Beech
Fagus grandifolia

Heritage River Birch
Betula nigra

Japanese Flowering Cherry
Prunus serrulata

Crabapple
Malus

Dogwood
Cornus florida

White Fringe Tree
Chionanthus virginicus

Ginkgo
Ginkgo biloba

Hawthorn
Crataegus viridus

Littleleaf Linden
Tilia cordata

Saucer Magnolia
Magnolia x soulangiana

Japanese Maple
Acer palmatum

Red Maple
Acer rubrum

Sugar Maple
Acer saccharum

Pin Oak
Quercus palustris

Bradford Pear
Pyrus calleryana

Tulip Poplar
Liriodendron tulipifera

Redbud
Cercis canadensis

Serviceberry
Amelanchier arborea

Carolina Silverbell
Halesia carolina

Sourwood
Oxydendrum arboreum

Sweet Gum
Liquidambar styraciflua

American Yellowwood
Cladrastis kentukea

Japanese Zelkova
Zelkova serrata

Eastern Red Cedar
Juniperus virginiana

EVERGREENS

Leyland Cypress
Cupressocyparis leylandii

Hemlock
Tsuga canadensis

Chinese Juniper
Juniperus chinensis

Eastern White Pine
Pinus strobus

Japanese Black Pine
Pinus thunbergiana

Loblolly Pine
Pinus taeda

Southern Magnolia
Magnolia grandiflora

Colorado Spruce
Picea pungens

Norway Spruce
Picea abies

The things

we learn only

make a difference

when we put them

into action.

Shrubs

$\mathcal{I}$t is easy to become overwhelmed when trying to decide on which shrubs to plant around front and backyard home landscapes in Tennessee. The lawn and garden landscape is simply not complete if it lacks the seasonal interest that assorted shrubs can offer.

Witchhazel has actually bloomed in December and January, surprising us with rare color during those unpredictable Tennessee Winters. And Forsythia has been known to break dormancy very early, spreading golden cheer in late January and February.

In the days of Summer, hardly anything will compare to the huge blooms of the Butterfly Bush, or Buddleia, that is similar to the old-fashioned Lilac. Some folks even call the Crape Myrtle a tree instead of a shrub for the grand potential of its height and spread.

C H A P T E R   T E N

The Fall color of Tennessee shrubs goes a long way in helping brighten the bleak gray days of Winter. The Nandina is not only a visual delight with its bronze-red color, but its bright red berries find their way into Christmas decorations, if not into a bird's mouth first.

There are several shrubs that have an array of seasonal interest, such as the Itea or Virginia Sweetspire, which produces glorious blooms, then bears a gorgeous show of foliage in the Fall.

Fragrant Gardening has increased in popularity recently, which opens up all kinds of choices. Everyone is familiar with the old-fashioned, fragrant Lilac. This was my Grandmother Harbaugh's favorite.

With the variety of shrubs available, Tennessee boasts the possibility of interesting color all year round, declared through blooms, bark, or foliage.

Abelia

Abelia x grandiflora

Maturing to a size of 3-6 feet in height, Abelias are semi-evergreens of small to medium stature which freely bear a beautiful white flower, and are usually grown as hedges or shrub borders. The cultivar, 'Edward Goucher,' is a splendid alternate choice, known for pink blooms. The Abelia is the answer to the request for an evergreen shrub that will bloom throughout the Summer season.

WHEN TO PLANT:
Container-grown plants may be planted year round as soil conditions permit.

WHY YOU PLANT:
Abelias are tough, durable, and very tolerant of heat and humidity. Continuous, all-Summer blooming is the primary reason this evergreen shrub is so desirable.

WHERE YOU PLANT:
Abelias grow best in full sunlight, but will tolerate shade. For optimum performance, place them in well-drained, moist, acidic soil (pH 6-6.5).

HOW YOU PLANT:
Loosen the roots of plants grown in pots... thoroughly!
Prepare a wide, shallow hole 3/4 as deep and 2 times as wide as the root ball. Make a mix of 1/3 soil, 1/3 coarse sand, and 1/3 peat moss, organic humus, or commercial planting mix. Pack firmly around sides of root ball. Add 1-3" of mulch on top, staying clear of the crown of the plant. Then water well with a root stimulator fertilizer. *Note: Avoid planting when soil is frozen 1" deep, or when soil is wet enough to form a mudball in your fist.*

WHEN YOU WATER:

For newly planted shrubs, use a hand-held, open-ended hose, watering plants directly. Do this until the shrub's roots are established, generally one growing season, or when new growth is evident. Light, frequent watering is preferred over heavy watering. When in doubt, check soil wetness with a moisture meter before watering.

HOW/WHEN YOU PRUNE:

Pruning is only required to remove dead wood, then mostly to maintain the desired size. Spring is the best time for trimming.

HOW/WHEN YOU FERTILIZE:

In Spring and early Fall, select a well-balanced, slow-release granular fertilizer at the rate of one-half cup per 10 square feet and broadcast it under the canopy of the shrub and a little beyond.

ADDITIONAL ADVICE FOR PROPER CARE:

With Abelias, you may find some Leaf Spot damage, but nothing serious is expected.

Althea (Rose of Sharon)
Hibiscus syriacus

The Rose of Sharon matures to a height of 8-10 feet and is a deciduous shrub of medium stature. It produces large, 4" flowers in a splendid range of colors, blooming from mid-Summer into early Fall. The blooms are similar to the old-fashioned Hollyhock, and from rose to purple to white, they support the pleasant mood that this shrub's name implies.

WHEN TO PLANT:

The Rose of Sharon is easily transplantable at any time of the year, unless the soil is frozen or too wet.

WHY YOU PLANT:

This plant should be considered for its late season blooming in July, August, and September. We have observed it used mostly as a property border, screening shrub, and as a hedge.

WHERE YOU PLANT:

The Rose of Sharon may be planted in full sun to light shade, and is very tolerant of most soil conditions.

HOW YOU PLANT:

Loosen the roots of plants grown in pots... thoroughly! Prepare a wide, shallow hole 3/4 as deep and 2 times as wide as the root ball. Make a mix of 1/3 soil, 1/3 coarse sand, and 1/3 peat moss, organic humus, or commercial planting mix. Pack firmly around sides of root ball. Add 1-3" of mulch on top, staying clear of the crown of the plant. Then water well with a root stimulator fertilizer. *Note: Avoid planting when soil is frozen 1" deep or when soil is wet enough to form a mudball in your fist.*

WHEN YOU WATER:

Water immediately after planting. Slowly trickle water from the open end of hose approximately one minute per inch diameter of the root ball. Repeat three times the first week, two times the second week, and then once per week until the tree's roots are established, generally one growing season, or until new growth has appeared. When in doubt, check soil wetness with a moisture meter before watering.

HOW/WHEN YOU PRUNE:

To produce larger flowers, prune heavily in the Spring to just two or three buds. This is a practice that few gardeners perform, but rewards the effort with a beautiful payoff.

HOW/WHEN YOU FERTILIZE:

Select a well-balanced, slow-release granular fertilizer at the rate of one-half cup per 10 square feet and broadcast it under the canopy of the shrub and a little beyond.

ADDITIONAL ADVICE FOR PROPER CARE:

Common diseases and insects include Leaf Spot, Aphids, and White Flies. Look for Aphid concentration on newly opening buds, and watch for White Flies on the inner leaves and branches. Consult your local garden center for treatment if you see these problems arise.

Andromeda
Pieris japonica

This evergreen plant is often described as the "Lily of the Valley" shrub. It grows to a height of 6–8 feet and slightly less in width. This shrub features racemes of fragrant, urn-shaped, white flowers which cascade beautifully over the plant's foliage in the early Spring. There are many cultivars to choose from, most exhibiting bright red leaves, such as 'Mountain Fire,' which grows hardy and healthy in protected shade gardens.

WHEN TO PLANT:

Transplant this shrub Spring through Fall as soil conditions permit.

WHY YOU PLANT:

Andromeda is primarily used as a specimen or shrub border. It is a very striking plant, recently growing in popularity because of new interest in shade gardens. The Pieris japonica offers landscape features during all seasons with its evergreen foliage, Spring-blooming and showy new Summer growth.

WHERE YOU PLANT:

Place this variety in areas of partial shade. It likes moist, well-draining soil that is high in organic matter. And it looks wonderful when mixed with shade-loving perennials and ground covers. Andromeda may even be grown successfully in containers.

HOW YOU PLANT:

Loosen the roots of plants grown in pots... thoroughly! Prepare a wide, shallow hole 3/4 as deep and 2 times as wide as the root ball. Make a mix of 1/3 soil, 1/3 coarse sand, and 1/3 peat moss, organic humus, or commercial planting mix. Pack firmly around sides of root ball. Add 1-3" of mulch on top, staying clear of the crown of the plant. Then water well with a root stimulator fertilizer. *Note: Avoid planting when soil is frozen 1" deep or when soil is wet enough to form a mudball in your fist.* Note that additional sphagnum peat moss is recommended in the soil planting mix-ratio of 50 percent peat and 50 percent planting mix.

WHEN YOU WATER:

For newly planted shrubs, use a hand-held, open-ended hose, watering plants directly. Do this until the shrub's roots are established, generally one growing season, or when new growth is evident. Light, frequent watering is preferred over heavy watering. When in doubt, check soil wetness with a moisture meter before watering.

HOW/WHEN YOU PRUNE:

Prune immediately after flowering, by cutting back individual stems to maintain the natural pyramidal form of this shrub.

HOW/WHEN YOU FERTILIZE:

Select a well-balanced, slow-release granular fertilizer at the rate of one-half cup per 10 square feet and broadcast it under the canopy of the shrub and a little beyond.

ADDITIONAL ADVICE FOR PROPER CARE:

Watch for Leaf Spot on this plant, and check for Lace Bugs, which suck juices from the plant and cause foliage discoloration.

This causes the undersides of the leaves to look muddy, but with a spraying of a quality dormant oil in late Winter or early Spring, you may avoid this problem altogether.

Aucuba
Aucuba japonica

The Aucuba matures to 6-10 feet in height and only slightly less in width, with large, attractive, red fruit usually obscured by its thick and heavy foliage. The cultivars vary from green to spotted, 'Gold Dust', to eye-catching yellow splotches. This plant has a distinctively tropical look, and at first glance appears to be better suited to the Florida landscape, but it should do just fine in protected, shady areas in Tennessee.

WHEN TO PLANT:
You can plant Aucuba Spring through Fall as soil conditions permit, as long as the ground is not frozen or too wet.

WHY YOU PLANT:
This is a great shrub to consider when looking for a plant that does well in deep shade, while also producing beautifully colored foliage.

WHERE YOU PLANT:
Plant in shade areas with well-draining soil. The Aucuba does best in West Tennessee rather than the East, because of its warm-blooded nature. In the eastern part of the state, it also runs the risk of frost damage to the leaves.

HOW YOU PLANT:
Loosen the roots of plants grown in pots... thoroughly! Prepare a wide, shallow hole 3/4 as deep and 2 times as wide as the root ball. Make a mix of 1/3 soil, 1/3 coarse sand, and 1/3 peat moss,

organic humus, or commercial planting mix. Pack firmly around sides of root ball. Add 1-3" of mulch on top, staying clear of the crown of the plant. Then water well with a root stimulator fertilizer. *Note: Avoid planting when soil is frozen 1" deep or when soil is wet enough to form a mudball in your fist.*

WHEN YOU WATER:
For newly planted shrubs, use a hand,-held open-ended hose, watering plants directly. Do this until the shrub's roots are established, generally one growing season, or when new growth is evident. Light, frequent watering is preferred over heavy watering. When in doubt, check soil wetness with a moisture meter before watering.

HOW/WHEN YOU PRUNE:
Prune during the Spring to shape and remove any Winter-damaged stems.

HOW/WHEN YOU FERTILIZE:
Select a well-balanced, slow-release granular fertilizer at the rate of one-half cup per 10 square feet and broadcast it under the canopy of the shrub and a little beyond.

ADDITIONAL ADVICE FOR PROPER CARE:
You should not expect any special problems particular to Aucuba, and the addition of this plant will signal that the Caribbean has come to you.

Azalea, Exbury
Hybrids

This particular Azalea matures 6-10 feet in height and 2-3 feet in width. Upright in growth, this deciduous shrub has light-green foliage turning yellow to orange during the Fall. Blossoms of the Exbury Azalea run a full range of color: from pink, cream, orange, rose, red, yellow to white. This Azalea best typifies the native ones found dotting the East Tennessee countryside. Rarely are any natural Azaleas found growing in the woods of Middle Tennessee, but this does not mean they won't do well in yards spanning the state, if only given a little tender loving care.

WHEN TO PLANT:
Plant this Azalea Spring through Fall, as soil conditions permit.

WHY YOU PLANT:
The Exbury Azalea thrives in the cold and has a wide variety of blooming colors. This deciduous variety will tolerate more direct sun and varying soil conditions than most Azaleas, and the Exbury is particularly suited for good growth in the chillier temperatures of East Tennessee.

WHERE YOU PLANT:
Plant in sun or shade in well-draining, moist, acidic soil (pH 5.0- 6.0).

HOW YOU PLANT:
Loosen the roots of plants grown in pots... thoroughly! Prepare a wide, shallow hole 3/4 as deep and 2 times as wide as the root ball. Make a mix of 1/3 soil, 1/3 coarse sand, and 1/3 peat moss, organic humus, or commercial planting mix. Pack firmly around sides of root ball. Add 1-3" of mulch on top, staying clear of the crown of the plant. Then water well with a root stimulator fer-tilizer. *Note: Avoid planting when soil is frozen 1" deep or when soil is wet enough to form a mudball in your fist.*

WHEN YOU WATER:
For newly planted shrubs, use a hand-held, open-ended hose, watering plants directly. Do this until the shrub's roots are established, generally one growing season, or when new growth

is evident. Light, frequent watering is preferred over heavy watering. When in doubt, check soil wetness with a moisture meter before watering.

HOW/WHEN YOU PRUNE:
Prune after flowering, sometime during the Spring, and trim out individual branches to maintain a natural appearance. This plant may also be "headed-back" to keep a desired height.

HOW/WHEN YOU FERTILIZE:
Feed Azaleas immediately after blooming ceases, and then again 6-8 weeks later. Fertilization should be stopped after July. Use specially formulated plant foods for Azaleas, and consider using a new combination Azalea fertilizer with systemic insecticide for insect protection.

ADDITIONAL ADVICE FOR PROPER CARE:
You may expect very few problems, with Powdery Mildew being the only significant exception. Otherwise, the Exbury should provide some of the most beautiful flowers in the world of shrubs.

Azalea, Girard
Hybrids

Maturing to 3-5 feet in height, Girard Hybrids are usually selected for their cold-hardiness and large flowers produced in mid-Spring. Cultivar colors vary from 'Girard's Hot Shot,' 'Girard's Purple,' to 'Girard's Rose,' all riddled with various splashes of color. Recently, Girards have gained popularity in Tennessee landscapes due to their late-blooming hardiness, and fashionable colors. Girards are perfect to consider if you worry about Jack Frost nipping at your plants.

WHEN TO PLANT:
Container shrubs of this variety may be planted Spring through Fall.

WHY YOU PLANT:
This is an excellent, large-flowering, evergreen Azalea which will tolerate temperatures as low as -5 degrees to -15 degrees Fahrenheit.

WHERE YOU PLANT:
Girard Hybrids do well when planted in shade. Partial shade is the best landscape location, but they will perform satisfactorily in full sun as well. Place them in well-drained, highly organic, moist soils with an acidic range of 5.0-6.0 pH.

HOW YOU PLANT:
Loosen the roots of plants grown in pots... thoroughly! Prepare a wide, shallow hole 3/4 as deep and 2 times as wide as the root ball. Make a mix of 1/3 soil, 1/3 coarse sand, and 1/3 peat moss, organic humus, or commercial planting mix. Pack firmly around sides of root ball. Add 1-3" of mulch on top, staying clear of the crown of the plant. Then water well with a root stimulator fertilizer. *Note: Avoid planting when soil is frozen 1" deep or when soil is wet enough to form a mudball in your fist.*

WHEN YOU WATER:
For newly planted shrubs, use a hand-held, open-ended hose, watering plants directly. Do this until the shrub's roots are established, generally one growing season, or when new growth is evident. Light, frequent watering is preferred over heavy watering. When in doubt, check soil wetness with a moisture meter before watering.

HOW/WHEN YOU PRUNE:
Preferably, Azaleas are to be pruned by the "reach and cut" method, which trims individual branches when the natural

growing appearance is desired. The plant may also be maintained in a "Boxwood shape" by shearing, and should be pruned
immediately after blooming.

HOW/WHEN YOU FERTILIZE:
Fertilize immediately after blooming by broadcasting granular
Azalea food to the base of the plants, and repeat this process in
6-8 weeks. The one thing to avoid is late Summer fertilization.
If shrubs show yellowing, supplement feeding with an iron
fertilizer.

ADDITIONAL ADVICE FOR PROPER CARE:
Crown Rot, Powdery Mildew, Aphids, and Azalea Stem Borers
are only a few of the many diseases and pests to attack these
shrubs. Most recently, Azalea Lace Bugs have been active in
Tennessee plantings. Consult your local garden center to combat these problems before they arise, leaving the blooms for
your enjoyment... not the bugs'.

Azalea, Glenn Dale
Hybrids

*Glenn Dale Hybrids mature to a height of 4-6 feet, featuring the cold-hardi-
ness of the Girard cultivars, and flowers as large and varied as the Indica
Types. Popular hybrids come dressed as follows: 'H. H. Hume' in white,
'Fashion' in orange-red, and 'Delaware Valley' in white. The Glenn Dale
Hybrids grow more open and less compact than the Kurume Azaleas, and
combine many features of other hybrids, to offer several desirable growth
characteristics in one beautiful variety.*

WHEN TO PLANT:
Container shrubs of this variety may be planted Spring through
Fall, as soil conditions permit.

WHY YOU PLANT:

This is an excellent, large-flowering evergreen plant which will tolerate temperatures as low as -5 degrees to -15 degrees Fahrenheit.

WHERE YOU PLANT:

Glenn Dale Hybrids do well when planted in shade, and although partial shade is the best landscape location, they will perform satisfactorily in full sunlight. Place them in well-drained, highly organic, moist soils with an acidic range of 5.0-6.0 pH.

HOW YOU PLANT:

Loosen the roots of plants grown in pots... thoroughly! Prepare a wide, shallow hole 3/4 as deep and 2 times as wide as the root ball. Make a mix of 1/3 soil, 1/3 coarse sand, and 1/3 peat moss, organic humus, or commercial planting mix. Pack firmly around sides of root ball. Add 1-3" of mulch on top, staying clear of the crown of the plant. Then water well with a root stimulator fertilizer. *Note: Avoid planting when soil is frozen 1" deep or when soil is wet enough to form a mudball in your fist.*

WHEN YOU WATER:

For newly planted shrubs, use a hand-held, open-ended hose, watering plants directly. Do this until the shrub's roots are established, generally one growing season, or when new growth is evident. Light, frequent watering is preferred over heavy watering. When in doubt, check soil wetness with a moisture meter before watering.

HOW/WHEN YOU PRUNE:

Preferably, Azaleas are to be pruned by the "reach and cut" method, which trims individual branches when the natural growing appearance is desired. Also, the plant may be maintained in a "Boxwood shape" by shearing. Always prune shortly after blooming.

How/When you fertilize:

Fertilize immediately after blooming by broadcasting granular Azalea food to the base of plants. Repeat this process in 6-8 weeks. Avoid late Summer fertilization, and if shrubs show yellowing, supplement feeding with an iron fertilizer.

Additional advice for proper care:

Crown Rot, Powdery Mildew, Aphids, and Azalea Stem Borers are only a few of the many diseases and pests to attack these shrubs. Most recently, Azalea Lace Bugs have been active in Tennessee plantings, so keep an eye out for them and consult your local garden center at first spotting.

Azalea, Gumpo
Satsuki

Maturing to 2 feet in height and 3 feet in width, the Gumpo blooms late, during May and June, in a variety of soft pink and white blooms. We predict the Satsuki, particularly the 'Robin Hill' series, will gain popularity in Tennessee gardens for its tolerance of sun and hot temperatures, as well as cold resistance. In the past, the Gumpo Azalea has been overlooked as a wise choice for Tennessee landscapes, but it reflects the softness and strength of many a Southern lady, with beauty and boldness wonderfully intertwined.

When to plant:

Container shrubs of this variety may be planted Spring through Fall.

Why you plant:

The Gumpo Azalea offers the option of extended mid-to-late blooming, rounding off the season with color.

WHERE YOU PLANT:

The low-spreading habit makes this Azalea an excellent choice for borders and areas with more sun than others, since it features more heat tolerance than other varieties.

HOW YOU PLANT:

Loosen the roots of plants grown in pots... thoroughly! Prepare a wide, shallow hole 3/4 as deep and 2 times as wide as the root ball. Make a mix of 1/3 soil, 1/3 coarse sand, and 1/3 peat moss, organic humus, or commercial planting mix. Pack firmly around sides of root ball. Add 1-3" of mulch on top, staying clear of the crown of the plant. Then water well with a root stimulator fertilizer. *Note: Avoid planting when soil is frozen 1" deep or when soil is wet enough to form a mudball in your fist.*

WHEN YOU WATER:

For newly planted shrubs, use a hand-held, open-ended hose, watering plants directly. Do this until the shrub's roots are established, generally one growing season, or when new growth is evident. Light, frequent watering is preferred over heavy watering. When in doubt, check soil wetness with a moisture meter before watering.

HOW/WHEN YOU PRUNE:

Preferably, Azaleas are to be pruned by the "reach and cut" method, which trims individual branches when the natural growing appearance is desired. The plant can also be maintained in a "Boxwood shape" by shearing, and should always be pruned shortly after blooming.

HOW/WHEN YOU FERTILIZE:

Feed Azaleas immediately after blooming ceases, and then again 6-8 weeks later. Fertilization should be stopped after July. Use specially formulated plant foods for Azaleas, and consider using a new combination Azalea fertilizer with systemic insecticide for insect protection.

Crown Rot, Powdery Mildew, Aphids, and Azalea Stem Borers are only a few of the many diseases and pests to attack these shrubs. Most recently, Azalea Lace Bugs have been active in Tennessee plantings, so be aware of them if you consider planting this sleeper variety in your own lawn or garden. Your garden center can be of assistance with the control of Azalea pests.

Azalea, Indica
Hybrids

These types are commonly known as the "Southern Indian Hybrids," maturing to a height of 3-6 feet. Indicas are typically large shrubs, with wonderful 2-3 1/2" flowers. The white bloomers are the most tolerant of sun areas, but less tolerant of cold temperatures. When thinking of the lush, rich floral color at The Masters golf tournament, you are seeing an impressive array of Azaleas, like the Indica types. This variety does best in West Tennessee, and other warmer climates, such as central Georgia, site of The Masters.

WHEN TO PLANT:
Plant this variety Spring through Fall, as soil conditions permit.

WHY YOU PLANT:
This is an excellent, large-flowering, evergreen shrub. This variety will accept full sun areas, where most Azaleas do not grow particularly well.

WHERE YOU PLANT:
You might want to consider Indicas over Kurume and Glenn Dale varieties if sun is a significant factor in your landscape. Indica's cold-hardiness is limited and they will perform best if grown in the warmer parts of the state.

HOW YOU PLANT:

Loosen the roots of plants grown in pots... thoroughly! Prepare a wide, shallow hole 3/4 as deep and 2 times as wide as the root ball. Make a mix of 1/3 soil, 1/3 coarse sand, and 1/3 peat moss, organic humus, or commercial planting mix. Pack firmly around sides of root ball. Add 1-3" of mulch on top, staying clear of the crown of the plant. Then water well with a root stimulator fertilizer. *Note: Avoid planting when soil is frozen 1" deep or when soil is wet enough to form a mudball in your fist.*

WHEN YOU WATER:

For newly planted shrubs, use a hand-held, open-ended hose, watering plants directly. Do this until the shrub's roots are established, generally one growing season, or when new growth is evident. Light, frequent watering is preferred over heavy watering. When in doubt, check soil wetness with a moisture meter before watering.

HOW/WHEN YOU PRUNE:

Prune Indicas after flowering occurs during the Spring. Trim out the individual branches to maintain a natural appearance. This plant may also be "headed-back" to keep a desired height.

HOW/WHEN YOU FERTILIZE:

Feed Azaleas immediately after blooming ceases, and then again 6-8 weeks later. Fertilization should be stopped after July. Use specially formulated plant foods for Azaleas, and consider using a new combination Azalea fertilizer with systemic insecticide for insect protection.

ADDITIONAL ADVICE FOR PROPER CARE:

You can expect very few problems from this variety, with Powdery Mildew being the only exception. Unlike its other colder brothers, Indica does not seem to suffer as much from Lace Bug infestation.

Azalea, Kurume

Hybrids

Maturing to 3-6 feet in height, this variety bears the distinction of being the most popular in the state of Tennessee. We find this somewhat surprising, since their early blooming habits prior to the Spring frost make them unreliable Spring performers. Kurume Azaleas are extremely floriferous Azaleas of medium stature, and may even be maintained as small shrubs. The cultivars are as interesting and expressive as their names: 'Hershey Red,' 'Coral Bell Pink,' 'Hinodegiri,' 'Lipstick Red,' 'Mothers Day,' and 'Ruby Red.' How can you be anything but popular with names like these?

WHEN TO PLANT:
Container shrubs of this variety may be planted Spring through Fall, as soil conditions allow.

WHY YOU PLANT:
This is an excellent multi-flowering, evergreen shrub which will tolerate temperatures as low as -5 degrees to -15 degrees Fahrenheit.

WHERE YOU PLANT:
Kurume Azaleas do well when planted in shade, although partial shade is the best landscape location, and they will even perform satisfactorily in full sunlight. Be sure to place the plants in well-drained, highly organic, moist soils with an acidic range of 5.0-6.0 pH.

HOW YOU PLANT:
Loosen the roots of plants grown in pots... thoroughly! Prepare a wide, shallow hole 3/4 as deep and 2 times as wide as the root ball. Make a mix of 1/3 soil, 1/3 coarse sand, and 1/3 peat moss, organic humus, or commercial planting mix. Pack firmly around sides of root ball. Add 1-3" of mulch on

top, staying clear of the crown of the plant. Then water well with a root stimulator fertilizer. *Note: Avoid planting when soil is frozen 1" deep or when soil is wet enough to form a mudball in your fist.*

WHEN YOU WATER:

For newly planted shrubs, use a hand-held, open-ended hose, watering plants directly. Do this until the shrub's roots are established, generally one growing season or when new growth is evident. Light, frequent watering is preferred over heavy watering. When in doubt, check soil wetness with a moisture meter before watering.

HOW/WHEN YOU PRUNE:

Preferably, Azaleas are to be pruned by the "reach and cut" method, which trims individual branches when the natural growing appearance is desired. The plant may also be maintained in a "Boxwood shape" by shearing, and should always be pruned shortly after blooming.

HOW/WHEN YOU FERTILIZE:

Fertilize immediately after blooming by broadcasting granular Azalea food to the base of plants. Repeat this process in 6-8 weeks. Avoid a late-Summer fertilization, and if shrubs show yellowing, supplement feeding with an iron fertilizer.

ADDITIONAL ADVICE FOR PROPER CARE:

Crown Rot, Powdery Mildew, Aphids, and Azalea Stem Borers are only a few of the many diseases and pests to attack these shrubs. Most recently, Azalea Lace Bugs have been active in Tennessee plantings, so consult your local garden center for remedies to these potentially life-threatening pests.

Azalea, Robin Hill

Satsuki Hybrids

Maturing to 2-3 feet in height and width, this is a Japanese evergreen Azalea that blooms late during May and June, sporting several different options for flower color. We are predicting future stardom for this variety in Tennessee, since it combines talents of heat and cold tolerance, making it the landscape's all-weather, and not just fair-weather, friend.

WHEN TO PLANT:
Container shrubs of this variety may be planted Spring through Fall, as the soil conditions permit.

WHY YOU PLANT:
Plant the Robin Hill variety when you prefer a late-blooming, more compact, dwarf-type Azalea.

WHERE YOU PLANT:
Place this variety in full sunlight to partial shade. Planting in partial shade while avoiding the afternoon sun will prolong the blooming season.

HOW YOU PLANT:
Loosen the roots of plants grown in pots... thoroughly! Prepare a wide, shallow hole 3/4 as deep and 2 times as wide as the root ball. Make a mix of 1/3 soil, 1/3 coarse sand, and 1/3 peat moss, organic humus, or commercial planting mix. Pack firmly around sides of root ball. Add 1-3" of mulch on top, staying clear of the crown of the plant. Then water well with a root stimulator fertilizer. *Note: Avoid planting when soil is frozen 1" deep or when soil is wet enough to form a mudball in your fist.*

WHEN YOU WATER:
For newly planted shrubs, use a hand-held, open-ended hose, watering plants directly. Do this until the shrub's roots are

established, generally one growing season, or when new growth is evident. Light, frequent watering is preferred over heavy watering. When in doubt, check soil wetness with a moisture meter before watering.

HOW/WHEN YOU PRUNE:
Preferably, Azaleas are to be pruned by the "reach and cut" method, which trims individual branches when the natural growing appearance is desired. The plant can also be maintained in a "Boxwood shape" by shearing. Always prune shortly after blooming.

HOW/WHEN YOU FERTILIZE:
Feed Azaleas immediately after blooming ceases, and then again 6-8 weeks later. Fertilization should be stopped after July. Use specially formulated plant foods for Azaleas, and consider using a new combination Azalea fertilizer with systemic insecticide for insect protection.

ADDITIONAL ADVICE FOR PROPER CARE:
Crown Rot, Powdery Mildew, Aphids, and Azalea Stem Borers are only a few of the many diseases and pests to attack these shrubs. Most recently, Azalea Lace Bugs have been active in Tennessee plantings. Consult your local garden center for solutions if any of these problems arise.

Barberry, Crimson Pygmy
Berberis thunbergii (var. atropurpurea)

Maturing to 3-4 feet in height and width, this Barberry has a dense branching habit, giving it a full, thick appearance. It has a signature purple-red foliage all Summer long, which changes to deep amber with the onset of cooler weather. Because of the colorful Summer foliage, this deciduous plant is very popular during the Summer months.

WHEN TO PLANT:

This shrub is available mostly as a container-grown plant, making it possible to plant any time the soil is workable.

WHY YOU PLANT:

The Barberry is superb as a hedge, border, or in a mass grouping. It features a great color contrast to the background of the overall landscape.

WHERE YOU PLANT:

Plant this variety in full sun areas for the best growth and color intensity. It is very adaptable to a variety of soil and growing conditions.

WALT'S WISDOM

A little

kindess goes a

long way.

HOW YOU PLANT:

Loosen the roots of plants grown in pots... thoroughly! Prepare a wide, shallow hole 3/4 as deep and 2 times as wide as the root ball. Make a mix of 1/3 soil, 1/3 coarse sand, and 1/3 peat moss, organic humus, or commercial planting mix. Pack firmly around sides of root ball. Add 1-3" of mulch on top, staying clear of the crown of the plant. Then water well with a root stimulator fertilizer. *Note: Avoid planting when soil is frozen 1" deep or when soil is wet enough to form a mudball in your fist.*

WHEN YOU WATER:

For newly planted shrubs, use a hand-held, open-ended hose, watering plants directly. Do this until the shrub's roots are established, generally one growing season or when new growth is evident. Light, frequent watering is preferred over heavy watering. When in doubt, check soil wetness with a moisture meter before watering.

HOW/WHEN YOU PRUNE:

Pruning is only needed to shape or keep the plant to the desired size. This shrub may be trimmed at any time, but the time prior to new growth - in Winter and early Spring - is suggested.

How/When you fertilize:
Select a well-balanced, slow-release granular fertilizer at the rate of one-half cup per 10 square feet and broadcast it under the canopy of the shrub and a little beyond. Feed in the Spring.

Additional advice for proper care:
Diseases and insects are not expected to be serious with this variety, but a good spraying with a quality dormant oil prior to Spring growth will prevent possible Spider Mite infestation.

Barberry, Golden
Berberis Aurea

This plant grows in a dwarf, mound-type shape, and is similar in dimension and stature to the Crimson Barberry, except that the foliage is a bright yellow instead of a brilliant, deep red. The Golden Barberry is very striking during the Summer, especially when planted in mass groupings or used as a border. This is the one to consider for a glimpse of the hazy, golden days of Summer bursting forth in a backyard or garden setting.

When to plant:
This shrub is available mostly as a container-grown plant, and therefore, may be planted anytime the soil is workable.

Why you plant:
This variety is superb as a hedge, border, or in a mass grouping. It offers great color contrast, throughout the Spring, Summer and Fall.

WHERE YOU PLANT:

Plant in full sunlight areas for the best growth and color intensity. It is very adaptable to a variety of soil and growing conditions, so you can be creative in the placement to highlight areas of your yard.

HOW YOU PLANT:

Loosen the roots of plants grown in pots... thoroughly! Prepare a wide, shallow hole 3/4 as deep and 2 times as wide as the root ball. Make a mix of 1/3 soil, 1/3 coarse sand, and 1/3 peat moss, organic humus, or commercial planting mix. Pack firmly around sides of root ball. Add 1-3" of mulch on top, staying clear of the crown of the plant. Then water well with a root stimulator fertilizer. *Note: Avoid planting when soil is frozen 1" deep or when soil is wet enough to form a mudball in your fist.*

WHEN YOU WATER:

For newly planted shrubs, use a hand-held, open-ended hose, watering plants directly. Do this until the shrub's roots are established, generally one growing season or when new growth is evident. Light, frequent watering is preferred over heavy watering. When in doubt, check soil wetness with a moisture meter before watering.

HOW/WHEN YOU PRUNE:

Pruning is only needed to shape or keep the plant at a desired size. This shrub can be trimmed at any time, however, Winter to early Spring, (prior to new growth) is suggested.

HOW/WHEN YOU FERTILIZE:

Select a well-balanced, slow-release granular fertilizer at the rate of one-half cup per 10 square feet and broadcast it under the canopy of the shrub and a little beyond. Feed in the Spring.

ADDITIONAL ADVICE FOR PROPER CARE:

Diseases and insects are not expected to be serious with this variety, but a good spraying with a quality dormant oil prior to Spring growth will prevent possible Spider Mite infestation.

Boxwood, Common
Buxus sempervirens

Maturing to 10-15 feet in height, this is the aristocrat of all shrubs. When lined up in a hedge, it creates a look of distinction and historical importance. Boxwoods are synonymous with the great estates of Western civilization. They've been used throughout landscapes from the traditional English gardens to plantation estates of the New World, such as Mount Vernon, George Washington's home.

WHEN TO PLANT:
This shrub is very transplantable because of its fibrous root system, making it one of the few plants that can be dug and transplanted year-round with probable success.

WHY YOU PLANT:
The Common Boxwood lends to shaping in hedges, as a topiary, and as a specimen shrub. It is also used to anchor the ends of beds and to enhance the entrance to residences, creating quite a regal appearance.

WHERE YOU PLANT:
Locate this shrub in full sun to partial shade in well-draining soil for the best results.

HOW YOU PLANT:
Position root ball in a wide, shallow hole 3/4 as deep and 2 times as wide as the root ball. Cut twine around trunk and top of root ball, remove any nails, fold back burlap to the sides of

the root ball. Do not remove wire cage. No need to loosen
roots. Make a mix of 1/3 soil, 1/3 coarse sand, and 1/3 peat

moss, organic humus or commercial planting mix.
Pack firmly around sides of root ball. Add 2-3" of
mulch on top. Water well with a root stimulator
fertilizer. *Note: Avoid planting when soil is frozen 1" deep
or when soil forms mud balls.*

Always tell the

truth, then you

won't worry

over what

you've said.

WHEN YOU WATER:
Water immediately after planting. Slowly trickle
water from the open end of hose approximately
one minute per inch diameter of the root ball.
Repeat three times the first week, two times the
second week, and then once per week until the
tree's roots are established, generally one growing
season, or until new growth has appeared. When in
doubt, check soil wetness with a moisture meter
before watering.

HOW/WHEN YOU PRUNE:
The Common Boxwood is densely textured and
can be sheared almost any time of the year, but avoid late Fall
and late Spring trimming, when the light green, new growth is
present.

HOW/WHEN YOU FERTILIZE:
Fertilize during the Spring by applying one-half cup of well-
balanced, slow-release granular fertilizer per one foot height of
the shrub. Broadcast the plant food evenly under the dripline of
the shrub.

ADDITIONAL ADVICE FOR PROPER CARE:
Common diseases and insects include Canker Blight, Root Rot,
Scale, and Boxleaf Miner. Root Rot is a problem, and off-col-
ored foliage indicates the possibility of poorly drained soil.
Consult your local garden center for proper action to take.

Boxwood, Korean (Littleleaf)
Buxus microphylla

If the Common Boxwood is the most regal of its kind, then the Littleleaf must be "Prince" because of its smaller stature, but similar pedigree to its larger parent. This little fellow matures to 2-3 feet in height and is a much hardier variety, but there is a trade-off: the Littleleaf Boxwood's foliage discolors in cold Winter weather, but it will survive to -20 degrees.

WHEN TO PLANT:
This shrub is very transplantable because of its fibrous root system, making it one of the few plants that can be dug and transplanted year-round with probable success.

WHY YOU PLANT:
Littleleaf Boxwoods are planted for hardy formal hedging and landscape bordering. 'Wintergreen' and 'Winter Gem' are two of our favorite cultivars.

WHERE YOU PLANT:
Place this shrub in full sun to partial shade in well-draining soil.

HOW YOU PLANT:
Position root ball in a wide, shallow hole 3/4 as deep and 2 times as wide as the root ball. Cut twine around trunk and top of root ball, remove any nails, fold back burlap to the sides of the root ball. Do not remove wire cage. No need to loosen roots. Make a mix of 1/3 soil, 1/3 coarse sand, and 1/3 peat moss, organic humus or commercial planting mix. Pack firmly around sides of root ball. Add 2-3" of mulch on top. Water well with a root stimulator fertilizer. *Note: Avoid planting when soil is frozen 1" deep or when soil forms mud balls.*

WHEN YOU WATER:
Water immediately after planting. Slowly trickle water from the

open end of hose approximately one minute per inch diameter of the root ball. Repeat three times the first week, two times the second week, and then once per week until the tree's roots are established, generally one growing season, or until new growth has appeared. When in doubt, check soil wetness with a moisture meter before watering.

HOW/WHEN YOU PRUNE:
The Littleleaf Boxwood is of dense texture and may be sheared almost any time of the year, but do avoid late Fall and late Spring trimming, when the light green, new growth is present.

HOW/WHEN YOU FERTILIZE:
During the Spring, apply one-half cup of well balanced slow-release granular fertilizer per one foot height of the plant, and broadcast the plant food evenly under the dripline of the shrub.

ADDITIONAL ADVICE FOR PROPER CARE:
Common diseases and insects include Canker Blight, Root Rot, Scale, and Boxleaf Miner. Root Rot is a problem, and off-colored foliage indicates the possibility of poorly drained soil. Take care to plant in a well-drained area, or consider a transplant to a more suitable location for healthy growth, since it does survive transplanting well.

Butterfly Bush
Buddleia

As you might guess from the name, this shrub is a great attraction for butterflies. Maturing to a height of 5-10 feet, it is often referred to as Summer Lilac for the aromatic scent of the fragrant flowers which lure the butterflies its way. It may also lure you to plant it for the duration of blooms, which last from June until the first frost of the Fall.

WHEN TO PLANT:
Container-grown plants may be transplanted any time the soil conditions permit.

WHY YOU PLANT:
This shrub is valued for its Summer-long flowering and its ability to lure butterflies. The blooms range in several colors, from white, pink, red and lavender blue to even yellow.

WHERE YOU PLANT:
The Butterfly Bush is used as a border, in mass plantings, and as a single shrub in a Perennial garden. Plant in full sun areas, with well-drained, fertile soil.

HOW YOU PLANT:
Loosen the roots of plants grown in pots... thoroughly! Prepare a wide, shallow hole 3/4 as deep and 2 times as wide as the root ball. Make a mix of 1/3 soil, 1/3 coarse sand, and 1/3 peat moss, organic humus, or commercial planting mix. Pack firmly around sides of root ball. Add 1-3" of mulch on top, staying clear of the crown of the plant. Then water well with a root stimulator fertilizer. *Note: Avoid planting when soil is frozen 1" deep or when soil is wet enough to form a mudball in your fist.*

WHEN YOU WATER:
For newly planted shrubs, use a hand-held, open-ended hose, watering plants directly. Do this until the shrub's roots are established, generally one growing season, or when new growth is evident. Light, frequent watering is preferred over heavy watering. When in doubt, check soil wetness with a moisture meter before watering.

HOW/WHEN YOU PRUNE:
This vigorously growing shrub performs well when cut to the ground during the Spring, before new growth begins.

HOW/WHEN YOU FERTILIZE:

In early Spring prior to new growth, select a well-balanced, slow-release granular fertilizer at the rate of one-half cup per 10 square feet and broadcast it under the canopy of the shrub and a little beyond.

ADDITIONAL ADVICE FOR PROPER CARE:

No serious disease or insect problems are expected, making for virtually trouble-free enjoyment of blooms and butterflies all Summer long.

Camellia
Camellia japonica

Maturing to 6-7 feet in height, Camellias continue to be a favorite evergreen flowering shrub for Southern gardeners. It is known as the "Winter Rose Bush" because of its rose-like blossoms displayed from September to April. It does need reasonably gentle temperatures in the colder months to put on its rare Winter show. Bud damage can be a problem in the colder climate areas of East Tennessee, leaving better chances for success with Camellias to the West Tennessee gardener.

WHEN TO PLANT:

This container shrub may be planted any time of year that soil conditions permit.

WHY YOU PLANT:

Camellias are known for their delightful blooms during an otherwise drab time of Winter.

WHERE YOU PLANT:

Plant in full sun to light shade areas with a fertile, high humus,

well-draining, slightly acidic (pH 6.0-6.5) soil. Camelia
Japonica is limited to landscape use in West Tennessee, but
blooms from September through November and can be hardy in
Middle and East Tennessee.

HOW YOU PLANT:

Loosen the roots of plants grown in pots... thoroughly!
Prepare a wide, shallow hole 3/4 as deep and 2 times as wide
as the root ball. Make a mix of 1/3 soil, 1/3 coarse sand, and
1/3 peat moss, organic humus, or commercial planting mix.
Pack firmly around sides of root ball. Add 1-3" of mulch on
top, staying clear of the crown of the plant. Then water
well with a root stimulator fertilizer. *Note: Avoid planting when
soil is frozen 1" deep or when soil is wet enough to form a mudball in
your fist.*

WHEN YOU WATER:

For newly planted shrubs, use a hand-held, open-ended hose,
watering plants directly. Do this until the shrub's roots are
established, generally one growing season or when new growth
is evident. Light, frequent watering is preferred over heavy
watering. When in doubt, check soil wetness with a moisture
meter before watering.

HOW/WHEN YOU PRUNE:

Prune any time by the "reach and cut" method, by reaching
inside and trimming out single branches, and prune Camellia
shortly after flowering.

HOW/WHEN YOU FERTILIZE:

Select a well-balanced, slow-release granular fertilizer at the rate
of one-half cup per 10 square feet and broadcast it under the
canopy of the shrub and a little beyond.

ADDITIONAL ADVICE FOR PROPER CARE:

Common diseases and insects include Black Mold and physiological disorders such as Bud Drop and Sunburn Chlorosis. The

major insect to watch for is Scale, and you should consult your local garden center if any of these problems arise.

Cedar, Japanese
Cryptomeria japonica

This is a stately, upright shrub used to anchor, or attract the eye, towards a landscape setting you might want to highlight. This shrub has foliage which is best described as a contrasting kaleidoscope to the mood of the season, with a cool, blue-green color in the Summer, which turns to a warm, bronze tint to liven up the chill of Winter.

WHEN TO PLANT:
This shrub is transplantable any time the soil conditions will permit.

WHY YOU PLANT:
Japanese Cedar is used for the contrasting attention of the foliage. During the Summer, it displays a rich, bright, blue-green foliage which turns to a bronze hue in the Winter, making the Japanese Cedar appealing all year.

WHERE YOU PLANT:
Plant in full sun to light shade areas. This shrub enjoys a light, rich, deep soil with a pH of 6-6.5.

HOW YOU PLANT:
Loosen the roots of plants grown in pots... thoroughly! Prepare a wide, shallow hole 3/4 as deep and 2 times as wide as the root ball. Make a mix of 1/3 soil, 1/3 coarse sand, and 1/3 peat moss, organic humus, or commercial planting mix. Pack firmly around sides of root ball. Add 1-3" of mulch on top, staying clear of the

crown of the plant. Then water well with a root stimulator fertilizer. *Note: Avoid planting when soil is frozen 1" deep or when soil is wet
enough to form a mudball in your fist.*

WHEN YOU WATER:
For newly planted shrubs, use a hand-held, open-ended hose,
watering plants directly. Do this until the shrub's roots are
established, generally one growing season, or when new growth
is evident. Light, frequent watering is preferred over heavy
watering. When in doubt, check soil wetness with a moisture
meter before watering.

HOW/WHEN YOU PRUNE:
This variety may be pruned all during the year except for periods of single digit temperatures. Selective trimming is preferred
to maintain the pyramid shape, but shearing is acceptable with
a pair of quality pruning shears.

HOW/WHEN YOU FERTILIZE:
Fertilize during the early Spring by broadcasting an evergreen
fertilizer as directed to the base and outlying canopy of the
shrub.

ADDITIONAL ADVICE FOR PROPER CARE:
A common disease is Branch Die Back, which is a physiological
disorder caused by environmental conditions. As a remedy, cut
back the dead branches to stimulate new growth.

Chastetree

Vitex agnus-castus

*This plant is referred to as a tree, but in reality should be considered a large,
herbaceous perennial shrub. It develops a loosely branched, airy but open out-*

line, growing 5-10 feet high in Tennessee. The grey-green, five-lobed leaves are an attractive contrast to the rich, sky-blue flowers. The Chastetree blooms from mid-Summer into the Fall, and has been planted successfully in 30", or larger, clay pots with annual flowers surrounding the base.

WHEN TO PLANT:
This is a container-grown shrub and may be planted any time.

WHY YOU PLANT:
The Chastetree is a great selection if you want to lure butterflies to your garden. We've also seen Chastetrees planted on a 4-5 feet standard, like a tree rose, and then used to dress up a back-yard patio.

WHERE YOU PLANT:
Plant this variety in full sun in loose, moist, well-draining soil.

HOW YOU PLANT:
Loosen the roots of plants grown in pots... thoroughly! Prepare a wide, shallow hole 3/4 as deep and 2 times as wide as the root ball. Make a mix of 1/3 soil, 1/3 coarse sand, and 1/3 peat moss, organic humus, or commercial planting mix. Pack firmly around sides of root ball. Add 1-3" of mulch on top, staying clear of the crown of the plant. Then water well with a root stimulator fertilizer. *Note: Avoid planting when soil is frozen 1" deep or when soil is wet enough to form a mudball in your fist.*

WHEN YOU WATER:
Use a slow-trickle, open-end hose at the base of the plant. Water approximately one minute for each inch of diameter of the root ball. Repeat three times the first week, two times the second week, and then once per week until the tree's roots are established.
Note: When in doubt, check the soil's wetness with a moisture meter before watering.

How/When you prune:

During the Summer, trim off the spent flowers to induce more continuous blooms. In the Spring, you should prune all the way back to the live wood to enhance vigorous growth.

How/When you fertilize:

Broadcast a complete shrub or nursery fertilizer in granular slow-release form during the Spring. Apply at a rate equal to one pound per inch of tree diameter.

Additional advice for proper care:

The Chastetree may develop Leaf Spot and Root Rot, but these diseases are not too common. If you notice leaf damage or discoloration, consult your local garden center for proper advice. Otherwise, you will enjoy this little tree as a welcome addition to back porch or garden.

Cotoneaster
Cotoneaster dammeri

Maturing to only 1-2 feet in height and out to 5-10 feet in width, this is one of the best evergreens to use as a ground cover. The Cotoneaster features pink to white flowers, with striking Fall leaf color and red berries during the Winter. This spider-looking shrub features varieties from deciduous to semi-deciduous, and growth patterns ranging from spreading to upright, making it a great choice for filling planters and adding an interesting feature to slope or hillside.

When to plant:

Container-grown shrubs may be planted any time the soil conditions allow.

WHY YOU PLANT:

The Cotoneaster is an excellent choice for banks, borders, and mass plantings. It is quite fast-growing, and if planted on 3-feet centers, can cover the area in one year. The berries are a great source of color in Fall and Winter, a great source of food for the birds, and you can look forward to dainty, white flowers which form in the Spring.

WHERE YOU PLANT:

Place in full sun to partial shade. This plant is adaptable to a wide range of soil conditions, but prefers a well-draining soil. Cotoneaster may be planted along a high stone retaining wall with limbs cascading over and down, for a very striking landscape effect.

HOW YOU PLANT:

Loosen the roots of plants grown in pots... thoroughly! Prepare a wide, shallow hole 3/4 as deep and 2 times as wide as the root ball. Make a mix of 1/3 soil, 1/3 coarse sand, and 1/3 peat moss, organic humus, or commercial planting mix. Pack firmly around sides of root ball. Add 1-3" of mulch on top, staying clear of the crown of the plant. Then water well with a root stimulator fertilizer. *Note: Avoid planting when soil is frozen 1" deep or when soil is wet enough to form a mudball in your fist.*

WHEN YOU WATER:

For newly planted shrubs, use a hand-held, open-ended hose, watering plants directly. Do this until the shrub's roots are established, generally one growing season, or when new growth is evident. Light, frequent watering is preferred over heavy watering. When in doubt, check soil wetness with a moisture meter before watering.

HOW/WHEN YOU PRUNE:

Prune for shape and size by trimming one branch at a time, and prune after blooming has ceased.

HOW/WHEN YOU FERTILIZE:

Select a well-balanced, slow-release granular fertilizer at the rate of one-half cup per 10 square feet and broadcast it under the canopy of the shrub and a little beyond.

ADDITIONAL ADVICE FOR PROPER CARE:

There may be isolated cases of Fire Blight with these varieties, and Spider Mites and Aphids may also cause leaf drop and decline. Overall, these plants are quite hardy, and a good, soaking spray of dormant oil applied in the Spring, repeated again in early Summer, should take care of any insect problems.

Crape Myrtle
Lagerstroemia

Some varieties are dwarf cultivars at 2 feet, while regular varieties grow to be 15-20 feet in height. The Crape Myrtle is a beautiful, flowering mainstay of any Southern lawn or garden. Blooms range from white, pink, red to lavender, and can be wonderfully complemented by the mature bark, which turns an appealing mottled brown to tan shade. If there is not a Crape Myrtle in a landscape, it is usually assumed that the planting is not finished.

WHEN TO PLANT:

These plants may be transplanted any time Spring through Fall, as the soil conditions permit.

WHY YOU PLANT:

This plant makes a beautiful Summer flowering shrub or tree, blooming in a range of softer colors. The smooth brown bark is also a rather attractive feature.

WHERE YOU PLANT:
Place in full sun with moist, well-draining soil.

HOW YOU PLANT:
Loosen the roots of plants grown in pots... thoroughly! Prepare a wide, shallow hole 3/4 as deep and 2 times as wide as the root ball. Make a mix of 1/3 soil, 1/3 coarse sand, and 1/3 peat moss, organic humus, or commercial planting mix. Pack firmly around sides of root ball. Add 1-3" of mulch on top, staying clear of the crown of the plant. Then water well with a root stimulator fertilizer. *Note: Avoid planting when soil is frozen 1" deep or when soil is wet enough to form a mudball in your fist.*

WHEN YOU WATER:
For newly planted shrubs, use a hand-held, open-ended hose, watering plants directly. Do this until the shrub's roots are established, generally one growing season, or when new growth is evident. Light, frequent watering is preferred over heavy watering. When in doubt, check soil wetness with a moisture meter before watering.

WALT'S WISDOM

Swallowing

angry words is

a lot easier than

eating them.

HOW/WHEN YOU PRUNE:
To prune bush-form plants, cut back older stems to the ground during the Spring. To prune tree-form plants, cut back all but 3 to 5 stems, trimming off all lateral branches up to one-half the height of the plant, in the Spring.

HOW/WHEN YOU FERTILIZE:
Fertilize in the Spring with shrub fertilizer, and repeat in early Summer for vigorous growth to promote blooming.

ADDITIONAL ADVICE FOR PROPER CARE:
Common diseases and insects include Powdery Mildew, Sooty Mold, and Aphids on blooms. To avoid mildew and mold problems, try keeping the Crape Myrtle thinned out, and avoid water-

ing in the evening. Also remember that these are the last plants to start growing in the Spring. Don't give up if your Crape Myrtle hasn't shown signs of life in early Spring... it will grow!

Deutzia
Deutzia gracilis

Deutzia measures 2 feet in height and 5 feet in width, making it a squatty, low-spreading shrub that bears pure white flowers in the Spring. You might consider Deutzia for its beautiful contrast in the Fall when the foliage changes to a deep burgundy. Deutzia drops its leaves in the Winter.

WHEN TO PLANT:
Plant container-grown shrubs year round, as the soil conditions permit, although Spring transplantings are most favorable for this shrub.

WHY YOU PLANT:
Use Deutzia as a ground cover, in mass groupings, or in a mixed border.

WHERE YOU PLANT:
Plant in full sun to very light shade in a wide variety of soil conditions. Consider planting Deutzia near a patio or a vantage point for viewing from the indoors.

HOW YOU PLANT:
Loosen the roots of plants grown in pots... thoroughly! Prepare a wide, shallow hole 3/4 as deep and 2 times as wide as the root ball. Make a mix of 1/3 soil, 1/3 coarse sand, and 1/3 peat moss, organic humus, or commercial planting mix. Pack firmly around sides of root ball. Add 1-3" of mulch on top, staying clear of the crown of the plant. Then water well with a root stimulator fertilizer. *Note: Avoid planting when soil is frozen 1" deep or when soil is wet*

enough to form a mudball in your fist.

WHEN YOU WATER:
For newly planted shrubs, use a hand-held, open-ended hose, watering plants directly. Do this until the shrub's roots are established, generally one growing season, or when new growth is evident. Light, frequent watering is preferred over heavy watering. When in doubt, check soil wetness with a moisture meter before watering.

HOW/WHEN YOU PRUNE:
Extensive pruning may be required in the Fall after the foliage has dropped, and you may want to do some pruning and grooming during the Summer months.

HOW/WHEN YOU FERTILIZE:
When fertilizing in the Spring, select a well-blanced, slow-release granular fertilizer at the rate of one-half cup per 10 square feet and broadcast it under the canopy of the shrub and a little beyond.

ADDITIONAL ADVICE FOR PROPER CARE:
Common diseases and insects include Leaf Spot and Aphids, although these are not serious threats.

Dogwood, Bloodtwig
Cornus sanguinea

Maturing to 4-8 feet in height, the Bloodtwig Dogwood is a variety of one of the most popular trees in the state of Tennessee. This deciduous shrub grows in clumps with upright, spreading limbs originating from the base, and is best known for its profuse blooms bursting forth during May and June. However, it is best known for its shocking red twigs that contrast against the Winter landscape.

WHEN TO PLANT:

Plant any time the soil is workable during the Fall, Winter or Spring.

WHY YOU PLANT:

Bloodtwig Dogwood is excellent for landscaping. It is also effective as a bank cover, since it holds soil well. This variety has medium to dark green foliage in Spring and Summer, which turns purple to red in the Fall. This shrub also displays striking red branches in the Winter.

WHERE YOU PLANT:

Plant on banks for ground cover, in mass groupings, or in sets of three for accent color during Winter months. It is very adaptable to most soil conditions.

HOW YOU PLANT:

Loosen the roots of plants grown in pots... thoroughly! Prepare a wide, shallow hole 3/4 as deep and 2 times as wide as the root ball. Make a mix of 1/3 soil, 1/3 coarse sand, and 1/3 peat moss, organic humus, or commercial planting mix. Pack firmly around sides of root ball. Add 1-3" of mulch on top, staying clear of the crown of the plant. Then water well with a root stimulator fertilizer. *Note: Avoid planting when soil is frozen 1" deep or when soil is wet enough to form a mudball in your fist.*

WHEN YOU WATER:

Use a slow-trickle, open-end hose at the base of the plant. Water approximately one minute for every inch of diameter of the root ball. Repeat three times the first week, two times the second week, and then once per week until the shrub's roots are established.

Note: When in doubt, check the soil's wetness with a moisture meter before watering.

HOW/WHEN YOU PRUNE:

Prune older canes down to the ground during late Winter or early Spring.

HOW/WHEN YOU FERTILIZE:

When fertilizing in the Spring, select a well-balanced, slow-release granular fertilizer at the rate of one-half cup per 10 square feet and broadcast it under the canopy of the shrub and a little beyond.

ADDITIONAL ADVICE FOR PROPER CARE:

No serious diseases and insects are expected with this plant. The range of locations for planting this Dogwood allows for variety when designing it into your landscape.

Dogwood, Redtwig
Cornus sericea

The Redtwig and Yellowtwig Dogwoods are actually trees and not shrubs. These colorfully branched tree/shrubs light up the Winter with stalks arising from the base to form a large, vase-like shape. Each branch has minimal lateral stalks, giving this plant a rather linear, colorful pattern which adds contrast to the landscape.

WHEN TO PLANT:

Plant any time the soil is workable during the Fall, Winter or Spring.

WHY YOU PLANT:

Redtwig Dogwood is excellent for landscaping, and is also very effective as a bank cover since it holds soil well. It has medium to dark green foliage in Spring and Summer, which turns purple to red in the Fall. This shrub also displays striking red branches in the Winter.

WHERE YOU PLANT:

Plant on banks for ground cover, in mass groupings, or in sets of three for accent color during Winter months. It is very adaptable to most soil conditions.

HOW YOU PLANT:

Loosen the roots of plants grown in pots... thoroughly! Prepare a wide, shallow hole 3/4 as deep and 2 times as wide as the root ball. Make a mix of 1/3 soil, 1/3 coarse sand, and 1/3 peat moss, organic humus, or commercial planting mix. Pack firmly around sides of root ball. Add 1-3" of mulch on top, staying clear of the crown of the plant. Then water well with a root stimulator fertilizer. *Note: Avoid planting when soil is frozen 1" deep or when soil is wet enough to form a mudball in your fist.*

WHEN YOU WATER:

Use a slow-trickle, open-end hose at the base of the plant. Water approximately one minute for each inch of diameter of the root ball. Repeat three times the first week, two times the second week, and then once per week until the shrub's roots are established. *Note: When in doubt, check the soil's wetness with a moisture meter before watering.*

HOW/WHEN YOU PRUNE:

Prune older canes down to the ground during late Winter or early Spring.

HOW/WHEN YOU FERTILIZE:

Select a well-balanced, slow-release granular fertilizer at the rate of one-half cup per 10 square feet and broadcast it under the canopy of the shrub and a little beyond.

ADDITIONAL ADVICE FOR PROPER CARE:

Watch for Twig Blight (Canker), Scale, and Bagworms, which are not usually severe. Otherwise, no problems are expected to affect the health of your Redtwig.

Dogwood, Yellowtwig
Cornus lutea

Maturing to 3-6 feet in height, the Yellowtwig is a colorful variation on the closely related Redtwig. It is a deciduous tree which grows in a clump with upright, spreading limbs originating from the base. This is one to look forward to in the Winter landscape, when the green limbs turn a brilliant golden shade.

WHEN TO PLANT:
Plant any time the soil is workable during the Fall, Winter or Spring.

WHY YOU PLANT:
Yellowtwig Dogwood is excellent for landscaping. It is also very effective as a bank cover since it holds soil extremely well. The Yellowtwig features medium to dark green foliage in Spring and Summer, which turns purple to red in the Fall.

WHERE YOU PLANT:
Plant on banks for ground cover, in mass groupings, or in sets of three for accent color during Winter months. This variety is very adaptable to most soil conditions.

HOW YOU PLANT:
Loosen the roots of plants grown in pots... thoroughly! Prepare a wide, shallow hole 3/4 as deep and 2 times as wide as the root ball. Make a mix of 1/3 soil, 1/3 coarse sand, and 1/3 peat moss, organic humus, or commercial planting mix. Pack firmly around sides of root ball. Add 1-3" of mulch on top, staying clear of the crown of the plant. Then water well with a root stimulator fertilizer. *Note: Avoid planting when soil is frozen 1" deep or when soil is wet enough to form a mudball in your fist.*

WHEN YOU WATER:
Use a slow-trickle, open-end hose at base of plant. Water

approximately one minute for every inch of diameter of the root ball. Repeat three times the first week, two times the second week, and then once per week until the shrub's roots are established. *Note: When in doubt, check the soil's wetness with a moisture meter before watering.*

HOW/WHEN YOU PRUNE:
Prune older canes down to the ground during late Winter or early Spring.

HOW/WHEN YOU FERTILIZE:
In the Spring, select a well-balanced, slow-release granular fertilizer at the rate of one-half cup per 10 square feet and broadcast it under the canopy of the shrub and a little beyond.

ADDITIONAL ADVICE FOR PROPER CARE:
Watch for Twig Blight (Canker), Scale, and Bagworms, although no serious problems should affect the health of the Yellowtwig.

Firethorn
Pyracantha coccinea

Maturing from 6-18 feet in height and width, this is generally a large shrub, but varies according to the cultivar. Firethorn displays white flowers that produce differing colors of berries, depending on the cultivar: 'Mohave' in orange-red, 'Santa Cruz' in bright red, and 'Wonderberry' in bright orange-red. Pyracantha is extremely hardy, and sports sticky thorns on all branches for a unique visual appeal.

WHEN TO PLANT:
You may transplant Firethorn year round, as soil conditions permit.

WHY YOU PLANT:

This variety is planted mostly for its showy berries in Fall and Winter, and is used primarily on espaliers and for specimen plantings. The blooms are very tiny, yet because of the mass clusters, they are very showy during Spring blooming. The berries follow the bloom, and by the Fall and Winter, they are both flashy in appearance and functional as food for birds.

WHERE YOU PLANT:

Place in full sun or partial shade areas. The Firethorn grows quite well when placed on a southwest wall facing a brick or masonry wall. It will accept a wide range of well-draining soil conditions, but this variety is somewhat difficult to transplant; therefore, make your site selection with permanence in mind.

HOW YOU PLANT:

Loosen the roots of plants grown in pots... thoroughly! Prepare a wide, shallow hole 3/4 as deep and 2 times as wide as the root ball. Make a mix of 1/3 soil, 1/3 coarse sand, and 1/3 peat moss, organic humus, or commercial planting mix. Pack firmly around sides of root ball. Add 1-3" of mulch on top, staying clear of the crown of the plant. Then water well with a root stimulator fertilizer. *Note: Avoid planting when soil is frozen 1" deep or when soil is wet enough to form a mudball in your fist.*

WHEN YOU WATER:

For newly planted shrubs, use a hand-held, open-ended hose, watering plants directly. Do this until the shrub's roots are established, generally one growing season, or when new growth is evident. Light, frequent watering is preferred over heavy watering. When in doubt, check soil wetness with a moisture meter before watering. Once the Firethorn is established, it is very tolerant of dry conditions.

HOW/WHEN YOU PRUNE:

This plant is in the rosaceae (rose) family, so it will tolerate continual trimming. Use high quality pruning shears to create the shape you desire.

HOW/WHEN YOU FERTILIZE:
Select a well-balanced, slow-release granular fertilizer at the rate of one-half cup per 10 square feet and broadcast it under the canopy of the shrub and a little beyond.

ADDITIONAL ADVICE FOR PROPER CARE:
This plant is susceptible to Fire Blight and Rust. The most common pest is the Lace Bug, evidenced during the Summer by the discoloration of the leaves. This is preventable with an application of dormant oil in late Winter or early Spring, then repeated in early Summer. Be sure to check the product label for proper application.

Forsythia
Forsythia x intermedia

This easy to grow, most recognizable flowering shrub has become synonomous with the awakening of Spring. The flowering dates of other shrubs are actually expressed as to whether they happen before or after the Forsythia's blooming time. The distinctive yellow and yellow-gold blooms appear prior to the leaves and give vivid display on the upright, arching stems. Cultivars range in size from low and spreading to tall and upright. A feature often overlooked is the beautiful red to yellow-orange foliage which the Fall will bring.

WHEN TO PLANT:
Plant balled and burlaped specimens in the Fall, Winter or Spring. Container varieties may be planted any time the soil is workable.

WHY YOU PLANT:

The Border Forsythia displays very early Spring color, and is extremely adaptable, tolerating a wide range of soil conditions.

WHERE YOU PLANT:

Avoid foundation planting, that is, placing plants too close to the house, as they will spread too large as they grow. Use as a hedge, shrub border, in masses, and on banks. The latter, bank planting, is an overlooked usage which should be considered.

HOW YOU PLANT:

Balled and burlaped: Position rootball in a wide, shallow hole 3/4 as deep and 2 times as wide as the root ball. Cut twine around trunk and top of root ball, remove any nails, fold back burlap to the sides of the root ball. Do not remove wire cage. No need to loosen roots. Make a mix of 1/3 soil, 1/3 coarse sand, and 1/3 peat moss, organic humus or commercial planting mix. Pack firmly around sides of root ball. Add 2-3" of mulch on top. Water well with a root stimulator fertilizer. *Note: Avoid planting when soil is frozen 1" deep or when soil forms mud balls.* Container: Thoroughly loosen the roots of plants grown in pots, then follow balled and burlaped instructions.

WHEN YOU WATER:

Use a slow-trickle, open-end hose at the base of the plant. Water approximately one minute for each inch of diameter of the root ball. Repeat three times the first week, two times the second week, and then once per week until the shrub's roots are established.

Note: When in doubt, check the soil's wetness with a moisture meter before watering.

HOW/WHEN YOU PRUNE:
Prune any time after the Forsythia has finished blooming.

HOW/WHEN YOU FERTILIZE:
After pruning, select a well-balanced, slow-release granular fertilizer at the rate of one-half cup per 10 square feet and broadcast it under the canopy of the shrub and a little beyond.

ADDITIONAL ADVICE FOR PROPER CARE:
Crown Gall, Dieback, Leafspot, Weevils, and Spider Mites may present problems, although none are very troublesome to Forsythia. If any should arise, consult your local garden center.

Gold Thread or Mops
Chamaecyparis obtusa

This is a slow-growing shrub with a mounding, inverted "mop" look. The Gold Thread shrub supports thread-like weeping branches that are bright yellow on the tips and turn light-yellow to green at the base of the branches. This is an outstanding plant, particularly for the color it will offer a Winter landscape.

WHEN TO PLANT:
This shrub should be transplanted from a container and planted any time during the year, as soil conditions permit.

WHY YOU PLANT:
Gold Thread, or Mops, is definitely a specimen plant. These are wonderful selections for a perennial rock garden, where you may enjoy their cheerful burst of color, particularly in the Winter months.

WHERE YOU PLANT:

Place in full sun to partial shade areas of yard or garden. *Note: Shading will lessen the intensity of color.* They like moist, fertile soil and a moderately humid atmosphere.

HOW YOU PLANT:

Loosen the roots of plants grown in pots... thoroughly! Prepare a wide, shallow hole 3/4 as deep and 2 times as wide as the root ball. Make a mix of 1/3 soil, 1/3 coarse sand, and 1/3 peat moss, organic humus, or commercial planting mix. Pack firmly around sides of root ball. Add 1-3" of mulch on top, staying clear of the crown of the plant. Then water well with a root stimulator fertilizer. *Note: Avoid planting when soil is frozen 1" deep or when soil is wet enough to form a mudball in your fist.*

WHEN YOU WATER:

For newly planted shrubs, use a hand-held, open-ended hose, watering plants directly. Do this until the shrub's roots are established, generally one growing season, or when new growth is evident. Light, frequent watering is preferred over heavy watering. When in doubt, check soil wetness with a moisture meter before watering.

HOW/WHEN YOU PRUNE:

Prune to the desired shape at any time of the year. Some folks may want a formal, uniform appearance while others may like a more natural look. Take your pick and trim to your heart's desire.

HOW/WHEN YOU FERTILIZE:

Fertilize during the early Spring by broadcasting an evergreen fertilizer to the base and outlying canopy of the shrub.

ADDITIONAL ADVICE FOR PROPER CARE:

No serious diseases or insects are noted with this variety, and it should provide a great pocket of color in your garden for the seasons when many plants tend to be bleak.

Holly, American

Ilex opaca

Maturing at 40-50 feet in height and 20-40 feet in width, this pyramid-shaped Holly is really more a tree than a shrub, since it grows to a truly grand stature. This stately Holly, with the spiney-edged leaves, is the one to harken memories of Christmas Past, and visions of Christmas Future. It is a true mainstay of the yuletide season, and will lend a festive aspect to the land-scape all year long.

WHEN TO PLANT:

Transplant balled and burlaped specimens during the Spring, and container shrubs during the Spring or Fall.

WHY YOU PLANT:

The American Holly makes a great evergreen specimen tree for the lawn.

WHERE YOU PLANT:

Planted both in sun or shady areas, the American Holly prefers to be somewhat protected from dry, windy conditions. This plant will not tolerate poor-draining soils.

HOW YOU PLANT:

Position root ball in a wide, shallow hole 3/4 as deep and 2 times as wide as the root ball. Cut twine around trunk and top of root ball, remove any nails, fold back burlap to the sides of the root ball. Do not remove wire cage. No need to loosen roots. Make a mix of 1/3 soil, 1/3 coarse sand, and 1/3 peat moss, organic humus or commercial planting mix. Pack firmly around sides of root ball. Add 2-3" of mulch on top. Water well with a root stimulator fertilizer. *Note: Avoid planting when soil is frozen 1" deep or when soil forms mud balls.*

WHEN YOU WATER:

Water immediately after planting. Slowly trickle water from the open end of hose approximately one minute per inch diameter of the root ball. Repeat three times the first week, two times the second week, and then once per week until the tree's roots are established, generally one growing season, or until new growth has appeared. When in doubt, check soil wetness with a moisture meter before watering.

HOW/WHEN YOU PRUNE:

Prune the American Holly during the Winter months and perform selective trimming by cutting back branches to maintain the desired shape.

HOW/WHEN YOU FERTILIZE:

Once in the Spring, select a well-balanced, slow-release granular fertilizer at the rate of one-half cup per 10 square feet and broadcast it under the canopy of the shrub and a little beyond.

ADDITIONAL ADVICE FOR PROPER CARE:

There are many leaf disorders that may occur with this species, plus the threat of Holly Leaf Miners. Watch for Leaf Scorch and also Leaf Anthracnose, and consult with your local garden center for proper care. *Note: Most of these problems are cosmetic and not terminal.*

Holly, Chinese
Ilex cornuta

Maturing at 8-10 feet in height, the Chinese Holly has glossy foliage that typifies the lacquer look of a Holly leaf. During the Spring, tiny fragrant flowers come forth and turn to red berries in the Winter. Cultivars provide quite a variety of growth heights, so you have the choice of creating a visually staggered look. The Chinese Holly is available in: 'Burford' at 8-10 feet, 'Dwarf Burford' at 6-10 feet, 'Needlepoint' at 4-6 feet, and 'Carrisa' at 2-3 feet.

WHEN TO PLANT:

Transplant Spring through Fall, as the soil conditions permit.

WHY YOU PLANT:

This plant has a great tolerance for heat and drought. The rich, lustrous green foliage and clusters of red berries make this plant a favorite in Tennessee.

WHERE YOU PLANT:

Chinese Holly prefers full sun, but has a tolerance for shade, and it may be used in various landscape applications.

HOW YOU PLANT:

Loosen the roots of plants grown in pots... thoroughly! Prepare a wide, shallow hole 3/4 as deep and 2 times as wide as the root ball. Make a mix of 1/3 soil, 1/3 coarse sand, and 1/3 peat moss, organic humus, or commercial planting mix. Pack firmly around sides of root ball. Add 1-3" of mulch on top, staying clear of the crown of the plant. Then water well with a root stimulator fertilizer. *Note: Avoid planting when soil is frozen 1" deep or when soil is wet enough to form a mudball in your fist.*

WHEN YOU WATER:

For newly planted shrubs, use a hand-held, open-ended hose, watering plants directly. Do this until the shrub's roots are established, generally one growing season, or when new growth is evident. Light, frequent watering is preferred over heavy watering. When in doubt, check soil wetness with a moisture meter before watering. *Note: Although this plant is heat and drought tolerant, frequent watering is required when it is transplanted.*

HOW/WHEN YOU PRUNE:

Prune any time in Spring through the early Fall, although heavy trimming during the Fall may result in fewer berries.

HOW/WHEN YOU FERTILIZE:

Select a well-balanced, slow-release granular fertilizer at the rate of one-half cup per 10 square feet and broadcast it under the canopy of the shrub and a little beyond.

ADDITIONAL ADVICE FOR PROPER CARE:

Chinese Holly is relatively free of problems, but watch for Scale on stems and branches. If this condition develops, consult your local garden center.

Holly, Foster
Ilex x attenuata 'Fosteri'

The Foster Holly matures to a height of 20-30 feet and a width of 10-15 feet, making it a beautiful mid-size Holly that bridges the gap between shrub and tree. It is a hybrid variety with the trademark rich, green foliage and berries in the Winter months. The advantage of the Foster Holly is the way it can be grouped or used to draw attention to corners.

WHEN TO PLANT:

Foster Holly should be transplanted during early Fall or Spring.

WHY YOU PLANT:

The Foster Holly's most popular use is as accent for corners of residences, although this practice is somewhat overdone. We suggest planting a grouping of 3-5 trees for a more pleasing effect.

WHERE YOU PLANT:

Plant in sun or partial shade areas, with fertile, moist, well-draining soil with a pH of 6.0-7.0.

HOW YOU PLANT:

Position root ball in a wide, shallow hole 3/4 as deep and 2 times as wide as the root ball. Cut twine around trunk and top of root ball, remove any nails, fold back burlap to the sides of the root ball. Do not remove wire cage. No need to loosen roots. Make a mix of 1/3 soil, 1/3 coarse sand, and 1/3 peat moss, organic humus or commercial planting mix. Pack firmly around sides of root ball. Add 2-3" of mulch on top. Water well with a root stimulator fertilizer. *Note: Avoid planting when soil is frozen 1" deep or when soil forms mud balls.*

WHEN YOU WATER:

Water immediately after planting. Slowly trickle water from the open end of hose approximately one minute per inch diameter of the root ball. Repeat three times the first week, two times the second week, and then once per week until the tree's roots are established, generally one growing season, or until new growth has appeared. When in doubt, check soil wetness with a moisture meter before watering.

HOW/WHEN YOU PRUNE:

Prune the Foster Holly at any time of the year, although they prefer early Spring and/or late Summer trimming. Shape with a pair of quality hedging shears to promote a thicker and more attractive Foster Holly.

HOW/WHEN YOU FERTILIZE:

In the Spring, select a well-balanced, slow-release granular fertilizer at the rate of one-half cup per 10 square feet and broadcast it under the canopy of the shrub and a little beyond.

ADDITIONAL ADVICE FOR PROPER CARE:

There are many leaf disorders that come along with this species. The major trouble is Holly Leaf Miners, but you also should watch for Leaf Scorch and Leaf Anthracnose. *Note: Most of these problems are cosmetic and not terminal, but you should consult your local garden center for possible solutions.*

Holly, Japanese
Ilex crenata

This plant has smaller, rounder, spineless leaves, differentiating it from the Chinese Holly. The Japanese Holly is a fine-textured, glossy evergreen that tolerates any degree of pruning. Often referred to as the "poor man's Boxwood," it is an interesting choice, with an interesting look for those gardeners who want to incorporate another Holly into their garden landscape.

WHEN TO PLANT:
Container plants may be transplanted Spring through Fall, but we suggest that balled and burlaped plants be transplanted from Fall through Spring.

WHY YOU PLANT:
Versatility makes this variety a popular planting choice, since the Japanese Holly will grow in either sun or shade, and cultivar shapes range from flat, rounded, pyramidal, to low, fat and spreading forms.

WHERE YOU PLANT:
Plant in full sun to partial shade areas, though it prefers well-draining, moist, slightly acidic pH, medium-textured soil.

HOW YOU PLANT:
Loosen the roots of plants grown in pots... thoroughly! Prepare a wide, shallow hole 3/4 as deep and 2 times as wide as the root ball. Make a mix of 1/3 soil, 1/3 coarse sand, and 1/3 peat moss, organic humus, or commercial planting mix. Pack firmly around sides of root ball. Add 1-3" of mulch on top, staying clear of the crown of the plant. Then water well with a root stimulator fertilizer. *Note: Avoid planting when soil is frozen 1" deep or when soil is wet enough to form a mudball in your fist.*

WHEN YOU WATER:

For newly planted shrubs, use a hand-held, open-ended hose, watering plants directly. Do this until the shrub's roots are established, generally one growing season, or when new growth is evident. Light, frequent watering is preferred over heavy watering. When in doubt, check soil wetness with a moisture meter before watering.

Note: The Japanese Holly is the plant most frequently replaced by nurseries, simply because it requires light, frequent watering for its continued growth.

HOW/WHEN YOU PRUNE:

This variety may be pruned any time of the year, avoiding periods of sub-freezing temperatures. Be sure to use sharp hedge shears when trimming.

HOW/WHEN YOU FERTILIZE:

In the Spring, select a well-balanced, slow-release granular fertilizer at the rate of one-half cup per 10 square feet and broadcast it under the canopy of the shrub and a little beyond.

ADDITIONAL ADVICE FOR PROPER CARE:

Spider Mites are a definite problem . . . it's not IF but WHEN they will invade. Therefore, we suggest preventive measures, such as dormant oil spray. Contact your local garden center or nursery for recommendations.

Holly, Winterberry
Ilex verticillata

Maturing to 6-10 feet in height, this upright, deciduous Holly has an unsurpassed display of red berries. From a distance during the Winter, the berries appear to be hanging in space because of the stark, leafless branches, making for quite a dramatic effect. One hybrid award-winner to consider for use in your own garden is 'Sparkleberry.'

WHEN TO PLANT:
You may transplant year round, as soil conditions permit.

WHY YOU PLANT:
Widely used for its striking Winter color, the Winterberry Holly is planted in mass groupings or as a single specimen, bearing some resemblance to the Crape Myrtle, but much smaller in height, at 6-8 feet.

WHERE YOU PLANT:
Place the Winterberry Holly in full sun or partial shade areas. This shrub tolerates wet soil, and may be planted in either light or heavy soil with a pH of 4.5-6.5, but it will develop Chlorosis if planted in an alkaline soil, pH 6.5-7.5.

HOW YOU PLANT:
Balled and Burlaped: Position root ball in a wide, shallow hole 3/4 as deep and 2 times as wide as the root ball. Cut twine around trunk and top of root ball, remove any nails, fold back burlap to the sides of the root ball. Do not remove wire cage. No need to loosen roots. Make a mix of 1/3 soil, 1/3 coarse sand, and 1/3 peat moss, organic humus or commercial planting mix. Pack firmly around sides of root ball. Add 2-3" of mulch on top. Water well with a root stimulator fertilizer. *Note: Avoid planting when soil is frozen 1" deep or when soil forms mud balls.* Container: Loosen the roots of plants grown in pots, then follow balled and burlaped instructions.

WHEN YOU WATER:
Water immediately after planting. Slowly trickle water from the open end of hose approximately one minute per inch diameter of the root ball. Repeat three times the first week, two times the second week, and then once per week until the shrub's roots are

established, generally one growing season, or until new growth has appeared. When in doubt, check soil wetness with a moisture meter before watering.

Note: This variety is tolerant of overwatering.

HOW/WHEN YOU PRUNE:

Winterberry may be pruned any time of year, avoiding periods of sub-freezing temperatures. If a tree-form is desired, remove the lower, vertical branches. As the plant grows, maintain a clean trunk on the lower section of the tree.

HOW/WHEN YOU FERTILIZE:

Select a well-balanced, slow-release granular fertilizer at the rate of one-half cup per 10 square feet and broadcast it under the canopy of the shrub and a little beyond.

ADDITIONAL ADVICE FOR PROPER CARE:

Common diseases include Powdery Mildew and Leaf Spot, although these are not serious problems.

Holly, Yaupon
Ilex vomitoria

The Yaupon Holly matures to 15-20 feet in height and 10-12 feet in width, and is very adaptable to Southeast conditions, making it a well-suited choice for the Tennessee gardener. The foliage is a subdued grey-green and this plant is tolerant of heavy pruning, so it can be shaped in creative forms without harming the plant. We have seen it sculpted in sizes ranging from 2-3 feet up to 6 feet tall and 8 feet wide, so prune away!

WHEN TO PLANT:

Yaupon Holly may be planted year round, as the soil conditions allow.

WHY YOU PLANT:

There are many uses for the Yaupon Holly, such as foundation planting, borders, specimen, topiary, and espalier.

WHERE YOU PLANT:

Place this variety in sun or shade areas. It is adaptable to dry or wet soils and tolerant of a wide range of conditions, making it different from other Holly varieties. Its particular heat tolerance makes it more adaptable to West and Middle Tennessee.

HOW YOU PLANT:

Loosen the roots of plants grown in pots... thoroughly! Prepare a wide, shallow hole 3/4 as deep and 2 times as wide as the root ball. Make a mix of 1/3 soil, 1/3 coarse sand, and 1/3 peat moss, organic humus, or commercial planting mix. Pack firmly around sides of root ball. Add 1-3" of mulch on top, staying clear of the crown of the plant. Then water well with a root stimulator fertilizer. *Note: Avoid planting when soil is frozen 1" deep or when soil is wet enough to form a mudball in your fist.*

WHEN YOU WATER:

For newly planted shrubs, use a hand-held, open-ended hose, watering plants directly. Do this until the shrub's roots are established, generally one growing season, or when new growth is evident. Light, frequent watering is preferred over heavy watering. When in doubt, check soil wetness with a moisture meter before watering.

HOW/WHEN YOU PRUNE:

Prune at any time year, avoiding periods of sub-freezing temperatures.

HOW/WHEN YOU FERTILIZE:

Once in the Spring, select a well-balanced, slow-release granular fertilizer at the rate of one-half cup per 10 square feet and broadcast it under the canopy of the shrub and a little beyond.

ADDITIONAL ADVICE FOR PROPER CARE:

No serious disease and insect threats are noted with the Yaupon Holly, so trim to your heart's desire and enjoy.

Hydrangea, Big Leaf
Hydrangea macrophylla

Maturing to 3-6 feet in height and 10 feet in width, this Hydrangea produces large clusters of red, pink, blue, or white flowers. The color you can expect depends largely on the particular cultivar and the pH of the soil. Big Leaf Hydrangea sports large, toothed leaves and oblong, rounded flowers which give this shrub a dense look when in full bloom.

WHEN TO PLANT:

Plant this variety Spring through Fall, as the soil conditions permit.

WHY YOU PLANT:

This Big Leaf Hydrangea has very rich, green foliage and is unsurpassed in the beauty of its flowers. The cultivars of choice are 'Candied' (dark pinkish-red), 'Glory Blue' (great blue flowers), 'Sister Theresa' (white flowers), and 'Merrits Supreme' (bright pink).

WHERE YOU PLANT:

Most cultivars prefer partial shade, except 'Niko Blue,' which prefers full sunlight. When grown in a low soil pH of 5.0-5.5, flowers tend to highlight the blue coloring, while a higher pH of 6.5-7.0 helps bring out the pink to red colors.

HOW YOU PLANT:

Loosen the roots of plants grown in pots... thoroughly! Prepare a wide, shallow hole 3/4 as deep and 2 times as wide as the root ball. Make a mix of 1/3 soil, 1/3 coarse sand, and 1/3 peat moss, organic humus, or commercial planting mix. Pack firmly around sides of root ball. Add 1-3" of mulch on top, staying clear of the crown of the plant. Then water well with a root stimulator fertilizer. *Note: Avoid planting when soil is frozen 1" deep or when soil is wet enough to form a mudball in your fist.*

WHEN YOU WATER:
For newly planted shrubs, use a hand-held, open-ended hose, watering plants directly. Do this until the shrub's roots are established, generally one growing season, or when new growth is evident. Light, frequent watering is preferred over heavy watering. When in doubt, check soil wetness with a moisture meter before watering.

HOW/WHEN YOU PRUNE:
Any pruning on the Big Leaf Hydrangea should be performed immediately after blooming. This species flowers from buds set on the last season's growth. It is somewhat of an art form to trim out old wood and leave developing wood for next year's blooms.

HOW/WHEN YOU FERTILIZE:
Select a well-balanced, slow-release granular fertilizer at the rate of one-half cup per 10 square feet and broadcast it under the canopy of the shrub and a little beyond.

ADDITIONAL ADVICE FOR PROPER CARE:
Bud Blight, Leaf Spot, Mildew, Rust, Aphids, and Scale may present some problems, although none are serious threats. Otherwise, enjoy the Hydrangea's big, bulbous blooms.

Hydrangea, Oak Leaf
Hydrangea quercifolia

Maturing 4-6 feet in height and width, this was once, in our eyes, the ugly stepchild of shrubs. We saw it as an unattractive, scraggly plant, but now realize that it has a distinct beauty all its own. Oak Leaf Hydrangea displays large, showy panicles of white flowers during May and June. Its coarsely textured foliage has an Oak-like shape which becomes reddish-purple in the Fall. Also, it has outstanding cinnamon exfoliating bark on spindly, crooked stems.

WHEN TO PLANT:
Plant this variety year round, as the soil conditions permit.

WHY YOU PLANT:
Several years ago, this plant was not on any list of mine. However, an article in *Southern Living* stimulated gardeners' interest and the rest is history. Now the Oak Leaf Hydrangea is one of our most-recommended shrubs.

WHERE YOU PLANT:
Place this plant in partial shade areas with moist, fertile, well-draining soil. This shrub is a candidate for mass bank plantings due to its fibrous roots which tend to sucker and spread.

HOW YOU PLANT:
Position root ball in a wide, shallow hole 3/4 as deep and 2 times as wide as the root ball. Cut twine around trunk and top of root ball, remove any nails, fold back burlap to the sides of the root ball. Do not remove wire cage. No need to loosen roots. Make a mix of 1/3 soil, 1/3 coarse sand, and 1/3 peat moss, organic humus or commercial planting mix. Pack firmly around sides of root ball. Add 2-3" of mulch on top. Water well with a root stimulator fertilizer. *Note: Avoid planting when soil is frozen 1" deep or when soil forms mud balls.*

WHEN YOU WATER:

Water immediately after planting. Slowly trickle water from the open end of hose approximately one minute per inch diameter of the root ball. Repeat three times the first week, two times the second week, and then once per week until the tree's roots are established, generally one growing season, or until new growth has appeared. When in doubt, check soil wetness with a moisture meter before watering.

HOW/WHEN YOU PRUNE:

Prune just after blooming is finished by cutting back the spent blooms.

HOW/WHEN YOU FERTILIZE:

In Spring and Fall, select a well-balanced, slow-release granular fertilizer at the rate of one-half cup per 10 square feet and broadcast it under the canopy of the shrub and a little beyond.

ADDITIONAL ADVICE FOR PROPER CARE:

The Oak Leaf Hydrangea is quite worry-free, making it an even more appealing alternative for the Tennessee gardener.

Hydrangea, Smooth Leaf
Hydrangea arborescens

Smooth Leaf Hydrangea matures to 3-5 feet in height and some what larger in width. If pruned after the first flush of growth, this Hydrangea will display very showy flowers from June to September. This plant is often given as a gift in a flower arrangement and winds up in the garden landscape. When Hydrangeas are mentioned, we tend to think of Grandmother's garden. Just as neckties go in and out of style, Hydrangea's popularity peaks and ebbs. Today, Hydrangeas are back!

WHEN TO PLANT:

Plant this variety year round, as the soil conditions permit.

WHY YOU PLANT:

The Smooth Leaf Hydrangea is one of only a few Summer-flowering shrubs which can be successfully grown in shade. 'Annabelle' is this variety's most popular cultivar.

WHERE YOU PLANT:

You may plant this variety in sun or shade, but this shrub prefers partial shade in rich, deep, well-drained, moist soil. It tolerates a wide range of pH soil levels.

HOW YOU PLANT:

Position root ball in a wide, shallow hole 3/4 as deep and 2 times as wide as the root ball. Cut twine around trunk and top of root ball, remove any nails, fold back burlap to the sides of the root ball. Do not remove wire cage. No need to loosen roots. Make a mix of 1/3 soil, 1/3 coarse sand, and 1/3 peat moss, organic humus or commercial planting mix. Pack firmly around sides of root ball. Add 2-3" of mulch on top. Water well with a root stimulator fertilizer. *Note: Avoid planting when soil is frozen 1" deep or when soil forms mud balls.*

WHEN YOU WATER:

Water immediately after planting. Slowly trickle water from the open end of hose approximately one minute per inch diameter of the root ball. Repeat three times the first week, two times the second week, and then once per week until the tree's roots are established, generally one growing season, or until new growth has appeared. When in doubt, check soil wetness with a moisture meter before watering.

HOW/WHEN YOU PRUNE:

Prune back to ground during the late Fall or early Spring to encourage next season's growth.

How/When you fertilize:

Select a well-balanced, slow-release granular fertilizer at the rate of one-half cup per 10 sq. ft. and broadcast it under the canopy of the shrub and a little beyond.

Additional advice for proper care:

Bud Blight, Powdery Mildew, Aphids, and Scale are problems, although none are too serious. Otherwise, enjoy the blooms of the Hydrangea, and be reminded of times when "To Grandma's House We Go."
Note: Leaves will appear "dog-eared" under drought stress.

Inkberry
Ilex glabra

Maturing to 6-8 feet in height and 8-10 feet in width, the Inkberry, like the Japanese Holly, is a very trimmable shrub. The Inkberry features a rounded appearance with small Boxwood-shaped leaves that are a shiny, light to medium green. As the name suggests, this shrub produces small, dark berries that make it appear as if the foliage has been dotted with an artist's ink pen.

When to plant:

Plant Inkberry Spring through Fall, as the soil conditions allow.

Why you plant:

We suggest that you consider this plant as a substitute for the Japanese Holly when your landscape site is shady, very moist, or wet. Some cultivars bear a foliage change to a rich burgundy in the Fall, which makes a rather stunning Autumn variety.

Where you plant:

Plant either in sun or shade areas, noting that the Inkberry prefers very moist soils, and thrives in swampy areas of its natural habitat.

HOW YOU PLANT:

Loosen the roots of plants grown in pots... thoroughly! Prepare a wide, shallow hole 3/4 as deep and 2 times as wide as the root ball. Make a mix of 1/3 soil, 1/3 coarse sand, and 1/3 peat moss, organic humus, or commercial planting mix. Pack firmly around sides of root ball. Add 1-3" of mulch on top, staying clear of the crown of the plant. Then water well with a root stimulator fertilizer. *Note: Avoid planting when soil is frozen 1" deep or when soil is wet enough to form a mudball in your fist.*

WHEN YOU WATER:

This plant is one which will grow in swampy areas, making overwatering a difficult possibility. Inkberry should be maintained in a high organic, moist soil.

HOW/WHEN YOU PRUNE:

The Inkberry will tolerate heavy pruning—even totally cutting back the older plant to regenerate fresh growth. Trim any time of year, avoiding only sub-freezing periods.

HOW/WHEN YOU FERTILIZE:

Once in the Spring, select a well-balanced, slow-release granular fertilizer at the rate of one-half cup per 10 square feet and broadcast it under the canopy of the shrub and a little beyond.

ADDITIONAL ADVICE FOR PROPER CARE:

A common disease is Leaf Spot, but it shouldn't present a serious problem. Contact your local garden center for advice.

Jasmine, Winter
Jasminum nudiflorum

Maturing to a height of 3-4 feet and a width of 4-7 feet Winter Jasmine is a favorite choice for those of us who think we have a "Black Thumb." This shrub is absolutely tenacious in its will to live, and defines the term "low-maintenance." It will signal the arrival of new foliage with great yellow flowers as an announcement in February.

WHEN TO PLANT:
Plant during any season, as the soil conditions permit.

WHY YOU PLANT:
The Winter Jasmine blooms in late Winter to early Spring with unusual drooping branches. This is near the top of the list for the most "fool-proof" shrub.

WHERE YOU PLANT:
Use in mass groupings, as a ground cover, and above retaining walls. When used on walls, allow the branches to hang or grow down the sides. Winter Jasmine tolerates almost any soil condition and can be planted in sun or shade areas.

HOW YOU PLANT:
Loosen the roots of plants grown in pots... thoroughly! Prepare a wide, shallow hole 3/4 as deep and 2 times as wide as the root ball. Make a mix of 1/3 soil, 1/3 coarse sand, and 1/3 peat moss, organic humus, or commercial planting mix. Pack firmly around sides of root ball. Add 1-3" of mulch on top, staying clear of the crown of the plant. Then water well with a root stimulator fertilizer. *Note: Avoid planting when soil is frozen 1" deep or when soil is wet enough to form a mudball in your fist.*

WHEN YOU WATER:
For newly planted shrubs, use a hand-held, open-ended hose, watering plants directly. Do this until the shrub's roots are established, generally one growing season, or when new growth is evident. Light, frequent watering is preferred over heavy watering. When in doubt, check soil wetness with a moisture meter before watering.

How/When you prune:
You should prune back to within 6" of the ground every couple of years.

How/When you fertilize:
Select a well balanced slow-release granular fertilizer at the rate of one-half cup per 10 sq. ft. and broadcast it under the canopy of the shrub and a little beyond.

Additional advice for proper care:
No common diseases or insects should be expected with this variety, and even if there were any, the Winter Jasmine would take 'em on.

Laurel (Cherrylaurel), English
Prunus laurocerasus

Matures to 10-15 feet in height and spreading even more in width, English Laurel features a dark green foliage with small white flowers in the Spring. The bloom is not among the most spectacular, but the plant does offer good use as a hedge in shady areas. Recently the English Laurel has gained in popularity by replacing the Holly with a softer, more dense look to frame a home's foundation.

When to plant:
Plant English Laurel year round, as the soil conditions permit.

Why you plant:
Used as a moderate to fast-growing hedge plant, it lends a very elegant look. Planted in partial to deeply shaded areas, the foliage provides a "country-inn" look to cut arrangements.

WHERE YOU PLANT:

The English Laurel may be placed in sun or shade, but it prefers moist, well-draining soil of a moderate acidic value, pH 5.5 to 7.0. Avoid planting in areas which tend to stay wet. English Laurel is a wonderful choice to plant around large shade trees if you choose to frame the base of the trunk with greenery. To avoid problems with windburn, plant in protected areas.

HOW YOU PLANT:

Balled and burlaped: Position root ball in a wide, shallow hole 3/4 as deep and 2 times as wide as the root ball. Cut twine around trunk and top of root ball, remove any nails, fold back burlap to the sides of the root ball. Do not remove wire cage. No need to loosen roots. Make a mix of 1/3 soil, 1/3 coarse sand, and 1/3 peat moss, organic humus or commercial planting mix. Pack firmly around sides of root ball. Add 2-3" of mulch on top. Water well with a root stimulator fertilizer. *Note: Avoid planting when soil is frozen 1" deep or when soil forms mud balls.* Container: Loosen the roots of plants grown in pots then follow balled and burlaped instructions.

WHEN YOU WATER:

Ball and burlap: Water immediately after planting. Slowly trickle water from the open end of hose approximately one minute per inch diameter of the root ball. Repeat three times the first week, two times the second week, and then once per week until the tree's roots are established, generally one growing season, or until new growth has appeared. When in doubt, check soil wetness with a moisture meter before watering. Do not overwater English Laurel, particularly if the soil does not drain properly. Container: For newly planted shrubs, use a hand-held, open-ended hose, watering plants directly. Do this until the shrub's roots are established, generally one growing season, or when new growth is evident. Light, frequent watering is preferred over heavy watering. When in doubt, check soil wetness with a moisture meter before watering.

HOW/WHEN YOU PRUNE:
Prune to the desired shape and size by either shearing or cutting back the individual branches. Once the plant is shaped to your individual taste, trim only in the Spring and Fall.

HOW/WHEN YOU FERTILIZE:
Feed with a dry, granular, time-released shrub fertilizer once during the Spring, but avoid excessive fertilization. Feeding is a relatively simple affair, calling for removing mulch and lightly scratching in the food, reapplying the mulch and then watering well.

ADDITIONAL ADVICE FOR PROPER CARE:
A bacterium called Shotgun Fungus can attack the leaves of this plant. It is not a true fungus, but it is difficult to control. It is a cosmetic nuisance more than a threat to the plant. Consult your local garden center for advice. If your English Laurel does not maintain a deep green color, you may consider supplement feeding with Ironite or a similar product.

Lilac, Common
Syringa vulgaris

The word Lilac itself is synonymous with sweet fragrance, lavender colors and the soft, familiar beauty of Grandmother's garden. This heirloom shrub is now available in a range of sizes from dwarf varieties of 3-4 feet to larger plants at 8-15 feet. Flower colors range the entire gamut: from white, pink, yellow, red and blue to combination colors displayed in both single and double blossoms. The shrub itself is not recommended for extensive use in a Tennessee landscape since it lacks form and foliage, but should be selected for blossom and fragrance, which it provides in abundance.

WHEN TO PLANT:
Plant the balled and burlaped varieties during the Fall, Winter, or Spring. Container plants may be planted any time the soil is workable.

WHY YOU PLANT:
This shrub is an old stand-by. Where the Forsythia announces Spring, the Common Lilac announces Spring's ending and Summer's beginning.

WHERE YOU PLANT:
Plant this variety in full sunlight areas. Use it as a border or as a backdrop in landscape settings. The Lilac prefers soil close to neutral in pH, 6.5-7.0.

HOW YOU PLANT:
Balled and Burlaped Plants: Position the root ball in a wide, shallow hole, three-fourths deep and 2 times as wide as the root ball. Cut twine around the trunk and top of root ball and remove any nails. Fold back burlap to the sides of the root ball. Do not remove the wire cage, and don't worry with loosening the roots. Make a mix of one-third soil, one-third sand, and one-third peat moss or organic humus. Pack the mixture firmly around the sides of the root ball, and water well with a starter fertilizer. Add 1-3" of mulch on top. Container: Loosen the roots of plants grown in pots, then follow balled and burlaped instructions.

WHEN YOU WATER:
Use a slow-trickle, open-end hose at the base of the plant. Water approximately one minute for each inch of diameter of the root ball. Repeat three times the first week, two times the second week, and then once per week until the shrub's roots are established.
Note: When in doubt, check the soil's wetness with a moisture meter before watering.

HOW/WHEN YOU PRUNE:
Snip off old flowers soon after they fade to maintain a healthy and tidy appearance.

HOW/WHEN YOU FERTILIZE:
Select a well-balanced, slow-release granular fertilizer at the rate of one-half cup per 10 square feet and broadcast it under the canopy of the shrub and a little beyond.

ADDITIONAL ADVICE FOR PROPER CARE:
Watch for Powdery Mildew and Borer with this variety, and otherwise, enjoy the sweet fragrance and wonderful blooms.

Lilac, Persian
Syringa x persica

Like the Common Lilac, the Persian Lilac holds a fragrance which has few rivals in the world of shrubs. The Persian Lilac lacks the flowering size and fragrance of the Common Lilac, but is very compact, making it more attractive after the aromatic, blue blooms have faded. Like Hyacinth's bloom, the Lilac's flower is very fragrant, yet quickly gone. But, "it is better to have loved and lost than never to have loved at all."

WHEN TO PLANT:
This variety is container-grown and may be planted any time the soil is workable.

WHY YOU PLANT:
This plant is a must for fragrant gardens, and patio areas where you can enjoy the wonderful fragrance.

WHERE YOU PLANT:
A great plant for use as a shrub border, it performs best in full sun-

light. Plant one near a window to create a pleasing aroma.

HOW YOU PLANT:

Loosen the roots of plants grown in pots... thoroughly! Prepare a wide, shallow hole 3/4 as deep and 2 times as wide as the root ball. Make a mix of 1/3 soil, 1/3 coarse sand, and 1/3 peat moss, organic humus, or commercial planting mix. Pack firmly around sides of root ball. Add 1-3" of mulch on top, staying clear of the crown of the plant. Then water well with a root stimulator fertilizer. *Note: Avoid planting when soil is frozen 1" deep or when soil is wet enough to form a mudball in your fist.*

WHEN YOU WATER:

Use a slow-trickle, open-end hose at base of plant. Water approximately one minute for each inch of diameter of the root ball. Repeat three times the first week, two times the second week, and then once per week until the shrub's roots are established.

Note: When in doubt, check the soil's wetness with a moisture meter before watering.

HOW/WHEN YOU PRUNE:

Prune after blooming in the Summer to the desired height and shape.

HOW/WHEN YOU FERTILIZE:

Select a well-balanced, slow-release granular fertilizer at the rate of one-half cup per 10 square feet and broadcast it under the canopy of the shrub and a little beyond.

ADDITIONAL ADVICE FOR PROPER CARE:

In Tennessee, Powdery Mildew may present a problem, particularly in shaded areas. Otherwise, you have nothing to worry about, with sweet-smelling results to enjoy.

WALT'S WISDOM

To hear God's voice, turn down the world's volume.

Mock Orange
Philadelphus coronarius

Mock Orange is another old-time favorite that lost its popularity, but is coming back now, because of new cultivars. The bold fragrance and ease of care have piqued gardeners' interest in the "antique" Mock Orange once again. The cultivar 'Natchez' is perhaps the handsomest of all varieties, displaying slightly fragrant, 1 1/2" diameter, pure white flowers that cover the leaves during May and June.

WHEN TO PLANT:
The Mock Orange will transplant easily into a wide range of soils. Container-grown plants may be planted year round, as the soil conditions allow.

WHY YOU PLANT:
Mock Orange adds wonderful fragrance to the landscape. Also, the blooming time of the brilliant white flowers fills a blooming void in the garden during the late Spring and early Summer.

WHERE YOU PLANT:
Plant this variety in full sunlight or light shade. This shrub prefers a moist, well-drained soil amended with sphagnum peat moss. One might consider planting this as a backdrop to Spring-blooming evergreen Azaleas.

HOW YOU PLANT:
Loosen the roots of plants grown in pots... thoroughly! Prepare a wide, shallow hole 3/4 as deep and 2 times as wide as the root ball. Make a mix of 1/3 soil, 1/3 coarse sand, and 1/3 peat moss, organic humus, or commercial planting mix. Pack firmly around sides of root ball. Add 1-3" of mulch on top, staying clear of the crown of the plant. Then water well with a root stimulator fertilizer. *Note: Avoid planting when soil is frozen 1" deep or when soil is wet enough to form a mudball in your fist.*

WHEN YOU WATER:

Use a slow-trickle, open-end hose at the base of the plant. Water approximately one minute for each inch of diameter of the root ball. Repeat three times the first week, two times the second week, and then once per week until the shrub's roots are established.

Note: When in doubt, check the soil's wetness with a moisture meter before watering.

HOW/WHEN YOU PRUNE:

Prune immediately after blooming by removing old wood or cutting back to the ground for total rejuvination.

HOW/WHEN YOU FERTILIZE:

Fertilize immediately after blooming with a well-balanced, slow -release granular fertilizer.

ADDITIONAL ADVICE FOR PROPER CARE:

No serious problems should be expected. Be sure you plant these close to your home so you may enjoy them fully.

Nandina

Nandina domestica

Maturing to a height of 6-8 feet and slightly less in width, the Nandina features light, airy foliage that resembles bamboo leaves. It displays small white flowers in the Spring which produce plentiful red berries during the Winter. The berries make a nice complement to the bright red-to-purple foliage that the Nandina sports as its Fall and Winter coat. Extremely graceful in texture, the Nandina is a must for any Tennessee landscape demanding year round appeal.

WHEN TO PLANT:

Nandinas may be transplanted all year, as the soil conditions permit.

WHY YOU PLANT:

Nandinas are recommended for the medley of color in the seasonal displays of foliage, and for their splendid berries. Used in foundation plantings, hedges, and mass groupings, this shrub is also available in dwarf cultivars selected particularly for size, shape, and shade of foliage. A few of these dwarf cultivars are 'Fire Power,' 'Harbour Dwarf,' and 'Moon Bay.' 'Fire Power' has a mounded growth habit, 1 1/2-3 feet, and is disease-resistant. 'Harbour Dwarf' has a compact form and grows in beauty with age. 'Moon Bay' is a very compact shrub, 1 1/2-2 1/2 feet at maturity. These dwarf varieties are wonderful for Winter color.

WHERE YOU PLANT:

This is a very adaptable plant and may be placed in either sun or shade areas; preferably in moist, well-draining soil.

HOW YOU PLANT:

Loosen the roots of plants grown in pots... thoroughly! Prepare a wide, shallow hole 3/4 as deep and 2 times as wide as the root ball. Make a mix of 1/3 soil, 1/3 coarse sand, and 1/3 peat moss, organic humus, or commercial planting mix. Pack firmly around sides of root ball. Add 1-3" of mulch on top, staying clear of the crown of the plant. Then water well with a root stimulator fertilizer. *Note: Avoid planting when soil is frozen 1" deep or when soil is wet enough to form a mudball in your fist.*

WHEN YOU WATER:

For newly planted shrubs, use a hand-held, open-ended hose, watering plants directly. Do this until the shrub's roots are established, generally one growing season, or when new growth is evident. Light, frequent watering is preferred over heavy watering. When in doubt, check soil wetness with a moisture meter before watering.

HOW/WHEN YOU PRUNE:

On the regular Nandina cultivar, cut individual older canes to the ground in the early Spring and look for new shoots to regenerate within one growing season. Instead of cutting all old canes to the ground, you may want to stagger the heights of the canes you are removing. On the cultivars 'Fire Power' and 'Nana Purpurea,' shear to the desired shape during the early Spring. With 'Moon Bay' and 'Harbour Dwarf,' cut back individual stems halfway to the ground.

HOW/WHEN YOU FERTILIZE:
Select a slow-release formulation of ratio 12-6-6 (or equal) at the rate of one-half cup per 10 square feet and broadcast it under the canopy of the shrub and a little beyond.

ADDITIONAL ADVICE FOR PROPER CARE:
Nandina is a pest-free shrub, and maintenance is limited mostly to proper pruning. Other than that, your only problem is deciding on which of these wonderful cultivars to plant.

Oregon Grape
Mahonia bealei

Maturing to 4-10 feet in height and 4-5 feet in width, this upright evergreen shrub supports large 3-6" sprigs of dark, glossy, green leaves. The flowers waft a lemon fragrance from February until April, when the blooms fruit into clusters of blue berries, much like grapes. When a request is made for a plant that can take deep shade and drought conditions, usually under an overhang of a roof line, the answer is always the Mahonia.

WHEN TO PLANT:
Container plants may be planted year round, as the soil conditions permit.

WHY YOU PLANT:

The leaves of this particular plant are pointed and sharp, which should be considered if children are present. This shrub will add interest to the landscape from February all the way through June. We have seen the plant used effectively in deep shade and to offset corners of the home in foundation plantings.

WHERE YOU PLANT:

This plant performs best in full sun areas with a moist, well-draining soil, but will adapt just fine to areas with a half-day of sun, or with filtered light. It does prefer a soil pH of 5.5 to 6.5.

HOW YOU PLANT:

Loosen the roots of plants grown in pots... thoroughly! Prepare a wide, shallow hole 3/4 as deep and 2 times as wide as the root ball. Make a mix of 1/3 soil, 1/3 coarse sand, and 1/3 peat moss, organic humus, or commercial planting mix. Pack firmly around sides of root ball. Add 1-3" of mulch on top, staying clear of the crown of the plant. Then water well with a root stimulator fertilizer. *Note: Avoid planting when soil is frozen 1" deep or when soil is wet enough to form a mudball in your fist.*

WHEN YOU WATER:

For newly planted shrubs, use a hand-held, open-ended hose, watering plants directly. Do this until the shrub's roots are established, generally one growing season, or when new growth is evident. Light, frequent watering is preferred over heavy watering. When in doubt, check soil wetness with a moisture meter before watering.

HOW/WHEN YOU PRUNE:

Prune by cutting the older canes back deep into the body of the shrub, or even to the ground. You need to trim the Oregon Grape after fruiting, but this can be done as late as the Fall.

HOW/WHEN YOU FERTILIZE:

Select a well-balanced, slow-release granular fertilizer at the rate of one-half cup per 10 square feet and broadcast it under the canopy of the shrub and a little beyond.

ADDITIONAL ADVICE FOR PROPER CARE:

Leaf Scorch, caused by Winter sun and wind, is a common problem, but there are no serious pest threats. We have never needed to do a supplemental spray or watering on our Mahonias, and they are still outstanding. Other than pruning, this shrub is basically care free.

Photina, Red-Tip
Photina x fraseri

This shrub matures to 6–10 feet in height, occasionally reaching up to 15 feet. This is a fast-growing, privet-like, evergreen shrub. It is best known and planted for the bright red growth showcased in the Spring and Fall. This plant performs very well as an accent, content to highlight a landscape and not steal the scene from the bigger show-offs of the garden.

WHEN TO PLANT:

Transplant this shrub Spring through Fall, as the soil conditions permit.

WHY YOU PLANT:

The Photina is mostly used as a hedge and for screening applications. With gorgeous, almost artificial-looking glossy leaves, this plant offers a great display of color when contrasted with other green shrubs and trees.

WHERE YOU PLANT:

Place in sun to light shade areas with a moist, fertile soil, avoiding chronically wet areas. *Note: The leaf color is diminished when grown in shady areas.*

HOW YOU PLANT:

Loosen the roots of plants grown in pots... thoroughly! Prepare a wide, shallow hole 3/4 as deep and 2 times as wide as the root ball. Make a mix of 1/3 soil, 1/3 coarse sand, and 1/3 peat moss, organic humus, or commercial planting mix. Pack firmly around sides of root ball. Add 1-3" of mulch on top, staying clear of the crown of the plant. Then water well with a root stimulator fertilizer. *Note: Avoid planting when soil is frozen 1" deep or when soil is wet enough to form a mudball in your fist.*

WHEN YOU WATER:

For newly planted shrubs, use a hand-held, open-ended hose, watering plants directly. Do this until the shrub's roots are established, generally one growing season, or when new growth is evident. Light, frequent watering is preferred over heavy watering. When in doubt, check soil wetness with a moisture meter before watering.

HOW/WHEN YOU PRUNE:

To encourage new red growth, the Red-Tip Photina may be pruned Spring through Fall with a pair of quality pruning shears. Cutting back individual branches will allow you to maintain the desirable shape and size.

HOW/WHEN YOU FERTILIZE:

Feed with a well-balanced, slow-release fertilizer high in nitrogen during the Spring and Fall. To feed, remove the mulch around the dripline and lightly scratch in the granular food. Replace mulch and then water well.

ADDITIONAL ADVICE FOR PROPER CARE:

Entommosporium maculatum (Leaf Spot) can be fatal to this plant, so keep a keen eye out for symptoms such as roundish lesions with a purple halo, which will result in partial to total leaf drop. Consult your local garden center or nursery for a very vigorous spraying schedule to ward off this potentially life-threatening disease.

Privet, Japanese
Ligustrum japonicum

Use of this favorite Southern plant is limited to West Tennessee, because it requires a warmer climate. It is noted for its fast growth and shiny green foliage. Japanese Privet typifies the wax-coated, broadleaf, hedge shrub classification and works well in a variety of applications, and rounds out a good landscape design.

WHEN TO PLANT:

Japanese Privet may be transplanted year round, as the soil conditions permit.

WHY YOU PLANT:

This shrub has many uses, from multi-tree forms, to topiaries, to hedges.

WHERE YOU PLANT:

The Japanese Privet may be used in either sun or shade, and in moist soil conditions. In fact, this shrub seems to survive with little or no care.

HOW YOU PLANT:

Loosen the roots of plants grown in pots... thoroughly! Prepare a wide, shallow hole 3/4 as deep and 2 times as wide as the root ball. Make a mix of 1/3 soil, 1/3 coarse sand, and 1/3 peat moss, organic humus, or commercial planting mix. Pack firmly around sides of root ball. Add 1-3" of mulch on top, staying clear of the crown of the plant. Then water well with a root stimulator fertilizer. *Note: Avoid planting when soil is frozen 1" deep or when soil is wet enough to form a mudball in your fist.*

WHEN YOU WATER:
For newly planted shrubs, use a hand-held, open-ended hose, watering plants directly. Do this until the shrub's roots are established, generally one growing season or when new growth is evident. Light, frequent watering is preferred over heavy watering. When in doubt, check soil wetness with a moisture meter before watering.

HOW/WHEN YOU PRUNE:
Prune any time during the year, avoiding periods of sub-freezing temperatures. The Japanese Privet will tolerate heavy trimming.

HOW/WHEN YOU FERTILIZE:
Select a well-balanced, slow-release granular fertilizer at the rate of one-half cup per 10 square feet and broadcast it under the canopy of the shrub and a little beyond.

ADDITIONAL ADVICE FOR PROPER CARE:
No serious diseases and insects should be expected, although we have noticed some Winter sunburn and Leaf Spot which can be pruned out in early Spring.

Quince, Flowering
Chaenomeles speciosa

This is a small, deciduous shrub which varies greatly in flower color and habit.

The Flowering Quince is an early bloomer. It has a rather common look all year, until late Winter when it announces the coming of Spring in a choice of colors ranging from red, white and pink to coral.

WHEN TO PLANT:
Flowering Quince should be planted Spring through Fall, as the soil conditions permit.

WHY YOU PLANT:
This shrub is not very attractive when not in bloom, although it maintains popularity for its late Winter flowering habits. It has a wide range of blossom color possibilities.

WALT'S WISDOM

Be careful what you pray for, you might get it.

WHERE YOU PLANT:
Planted in full sun to partial shade areas, this variety is adaptable to a wide range of soil conditions.

HOW YOU PLANT:
Balled and burlaped: Position root ball in a wide, shallow hole 3/4 as deep and 2 times as wide as the root ball. Cut twine around trunk and top of root ball, remove any nails, fold back burlap to the sides of the root ball. Do not remove wire cage. No need to loosen roots. Make a mix of 1/3 soil, 1/3 coarse sand, and 1/3 peat moss, organic humus or commercial planting mix. Pack firmly around sides of root ball. Add 2-3" of mulch on top. Water well with a root stimulator fertilizer. *Note: Avoid planting when soil is frozen 1" deep or when soil forms mud balls.* Container: Loosen the roots of plants grown in pots, then follow the balled and burlaped instructions.

WHEN YOU WATER:
Water immediately after planting. Slowly trickle water from the open end of hose approximately one minute per inch diameter of the root ball. Repeat three times the first week, two times the

second week, and then once per week until the tree's roots are established, generally one growing season, or until new growth has appeared. When in doubt, check soil wetness with a moisture meter before watering.

How/When you prune:
Immediately after blooming, in the Spring, prune out the old wood, or cut back 6-12" from the base of the shrub to stimulate new flowering growth.

When you fertilize:
Select a well-balanced, slow-release granular fertilizer at the rate of one-half cup per 10 square feet and broadcast it under the canopy of the shrub and a little beyond.

Additional advice for proper care:
Common diseases and insects include Leaf Spot, Rust, Aphids, Scales, and Mites, although none are serious threats to the late-Winter blooming of this shrub.

Rhododendron
Rhododendron

This evergreen shrub combines handsome leathery, dark green foliage with large 3-10" clusters of Orchid-like flowers. Spin the color wheel to decide what your yard will look like. Cultivar colors include white, pink, red, purple, blue, yellow and almost endless combinations of these. Our preferences include 'Roseum Elegans' in lavender, 'English Roseum' in light rose, 'Nova Zembla' in red, and 'Chionoides' in white.

When to plant:
Plant any time of the year that the soil conditions allow.

WHY YOU PLANT:

Rhododendron is widely acknowledged as America's most popular evergreen shrub, and its widespread use will continue with so many colors to choose from.

WHERE YOU PLANT:

Plant in areas ranging from light to full shade, since full sun tends to diminish the foliage color. Finding a location with well-drained acidic soil is the single most important factor to insure this plant's survival and healthy growth.

HOW YOU PLANT:

Loosen the roots of plants grown in pots... thoroughly! Prepare a wide, shallow hole 3/4 as deep and 2 times as wide as the root ball. Make a mix of 1/3 soil, 1/3 coarse sand, and 1/3 peat moss, organic humus, or commercial planting mix. Pack firmly around sides of root ball. Add 1-3" of mulch on top, staying clear of the crown of the plant. Then water well with a root stimulator fertilizer. *Note: Avoid planting when soil is frozen 1" deep or when soil is wet enough to form a mudball in your fist.* Use at least a 50 percent sphagnum peat moss mixture and place the shrub slightly higher than the existing ground surface.

WHEN YOU WATER:

For newly planted shrubs, use a hand-held, open-ended hose, watering plants directly. Do this until the shrub's roots are established, generally one growing season, or when new growth is evident. Light, frequent watering is preferred over heavy watering. When in doubt, check soil wetness with a moisture meter before watering.

HOW/WHEN YOU PRUNE:

DO NOT SHEAR THIS PLANT. Only prune by the "reach and cut" method, which trims individual branches to maintain a natural shape. Prune immediately after blooming.

HOW/WHEN YOU FERTILIZE:

Fertilize immediately after blooming by broadcasting granular Azalea/Rhododendron food to the base of the plants, and repeat the process in 6-8 weeks. Avoid late Summer fertilization. If your shrubs show some yellowing, supplement feeding with an iron fertilizer.

ADDITIONAL ADVICE FOR PROPER CARE:

Crown Rot, Powdery Mildew, Aphids, and Azalea Stem Borers are only a few of the many diseases and pests which may attack these shrubs. Also, Lace Bugs are now becoming common in Tennessee. These can be controlled with a late Winter or early Spring application of a quality dormant oil spray.

Rhododendron, 'P.J.M.'
Rhododendron

Maturing at only 3-6 ft. in height, this hybrid is smaller than the other Rhododendron species. It has a rounded plant-form, with leaves 1/2" wide and 1 1/2" long, and bears small flowers that are a vivid, bright lavender pink. The dark green foliage becomes purple during the Fall, and the Winter leaf color sets the plant apart as a star among the Rhododendron family.

WHEN TO PLANT:

Plant this variety any time of the year that soil conditions allow.

WHY YOU PLANT:

This plant is a heavy bloomer and tends to tolerate a wide range of landscape conditions, making it rather versatile. Consider it for that area where you want to make a special visual statement.

WHERE YOU PLANT:

Plant in shade to light shade. Full sunlight diminishes the foliage color. Placement in well-drained soil is most important to this shrub's survival.

HOW YOU PLANT:

Loosen the roots of plants grown in pots... thoroughly! Prepare a wide, shallow hole 3/4 as deep and 2 times as wide as the root ball. Make a mix of 1/3 soil, 1/3 coarse sand, and 1/3 peat moss, organic humus, or commercial planting mix. Pack firmly around sides of root ball. Add 1-3" of mulch on top, staying clear of the crown of the plant. Then water well with a root stimulator fertilizer. *Note: Avoid planting when soil is frozen 1" deep or when soil is wet enough to form a mudball in your fist, and use at least 50% Sphagnum Peat Moss mixture and place the shrub slightly higher than the existing ground surface.*

WHEN YOU WATER:

For newly planted shrubs, use a hand-held, open-ended hose, watering plants directly. Do this until the shrub's roots are established, generally one growing season, or when new growth is evident. Light, frequent watering is preferred over heavy watering. When in doubt, check soil wetness with a moisture meter before watering.

HOW/WHEN YOU PRUNE:

DO NOT SHEAR THIS PLANT. Only prune by the "reach and cut" method, which trims individual branches to maintain a natural shape. Pruning should take place immediately after blooming.

HOW/WHEN YOU FERTILIZE:

Fertilize immediately after blooming by broadcasting granular Azalea/Rhododendron food to the base of the plants. Repeat this process in 6-8 weeks. Avoid late Summer fertilization. If shrubs show yellowing, supplement feeding with an iron fertilizer.

ADDITIONAL ADVICE FOR PROPER CARE:
Crown Rot, Powdery Mildew, Aphids, and Azalea Stem Borers are only a few of the many diseases and pests which may attack these shrubs. Also, Lace Bugs are now becoming common in Tennessee. These can be controlled with a late Winter or early Spring application of a quality dormant oil spray.

Spirea, Japanese
Spirea x bumalda

The Japanese Spirea is responsible for increased interest in Spireas in Tennessee gardens. Unlike the old favorite, 'vanhouttei,' which has white flowers and is rather unpredictable in growth, the Japanese Spirea offers a selection of compact plants. It also has choices of white, red, or pink blossoms, with foliage of yellow to lime-green, creating a beautiful contrast. The flowers are borne above the foliage in small, fuzzy, flat-topped clusters. We should not forget to mention the outstanding Fall leaf color of the Spireas different varieties will turn orange-red, yellow-red or a brilliant bronze.

WHEN TO PLANT:
Plant this variety any time the soil is workable.

WHY YOU PLANT:
When you desire a shrub that has varying colors of leaves in Spring and Fall, as well as varying blooming periods in Spring and Summer, the Spirea fills the order.

WHERE YOU PLANT:
Use in masses, on banks, and as border in front of landscape groupings. Spirea is tolerant of most soil conditions, except very wet areas.

How you plant:

Loosen the roots of plants grown in pots... thoroughly! Prepare a wide, shallow hole 3/4 as deep and 2 times as wide as the root ball. Make a mix of 1/3 soil, 1/3 coarse sand, and 1/3 peat moss, organic humus, or commercial planting mix. Pack firmly around sides of root ball. Add 1-3" of mulch on top, staying clear of the crown of the plant. Then water well with a root stimulator fertilizer. *Note: Avoid planting when soil is frozen 1" deep or when soil is wet enough to form a mudball in your fist.*

When you water:

For newly planted shrubs, use a hand-held, open-ended hose, watering plants directly. Do this until the shrub's roots are established, generally one growing season or when new growth is evident. Light, frequent watering is preferred over heavy watering. When in doubt, check soil wetness with a moisture meter before watering.

How/When you prune:

Prune Spirea to shape in the early Spring prior to the breakthrough of foliage. Also, trim when Summer blooms start to diminish or fade away. Light shearing of old flowers will induce new blossom growth.

How/When you fertilize:

Select a well-balanced, slow-release granular fertilizer at the rate of one-half cup per 10 square feet and broadcast it under the canopy of the shrub and a little beyond.

Additional advice for proper care:

Spirea is in the Rosaceae, or Rose family, so Fire Blight, Rust, Mildew, Aphids, and Scale are likely to attack this plant, although none seems to prevail over the Spirea.

Viburnum

Viburnum

Viburnums once enjoyed popularity only in Northern climates, but have recently gained stature in Southern gardens for their cold-hardiness and tolerance of hot conditions. This group consists of 120 species, and the list of cultivars is being increased daily. Sizes range from 2-3 feet all the way to 30 feet, and fragrances range from some of the sweetest to others that, frankly, stink. Leaves can look willowy or even Maple-like, and flower colors range just as widely.

WHEN TO PLANT:

Plant the Viburnum any time of year that the soil conditions allow.

WHY YOU PLANT:

Use this plant when looking for Spring and Summer-fragrant flowers, followed by Fall and Winter berries. Viburnum is equally effective as a background plant, in mass plantings, or as a screen.

WHERE TO PLANT:

The Viburnum prefers sun or partial shade, and is adaptable to a wide range of soil types, except for very wet, poorly drained soils.

HOW TO PLANT:

Position root ball in a wide, shallow hole 3/4 as deep and 2 times as wide as the root ball. Cut twine around trunk and top of root ball, remove any nails, fold back burlap to the sides of the root ball. Do not remove wire cage. No need to loosen roots. Make a mix of 1/3 soil, 1/3 coarse sand, and 1/3 peat moss, organic humus or commercial planting mix. Pack firmly around sides of root ball. Add 2-3" of mulch on top. Water well with a root stimulator fertilizer. *Note: Avoid planting when soil is frozen 1" deep or when soil forms mud balls.*

WHEN TO WATER:
Water immediately after planting. Slowly trickle water from the open end of hose approximately one minute per inch diameter of the root ball. Repeat three times the first week, two times the second week, and then once per week until the shrub's roots are established, generally one growing season, or until new growth has appeared. When in doubt, check soil wetness with a moisture meter before watering.

HOW TO PRUNE:
Maintain the size and shape by pruning individual limbs and branches during the growing season, however, dormant pruning is preferred.

WALT'S WISDOM

When God forgives, it's time for us to forget.

HOW/WHEN TO FERTILIZE:
Select a well-balanced, slow-release granular fertilizer at the rate of one-half cup per 10 square feet and broadcast it under the canopy of the shrub and a little beyond.

ADDITIONAL ADVICE FOR PROPER CARE:
Nothing serious should affect the health of your Viburnum, but contact your local garden center if any problems arise.

Weigela
Weigela florida

Weigela may be considered as a replacement for Azalea when a more dependable, late-Spring bloomer is desired. The flowers are a clone of the Azalea's, borne in clusters backed by loose, rich, green foliage. Being a deciduous plant, the Weigela is not the most attractive during the Winter, but there is increased interest in Weigela, especially in the cultivars 'Minuet,' a dark red flowering dwarf, 'Red Prince,' with red flowers in both Spring and Fall, 'Variegata,' with soft pink, variegated foliage with creamy leaf margins.

WHEN TO PLANT:
Container-grown shrubs may be planted any time the soil is workable.

WHY YOU PLANT:
Weigela is planted to create shrub borders, groupings, or mass plantings, and is very care free from diseases and insects.

WHERE YOU PLANT:
Plant in almost any full sunlight area, since this shrub is very adaptable to various soil conditions.

HOW YOU PLANT:
Loosen the roots of plants grown in pots... thoroughly! Prepare a wide, shallow hole 3/4 as deep and 2 times as wide as the root ball. Make a mix of 1/3 soil, 1/3 coarse sand, and 1/3 peat moss, organic humus, or commercial planting mix. Pack firmly around sides of root ball. Add 1-3" of mulch on top, staying clear of the crown of the plant. Then water well with a root stimulator fertilizer. *Note: Avoid planting when soil is frozen 1" deep or when soil is wet enough to form a mudball in your fist.*

WHEN YOU WATER:
For newly planted shrubs, use a hand-held, open-ended hose, watering plants directly. Do this until the shrub's roots are established, generally one growing season, or when new growth is evident. Light, frequent watering is preferred over heavy watering. When in doubt, check soil wetness with a moisture meter before watering.

How/When you prune:
Consider pruning the die-back branches immediately after blooming has ceased.

How/When you fertilize:
Select a well-balanced, slow-release granular fertilizer at the rate of one-half cup per 10 square feet and broadcast it under the canopy of the shrub and a little beyond.

Additional advice for proper care:
No disease or insect problems are expected with this variety, and it should serve well in Tennessee gardens as a reliable, resilient border patrol.

Witchhazel, Common
Hamamelis virginiana

The Witchhazel is one of the best kept secrets of all the woody landscape plants. Imagine walking through this plant's natural habitat during the Fall, smelling a sweet scent of soap, and wondering what could be blooming at that time of year? Then, upon further investigation, you discover a 4-6 foot plant bearing yellow Fall foliage. Underneath its leaves, running up and down the limbs, are unusual, whimsical, spider-shaped yellow flowers. 'Hamamelis Mollis,' a cousin of the 'Virginiana,' blooms on leafless branches during the Winter months of January and February in Tennessee. Think about it... what other plant provides Fall color foliage and fragrant flowers in Fall, Winter or Spring?

When to plant:
Plant this variety in the Winter or Spring, as soil conditions allow.

WHY YOU PLANT:

This shrub is excellent for use as a hedge and it does not need pruning. Many arborists feel this plant is overlooked and should rank equal to, or ahead of the Forsythia, for value as a Spring-flowering plant.

WHERE YOU PLANT:

This variety tolerates a wide range of soil conditions, including gravel, moist, poorly-draining to clay. The key to its survival is moisture.

HOW YOU PLANT:

Position root ball in a wide, shallow hole 3/4 as deep and 2 times as wide as the root ball. Cut twine around trunk and top of root ball, remove any nails, fold back burlap to the sides of the root ball. Do not remove wire cage. No need to loosen roots. Make a mix of 1/3 soil, 1/3 coarse sand, and 1/3 peat moss, organic humus or commercial planting mix. Pack firmly around sides of root ball. Add 2-3" of mulch on top. Water well with a root stimulator fertilizer. Note: *Avoid planting when soil is frozen 1" deep or when soil forms mud balls.*

WHEN YOU WATER:

Use a slow-trickle, open-end hose at the base of the plant. Water approximately one minute for each inch of diameter of the root ball. Repeat three times the first week, two times the second week, and then once per week until the shrub's roots are established.
Note: When in doubt, check the soil's wetness with a moisture meter before watering.

HOW/WHEN YOU PRUNE:

Prune for shaping only, during the early Spring.

HOW/WHEN YOU FERTILIZE:

Select a well-balanced, slow-release granular fertilizer at the rate of one-half cup per 10 square feet and broadcast it under the canopy of the shrub and a little beyond.

ADDITIONAL ADVICE FOR PROPER CARE:
No serious disease or insect problems are expected with this variety, and it does, indeed, make a wonderful all-season statement.

Witchhazel, Intermedia
Hamamelis intermedia

Maturing at 10-15 feet in height, this plant is a hybrid cross of Chinese (Mollis) and Japanese (Japonica) cultivars. The flowers have beautiful variety of color, blooming forth in February and March, and sometimes in April. The Intermedia provides a nice medium size to consider for an appropriate spot in the landscape.

WHEN TO PLANT:
Plant this variety in the Winter or Spring, as soil conditions allow.

WHY YOU PLANT:
This shrub is excellent as a hedge that doesn't need pruning. Many arborists feel this plant is overlooked and should rank equal to, or ahead of the Forsythia as an important Spring-flowering plant.

WHERE YOU PLANT:
This variety tolerates a wide range of soil conditions including gravel, moist, poorly draining to clay. The key to its survival is moisture.

HOW YOU PLANT:
Position root ball in a wide, shallow hole 3/4 as deep and 2

times as wide as the root ball. Cut twine around trunk and top of root ball, remove any nails, fold back burlap to the sides of the root ball. Do not remove wire cage. No need to loosen roots. Make a mix of 1/3 soil, 1/3 coarse sand, and 1/3 peat moss, organic humus or commercial planting mix. Pack firmly around sides of root ball. Add 2-3" of mulch on top. Water well with a root stimulator fertilizer. *Note: Avoid planting when soil is frozen 1" deep or when soil forms mud balls.*

WHEN YOU WATER:

Use a slow-trickle, open-end hose at the base of the plant. Water approximately one minute for each inch of diameter of the root ball. Repeat three times the first week, two times the second week, and then once per week until the shrub's roots are established.

Note: When in doubt, check the soil's wetness with a moisture meter before watering.

HOW/WHEN YOU PRUNE:

Prune for shaping only, during the early Spring.

HOW/WHEN YOU FERTILIZE:

Select a well-balanced, slow-release granular fertilizer at the rate of one-half cup per 10 square feet and broadcast it under the canopy of the shrub and a little beyond.

ADDITIONAL ADVICE FOR PROPER CARE:

No serious disease or insect problems are expected with this variety, leaving you to enjoy its visual warmth as the seasons turn colder.

Witchhazel, Vernal
Hamamelis vernalis

Maturing to 6-10 feet in height, this native shrub is great for creating a truly natural look in the landscape. Witchhazels are valued for their off-season blooming and welcoming fragrance. Given the name Witchhazel, this shrub blooms at the appropriate time - Fall.

WHEN TO PLANT:
Plant this variety in Winter or Spring, as soil conditions permit.

WHY YOU PLANT:
This shrub is excellent as a hedge that doesn't need pruning. Many arborists feel this plant is overlooked and should rank equal to, or ahead of, the Forsythia for Spring-flowering value.

WHERE YOU PLANT:
This variety tolerates a wide range of soil conditions including gravel, moist, poorly draining, or clay. The key to its survival is moisture.

HOW YOU PLANT:
Position root ball in a wide, shallow hole 3/4 as deep and 2 times as wide as the root ball. Cut twine around trunk and top of root ball, remove any nails, fold back burlap to the sides of the root ball. Do not remove wire cage. No need to loosen roots. Make a mix of 1/3 soil, 1/3 coarse sand, and 1/3 peat moss, organic humus or commercial planting mix. Pack firmly around sides of root ball. Add 2-3" of mulch on top. Water well with a root stimulator fertilizer. *Note: Avoid planting when soil is frozen 1" deep or when soil forms mud balls.*

WHEN YOU WATER:
Use a slow-trickle, open-end hose at the base of the plant. Water approximately one minute for each inch of diameter of the root ball. Repeat three times the first week, two times the second week, and then once per week until the shrub's roots are established.
Note: When in doubt, check the soil's wetness with a moisture meter before watering.

How/When you prune:
Prune Vernal Witchhazel for shaping only, during the early Spring.

How/When you fertilize:
Select a well-balanced, slow-release granular fertilizer at the rate of one-half cup per 10 square feet and broadcast it under the canopy of the shrub and a little beyond.

Additional advice for proper care:
No serious disease or insect problems are expected with this variety, so sit back and enjoy its seasonal appeal.

Yucca (Adam's Needle)
Yucca filamentosa

Maturing to 2-4 feet in height, the Yucca is a warm-weather friend with unique appeal in Tennessee gardens. This evergreen shrub has sword-like leaves with upright flowers on a vertical stem. The Yucca blooms in the heat of the Summer and will lend a distinctively tropical, even desert-like look to poolside, patio, and garden areas alike.

When to plant:
Yucca may be transplanted year round, as the soil conditions allow.

Why you plant:
This plant is used as an accent or contrasting plant and is distinguished by its low-maintenance requirements. This plant can also be very effective in areas you wish to keep secure or secluded. Because of its sharp dagger-leaves, it discourages intruders and pets and is a safety hazard for children.

WHERE YOU PLANT:

This variety performs best in either sun or partial shade areas, accepting a wide range of soil conditions. It is very tolerant of drought conditions and may be grown year round in urns or planters, with or without other plants.

HOW YOU PLANT:

Loosen the roots of plants grown in pots... thoroughly! Prepare a wide, shallow hole 3/4 as deep and 2 times as wide as the root ball. Make a mix of 1/3 soil, 1/3 coarse sand, and 1/3 peat moss, organic humus, or commercial planting mix. Pack firmly around sides of root ball. Add 1-3" of mulch on top, staying clear of the crown of the plant. Then water well with a root stimulator fertilizer. *Note: Avoid planting when soil is frozen 1" deep or when soil is wet enough to form a mudball in your fist.*

WHEN YOU WATER:

For newly planted shrubs, use a hand-held open-ended hose, watering plants directly. Do this until the shrub's roots are established, generally one growing season, or when new growth is evident. Light, frequent watering is preferred over heavy watering. When in doubt, check soil wetness with a moisture meter before watering. Infrequent watering is needed after shrub is established.

HOW/WHEN YOU PRUNE:

Prune back the flower spikes after the seed heads have formed. *Note: This variety is so durable that it has been known to survive the severe treatment from a bushhogging.*

HOW/WHEN YOU FERTILIZE:

Perform a light to moderate feeding during the Spring with a slow-release fertilizer formulated for shrubs.

ADDITIONAL ADVICE FOR PROPER CARE:

No serious diseases or insects noted with Yucca, leaving you to enjoy its hot-weather attitude any time of year.

Notes:

Vines

*T*HE POPULARITY OF VINES HAS taken off as rapidly as the vines themselves. From flowering to evergreen, the vine has a place almost anywhere in the home landscape. Many a mail-box has become embellished with flowers and vines creating a welcome sight as you return home everyday. The vine is certainly a must to grow on a decorative arbor or trellis, where it creates a magical environment that adds distinction and interest.

From the native Honeysuckles, to the popular Clematis, to the more unusual Climbing Hydrangea, the vine gives you so much color. Even during dormancy, some vines lend a unique feeling and contribute visual effects in the landscape with their knarled skeletons and interesting exfoliating barks.

Choose several Tennessee vines and enjoy the benefits of seasonal interest with annual and perennial vines.

There are three

essentials of

happiness: something

to hope for;

something to love;

and something

to do.

Clematis

Clematis

This finely textured deciduous vine is extremely popular due to its wide range of flowering sizes, colors and color combinations. Different varieties bloom any time from Spring to Fall. The Clematis Vine can grace a mailbox or lamppost to give your home "curb appeal." Clematis can grow up to 15 feet high, and some have been known to spread even more.

WHEN TO PLANT:
Spring is the preferred time to transplant potted items such as Clematis.

WHY YOU PLANT:
Clematis is planted to "dress-up" trellises, fencing, walls or any vertical feature that would benefit from a cheery look. The choices in colors are phenomenal and there are even some with fragrance. The look of a Clematis in bloom is almost irresistible.

WHERE YOU PLANT:
Most Clematis varieties love full sun yet they all need their roots to be in the shade. Place plant so it is protected from the afternoon sun at the base of the plant. Clematis does well in loamy, moderately moist soil.

HOW YOU PLANT:
Prepare a wide, shallow hole 3/4 as deep and 2 times as wide as the root ball. Make a mix of 1/3 soil, 1/3 coarse sand, and 1/3 peat moss, organic humus, or commercial planting mix. Pack firmly around sides of root ball. Add 1-3" of mulch on top, staying clear of the crown of the plant. Then water well with a root stimulator fertilizer. *Note: Mulching around the plant to keep the roots cool is essential. Pine straw works well or place a few nice rocks to keep the base cool and damp. Be very careful in handling roots and stems when trans-*

planting. Avoid planting when soil is frozen 1" deep or when soil forms
mud balls.

WHEN YOU WATER:

For new plantings, use a hand-held, open-ended hose, watering
plants directly. Do this until the plant's roots are established,
generally one growing season, or when new growth is evident.
Light, frequent watering is preferred over heavy watering.
When in doubt, check the soil's wetness with a moisture meter
before watering. A moisture meter is a "must" for gardening
peace of mind. Avoid overwatering the Clematis after it is
established.

HOW/WHEN YOU PRUNE:

Clematis pruning techniques are crucial for a good performance
year after year. Check with your garden center about how and
when to prune your Clematis selection. Some Clematis ('Sweet
Autumn', for example) benefit from severe to-the-ground pruning in late Winter or early Spring. Others prefer to be left alone
to bloom on last year's old wood. There is another group which
requires selective pruning in Spring.

HOW/WHEN YOU FERTILIZE:

Fertilize in Spring and repeat in early Fall with a slow-release
granular balanced fertilizer. Scratch it in around the base of the
vine, being careful with the stems. Water it well after feeding.

ADDITIONAL ADVICE FOR PROPER CARE:

Leaf spot and stem rot can be serious. Watch for mites and
white flies. A thorough application of dormant oil is advised in
Spring after new growth has flushed out, yet before blooms
have appeared.

Cypress Vine

Ipomoea quamoclit

The expression of vines comes to mind when you see the growth habit of the Cypress Vine. It twists and turns all over itself and anything in its path. This vine is easy to grow, loves full sun and has bright red flowers that cover the fine thread-like ferny foliage. The blooms begin in Summer and continue until our first hard frost.

WHEN TO PLANT:
Start seeds saved from previous year indoors in February or early March. Transplant small starter plants outdoors after mid-April or after the last chance of a killing frost.

WALT'S WISDOM

Skip Spring weeding and you'll pay all Summer long.

WHY YOU PLANT:
Cypress Vine has gorgeous foliage that makes it a valued vine, even before it blooms. Once you begin getting blooms, they will continue until frost, as will the dozens of hummingbirds attracted by Cypress Vine.

WHERE YOU PLANT:
This plant is perfect for a fence, trellis, arbor, lattice, or even a mailbox. Since Cypress Vine is so good about attracting hummingbirds, you will want to plant it close to a window or patio for the best view of the "hummers."

HOW YOU PLANT:
Very easily scratch up your desired planting site with a tiller or rake. Scatter seed liberally, cover with one inch of soil and water well. If you are starting from a container plant, dig a hole larger than the root ball, then add peat moss. Plant and water well with a liquid root stimulator.

WHEN YOU WATER:
Water well two times a week until the vine is established. Water once a week when the vine is showing new growth. During extreme heat, water 2-3 times a week.

HOW/WHEN YOU PRUNE:
No need to prune unless your Cypress Vine becomes too aggressive on smaller trellises or arbors. After the first frost, remove any seed pods you would like to save for planting next year. Then remove the entire plant, root and all, and start over next year.

HOW/WHEN YOU FERTILIZE:
You may feed two times during the growing season, once in the Spring and again in the Summer. Utilize granular slow-release fertilizer that is high in phosphorus. Apply near the base and scratch into soil. Water well.

ADDITIONAL ADVICE FOR PROPER CARE:
Trim as needed or cut back if the vine gets a little out of hand. Very little care is necessary for a fast-growing Cypress Vine.

Honeysuckle
Lonicera sempervirens

A relative of our native Honeysuckle, these mature to 10-20 feet in height. It is a deciduous vine that features trumpet or tubular clusters of flowers. Depending on the hybrid, the blooms range in color from creamy white, to yellow, to gold, to orange, to pink or red. Some of the blooms are even available in color combinations. This is a great vine for the gardener who has a large area to devote to a vine. Honeysuckle will tolerate filtered light to full sun.

WHEN TO PLANT:
Plant Spring through Fall, as soil conditions permit.

WHY YOU PLANT:
Use as a vine for walls, trellises, fences, and mail box decorations. The Honeysuckle is desired for its long blooming period. There is a gold-colored cultivar that flowers from June to frost. The fragrance is unmistakable and many times can be reminiscent of early childhood memories. The vines with a little age can be cut and twisted into wreaths and decorative pieces.

WHERE YOU PLANT:
Place in sun or slightly shaded areas with moist, well-draining soil. Honeysuckle certainly can take over an area, therefore, be careful when selecting a spot. Think big . . . this is a rapid grower.

HOW YOU PLANT:
Loosen the roots of plants grown in containers...thoroughly! Prepare a wide, shallow hole 3/4 as deep and 2 times as wide as the root ball. Make a mix of 1/3 soil, 1/3 coarse sand, and 1/3 peat moss, organic humus, or commercial planting mix. Pack firmly around sides of root ball. Add 1-3" of mulch on top, staying clear of the crown of the plant. Then water well with a root stimulator fertilizer. *Note: Avoid planting when soil is frozen 1" deep or when soil forms mud balls.*

WHEN YOU WATER:
For new plantings, use a hand-held, open-ended hose, watering plants directly. Do this until the plant's roots are established, generally one growing season, or when new growth is evident. Light, frequent wate.ing is preferred over heavy watering. When in doubt, check the soil's wetness with a moisture meter before watering. A moisture meter is a "must" for gardening peace of mind.

HOW/WHEN YOU PRUNE:
Prune to control shape and size just after blooming has ceased.

Avoid Winter trimming or next year's flower buds may be removed.

How/When you fertilize:
Fertilize in Spring and repeat in early Fall with a slow-release granular balanced fertilizer. Scratch it in around the base of the vine, being careful with the stems. Water it well after feeding.

Additional advice for proper care:
Common diseases may include Powdery Mildew and Leaf Spot. No serious insects noted. If you suspect a problem, contact your garden center for proper advice.

Hyacinth Bean Vine
Lablab purpureus (Dolichos Lablab)

Hyacinth Bean Vine has several wonderful features. As the name implies, the vine sports a showy bean in the form of a slick, waxy, purple pod which is actually edible. Prior to the bean, you will find Sweet Pea-like blooms that range from lavender to pink all Summer. This vine is an annual in Tennessee, so you can gather the beans in late Summer and Fall, save them and replant in the Spring. This vine is very attractive and fast growing.

When to plant:
Start seeds saved from previous year indoors in February or early March. Transplant small starter plants outdoors after mid-April or after any chance of a killing frost.

Why you plant:
The Hyacinth Bean Vine is a real performer, because of its fast growth. It will fill up a small arbor or trellis in one season, so it is a good choice where quick coverage is needed. It has been used in conjunction with Wisteria to provide a nice look while

the Wisteria is getting established. Hyacinth Bean Vine blooms are reminiscent of Grandma's Sweet Pea vine. The actual bean is more than ornamental, and is suitable for stir-fry!

WHERE YOU PLANT:
Plant in a location that will provide a half day to full day of sun exposure. The Hyacinth Bean Vine needs moist, but well-drained soil. Plant on a fence, arbor, trellis or even a mailbox.

HOW YOU PLANT:
Just scratch up your desired site with a tiller or rake. Soak seeds overnight prior to sowing, then cover them with one inch of soil. If planting a container plant, dig a hole larger than the root ball, then add peat moss. Plant and water well with liquid root stimulator.

WHEN YOU WATER:
Water well two times a week initially, but be prepared to water three times a week during extreme heat.

HOW/WHEN YOU PRUNE:
No need to prune unless the vine becomes too aggressive on smaller trellises or arbors. After the first frost, remove any seed pods you would like to save for planting next year. Then remove the entire plant, root and all and add it to your compost pile. Use your seeds to start over next year.

HOW/WHEN YOU FERTILIZE:
You may feed two times during growing season, once in Spring and again in the Summer. Utilize a granular slow-release fertilizer that is high in phosphorus. Apply near the base and scratch into soil. Water well.

ADDITIONAL ADVICE FOR PROPER CARE:

Watch for aphids in Summer. You may spray for aphids or
release aphid-eating ladybugs which can be purchased at local
garden centers or even by mail order.

Hydrangea, Climbing
Hydrangea anomala subsp. petiolaris

*This is the "best of vines," as quoted by many horticulturalists. Excellent for
massive effect on walls, arbors, and trees, Climbing Hydrangea matures in
climbing height at 50-70 feet. It has outstanding foliage, flowers, and Winter
bark which make this species a four season plant.*

WHEN TO PLANT:

Plant Spring through Fall, as soil conditions permit. This
shrub/vine requires well-drained, rich, moist soil.

WHY YOU PLANT:

Many say, "There is no better climbing vine." It has clusters of
white snowball-type blooms in the Spring that are quite attractive. As a three-year-old, the Climbing Hydrangea's limbs
become cinnamon-brown and the bark exfoliates (or sheds), like
its cousin the Oak Leaf Hydrangea, making the vine most outstanding in the Winter.

WHERE YOU PLANT:

Climbing Hydrangea is quite adaptable, you can plant in full
sun or shaded areas. Place in an eastern or northern exposure,
being sure the trellis or support is substantial enough to withhold
vining.

HOW YOU PLANT:

If you are starting from a container plant, dig a hole larger than the root ball, then add peat moss. Plant and water well with a liquid root stimulator.

WHEN YOU WATER:

Water well two times a week initially, but be prepared to water three times a week during extreme heat.

HOW/WHEN YOU PRUNE:

Pruning is required only for shaping, after the blooms have faded.

HOW/WHEN YOU FERTILIZE:

You may feed two times during the growing season, once in Spring and again in Summer. Utilize a granular slow-release fertilizer that is high in phosphorus. Apply near the base and scratch into soil. Water well.

ADDITIONAL ADVICE FOR PROPER CARE:

No serious diseases or insects noted. Following recommended water and fertilization during the developing years will pay dividends in an outstanding plant later on.

Jessamine, Carolina
Gelsemium sempervirens

Matures 10-20 feet on a trellis and 3-4 feet in a mound without support. This is a glossy evergreen vine with yellow, fragrant flowers during the Spring. The blooms are small but make a great show because of the huge clusters. The Carolina Jessamine is a great choice for a vine in full sun. Its growth habits are not overly invasive. The fragrance is very distinct and makes a nice bouquet.

WHEN TO PLANT:
You can plant Spring through Fall, as soil conditions permit.

WHY YOU PLANT:
The Carolina Jessamine has many uses, such as mailbox decoration, on trellises, along fences, and even as a ground cover. The blooms in the Spring are a real treat with the fragrance in the garden.

WHERE YOU PLANT:
Place in sun or shade areas. This shrub is very adaptable, but prefers moist, highly organic soil. Plant where you can enjoy the spring color and fragrance up close. Draping over a wall or fence is very effective year round for a great look.

HOW YOU PLANT:
Loosen the roots of plants grown in containers...thoroughly! Prepare a wide, shallow hole 3/4 as deep and 2 times as wide as the root ball. Make a mix of 1/3 soil, 1/3 coarse sand, and 1/3 peat moss, organic humus, or commercial planting mix. Pack firmly around sides of root ball. Add 1-3" of mulch on top, staying clear of the crown of the plant. Then water well with a root stimulator fertilizer. *Note: Avoid planting when soil is frozen 1" deep or when soil forms mud balls.*

WHEN YOU WATER:
For new plantings, use a hand-held, open-ended hose, watering plants directly. Do this until the plant's roots are established, generally one growing season, or when new growth is evident. Light, frequent watering is preferred over heavy watering. When in doubt, check the soil's wetness with a moisture meter before watering. A moisture meter is a "must" for gardening peace of mind.

HOW/WHEN YOU PRUNE:
Prune to maintain size and shape of the Carolina Jessamine.

Perform your pruning after the blooming has occurred or during the late Summer or early Fall.

How/When you fertilize:
Fertilize in Spring and repeat in early Fall with a slow-release granular balanced fertilizer. Scratch it in around the base of the vine, being careful with the stems. Water it well after feeding.

Additional advice for proper care:
Very few problems exist. Do not be afraid to prune any time after it blooms and you can root the cuttings for planting yourself or share them with a friend.

Moonvine
Ipomoea alba

This interesting annual vine has the ability to grow over 20 feet in one season. It's saucer-sized white blooms open each night, hence the name. In fact, you can actually set your watch to its blooming time each evening. It's a real source of entertainment. The flower buds open within a matter of minutes to display huge beautiful blossoms each evening.

When to plant:
Seeds can be sown indoors in February or March, then transplanted outdoors after the last chance of frost.

Why you plant:
Like many annual vines, Moonvine is planted for its unique fragrance and for the sheer enjoyment of watching blooms open, an activity that can be enjoyed by the entire family. This fast-growing blooming vine is ideal for its showiness when entertaining in the evening under an arbor or trellis.

Where you plant:

Plant near a structure on which Moonvine can grow, such as trellis, arbor, fence, lattice, mailbox or even the "skeleton" of a dead shrub or tree. Plant in full sun or at least a half day of sun for best results.

How you plant:

Just scratch up the soil of your desired site with a tiller or rake. Soak seeds overnight prior to sowing. Cover with one inch of soil and water well. If you are starting with a plant, go ahead and dig a hole large enough to accommodate the root ball and add peat moss. Plant and water well with liquid root stimulator.

When you water:

Water well two times a week initially, and be prepared to water three times a week during extreme heat.

How/When you prune:

No need to prune unless the vine becomes too aggressive on a smaller trellis or arbor. After the first frost, remove any seed pods you would like to save for planting next year. Remove the entire plant, root and all, and add it to the compost pile. Use the seeds you saved to start over next year.

How/When you fertilize:

You may feed two times during growing season, once in Spring and again in the Summer. Utilize granular slow-release fertilizer that is high in phosphorus. Apply near the base and scratch into soil. Water well.

Additional advice for proper care:

Remove any yellowing leaves that result from lack of water or stress. When collecting seed pods for starting next year, make sure the pods are dry and no longer "green."

Morning Glory
Ipomoea

This wonderful vine is truly reminiscent of an old-fashioned scene featuring a white picket fence covered with this vine in full bloom. The Morning Glory is very easy to grow, does not like to be nurtured and will grow approximately 10-20 feet in one season. It's an annual vine that is available in red, purple, blue, white or pink blooms.

WALT'S WISDOM

If everything fails when using garden products, try reading the label.

WHEN TO PLANT:
Start seeds saved from previous year indoors in February or early March. Transplant small starter plants outdoors after mid-April or the last chance of a killing frost.

WHY YOU PLANT:
Morning Glory vine has a wonderful cheery bloom that will greet you each morning in early to late Summer. This plant is very aggressive and will fill up a bare area rather fast, so keep this in mind when selecting a location.

WHERE YOU PLANT:
Lamp posts, mailboxes, arbors, trellises, and lattice are all perfect for Morning Glories. Plant for bright morning sun, if not full sun. You also want to select a spot where you can comfortably enjoy it in the morning.

HOW YOU PLANT:
Very easily scratch up the soil of your desired site with a tiller or rake. Soak seeds overnight prior to sowing. Cover with one inch of soil and water well. If you are starting with a plant, go ahead and dig a hole large enough to accommodate root ball and add

peat moss. Plant and water well with liquid root stimulator.

WHEN YOU WATER:
Water well two times a week initially and be prepared to water three times a week during extreme heat.

HOW/WHEN YOU PRUNE:
No pruning necessary except after the first frost, when you may want to pull the vine down and place it on the compost pile. Also at this time, you may want to collect seed from dried seed heads for planting the following season.

HOW/WHEN YOU FERTILIZE:
Unless your soil is extremely poor, you do not want to fertilize. Heavy feeding will cause lots of foliage at the expense of the desirable blooms. However, if you have deficient soil, you may want to add a little super phosphate around the area where seeds will be sowed.

ADDITIONAL ADVICE FOR PROPER CARE:
Be very aware this plant can literally take over its location in the garden. This plant reseeds itself close to its original growing spot. Just be sure you have allowed for plenty of room before Morning Glory is planted. Also, you can transplant in late Spring and relocate Morning Glory to other desirable locations.

Sweet Pea
Lathyrus odoratus

As the name implies, this is a "sweet" vine, but it has an aggressive growth habit. These vines are available in perennial and annual form and some are very fragrant. The colors range from creamy white to pink and purple shades. This vine has an old-fashioned feel. It's curly, thread-like tendrils cling onto whatever is standing still. This vine will tolerate a half day of full sun, and blooms in Summer.

WHEN TO PLANT:

The annual Sweet Pea can be planted in early Spring by sowing the seeds directly in the garden. You many even scatter the seeds in a late-Winter snowfall. If planting a perennial Sweet Pea Vine that is already growing, do so in early to mid-Spring, or in the Fall.

WHY YOU PLANT:

Sweet Peas take you back in time to childhood memories of visiting grandma's garden. Also, these plants are great for a natural bouquet to bring indoors and share. Sweet Pea is a great choice to plant to cover a bare mailbox along with another vine that may have a later blooming time. This vine is very aggressive and can help take over an otherwise boring trellis, arbor or lattice work.

WHERE YOU PLANT:

You will find Sweet Peas appropriate anywhere you need a fast-growing, untamed vine. There are varieties that have fragrant blooms, making them ideal for placement near a patio or entrance. Plant in at least a half day of sun if not full sun and in soil that is moist, but well-drained.

HOW YOU PLANT:

Very easily scratch up the soil of your desired site with a tiller or rake. Soak seeds overnight prior to sowing. Cover with one inch of soil and water well. If you are starting with a plant, go ahead and dig a hole large enough to accommodate the root ball and add peat moss. Plant and water well with liquid root stimulator.

WHEN YOU WATER:

Water well two times a week and be prepared to water three times a week during extreme heat. Once it is established, little watering is required.

HOW/WHEN YOU PRUNE:

You may pick flowers for bouquets any time you desire. Prune any yellowing or brown foliage as needed. Cut to the ground after a hard frost.

HOW/WHEN YOU FERTILIZE:

You may feed two times during the growing season, once in Spring and again in the Summer. Utilize granular slow-release fertilizer that is high in phosphorus. Apply near the base and scratch into soil. Water well.

ADDITIONAL ADVICE FOR PROPER CARE:

Sweet Pea vines are usually care free. Sometimes during our wet Tennessee Springs, we can encounter Powdery Mildew on the foliage. You may choose to go organic and dust or spray with sulphur, or you may choose a stronger approach with a fungicide spray.

Trumpet Vine
Campsis radicans

Trumpet Vine matures at 30-40 feet in vining height. This rather woody, openly growing vine features orange and scarlet trumpet-shaped flowers. The blooms are 2 1/2-3" long and 1-2" wide at the mouth of the flower. The foliage takes on an informal ivy-look and can get aggressive in growth. This is a great perennial vine for Tennessee gardens.

WHEN TO PLANT:

Can transplant year round, as soil conditions permit.

WHY YOU PLANT:

This vine can fill an area in one growing season. As one of the easiest vines to become established, the Trumpet Vine will even grow out of masonry cracks. This plant is valued for its attraction of hummingbirds.

WHERE YOU PLANT:

Place in full sun to light shade. It does well in most soil conditions, but responds quite well with good soil and care. The Trumpet Vine is often used for covering fences and trellises, and homeowners have enjoyed gracing their lampposts and even mailboxes with Trumpet Vine.

HOW YOU PLANT:

Loosen the roots of plants grown in containers...thoroughly! Prepare a wide, shallow hole 3/4 as deep and 2 times as wide as the root ball. Make a mix of 1/3 soil, 1/3 coarse sand, and 1/3 peat moss, organic humus, or commercial planting mix. Pack firmly around sides of root ball. Add 1-3" of mulch on top, staying clear of the crown of the plant. Then water well with a root stimulator fertilizer. *Note: Avoid planting when soil is frozen 1" deep or when soil forms mud balls.*

WHEN YOU WATER:

For new plantings, use a hand-held, open-ended hose, watering plants directly. Do this until the plant's roots are established, generally one growing season, or when new growth is evident. Light, frequent watering is preferred over heavy watering. When in doubt, check the soil's wetness with a moisture meter before watering. A moisture meter is a "must" for gardening peace of mind. Once established, the Trumpet Vine needs very little watering.

How/When you prune:

Prune only to control the size and shape of the plant. Can be trimmed any time of the year, but avoid Summer pruning while the blooms are visible.

How/When you fertilize:

Fertilize in Spring and repeat in early Fall with a slow-release granular balanced fertilizer. Scratch it in around the base of the vine, being careful with the stems. Water it well after feeding.

Additional advice for proper care:

Very rarely does the Trumpet Vine ever have problems. This is another reason why it's such a great vine.

Wisteria, Japanese
Wisteria floribunda

When mature, Japanese Wisteria grows to 30 feet and up in height, but it has been known to vine up trees to 40 feet. This fast-growing deciduous vine develops a large diameter trunk that shows an attractive grey color. It features abundant grape-like hanging panicles of flowers which appear prior to foliage growth in the Spring. This makes a spectacular display. Cultivars come in blooming colors of blue, purple, pink or white.

When to plant:

Can be planted year round, as soil conditions permit.

Why you plant:

We suggest planting Japanese Wisteria to cover patio trellises or to climb trees. Any support used should be substantial to hold the weight of this large vine. Most often, Japanese Wisteria is planted because of the gorgeous blooms that are truly unmistakable. Japanese Wisteria blooms only 2-3 weeks out of the year.

This can be disappointing, so we suggest a combination of assorted vines with a variety of blooming times.

WHERE YOU PLANT:

Place in full sun areas with moist, organic, well-draining soil. The Japanese Wisteria prefers a high soil pH of 6.5 to 7.5. Check your soil pH level and add lime if recommended. This vine is so aggressive you must use good judgment when considering where to plant. Whatever support you decide on must be anchored well. We have seen small fencing and arbors destroyed by older Japanese Wisteria vines.

HOW YOU PLANT:

Avoid planting seeds or plants that have been grown from seeds. We have found that grafted cultivars bloom earlier and are more dependable bloomers. Loosen the roots of plants grown in containers...thoroughly! Prepare a wide, shallow hole 3/4 as deep and 2 times as wide as the root ball. Make a mix of 1/3 soil, 1/3 coarse sand, and 1/3 peat moss, organic humus, or commercial planting mix. Pack firmly around sides of root ball. Add 1-3" of mulch on top, staying clear of the crown of the plant. Then water well with a root stimulator fertilizer. *Note: Avoid planting when soil is frozen 1" deep or when soil forms mud balls.*

WHEN YOU WATER:

For new plantings, use a hand-held, open-ended hose, watering plants directly. Do this until the plant's roots are established, generally one growing season, or when new growth is evident. Light, frequent watering is preferred over heavy watering. When in doubt, check the soil's wetness with a moisture meter before watering. A moisture meter is a "must" for gardening peace of mind.

WALT'S WISDOM

An expanded mind never returns to its original size.

How/When you prune:

With Japanese Wisteria, prune in "self-defense" at any time during the year after blooming ceases. Trimming during the dormant season is preferable.

How/When you fertilize:

Fertilize very sparingly using a low-nitrogen, natural organic fertilizer. Superphosphate or bone meal may be used instead of the low nitrogen fertilizer. This can be done at least once in the Spring and repeated in the Fall. Simply work into ground around the plants.

Additional advice for proper care:

Common diseases and insects include Crown Gall, Stem Canker, Mealy Bugs, Fall Webworms, and more. However, none of these seem to slow down this hardy vine.

Notes:

_____

_____

_____

_____

_____

_____

_____

_____

_____

_____

_____

_____

_____

_____

_____

_____

Deciduous Trees

DECIDUOUS TREES, or those which drop their leaves, are responsible for making Tennessee one of the greenest states in "The Land of the Free." The choices are almost endless with the ornamental and practical shade trees that shelter the landscapes of Tennessee.

The Volunteer State is officially represented by the Tulip Poplar. Tennessee's namesake is a rapid-growing, Summerblooming, deciduous tree, and no doubt, this is why the sweltering city of Memphis has a main street bearing the name, Poplar Avenue.

Spring announces its arrival here with the fanfare and parade of Dogwoods and Redbuds in full, resplendent bloom. Knoxville's fabulous Dogwood Trail makes a Spring pilgrimage there well worth the trip. Other varieties really show off in the Fall and have a spectacular display that brings tourists from far and wide, to marvel in the Smoky Mountains or cruise down many Nashville backroads.

CHAPTER TWELVE

In the usual dormancy and dreariness of the frostier months, there are even deciduous ornamentals, such as Hawthorns, which muster little red berries in the dead of Winter to add brilliance to the bleakest of days.

One intriguing characteristic often overlooked among some deciduous trees is exfoliating bark. This visually appealing characteristic becomes apparent just as many others trees have gone dormant for the Winter season. You may be surprised at the emphasis placed on the Winter appearance of deciduous trees—many garden centers are helping homeowners appreciate this often overlooked benefit.

Shade and ornamental trees seem to outline a house as a beautiful frame enhances a lasting work of art. The careful selection of trees will transform your house into the enduring and comforting place you will gladly call "Home."

Beech, American
Fagus grandifolia

This beautiful tree will mature to a height of 50-70 feet. This sturdy tree features a short trunk and a large, arching canopy- making it a wonderful choice for a shade tree! Although deciduous, younger Beech trees will retain their leaves in the Winter. This is the tree that brings back the image of days gone by- a simpler time when we carved our girlfriends' initials in a tree to prove that our young love would last forever!

WHEN TO PLANT:
An American Beech should be planted in the Spring.

WHY YOU PLANT:
The trunk is short and sturdy with branches that fan out to create a large, wide canopy. In the wild, you can find American Beech trees growing in areas ranging from rocky outcroppings to creek banks.

WHERE YOU PLANT:
The vastness of natural settings where American Beech can be found benefits the gardener by allowing a wide range of tolerable soil conditions. This tree has a shallow root system, and that's why you may find it hard to grow grass beneath the tree's canopy. Best placement for the gardener may be in a rear corner of the yard, and at least 30 feet from any hard surface or residence.

HOW YOU PLANT:
1) Dig a hole that is twice as wide and 30% deeper than the diameter of the root ball. Example: A 24" ball's hole should be 48" wide and 30" deep.
2) Cut the twine from the trunk, but leave the burlap on the ball when you plant. There is no need to loosen the roots.

3) Make a mix of 1/3 course sand, 1/3 soil, and 1/3 peat moss, organic humus or commercial planting mix.
4) Pack firmly around the sides of the root ball.
5) Add 2-3" of mulch on top of the ball.
6) Water well with a root stimulator fertilizer.
Note: Avoid planting when the ground is frozen or muddy.

WHEN YOU WATER:
For a new tree, slowly trickle water from a hose for a period of time equal to one minute per inch of diameter of the root ball. Repeat three times the first week, twice the next week, and weekly thereafter until the tree is firmly established - which is usually one growing season. When in doubt, check the soil's moisture with a moisture meter before watering.

HOW/WHEN YOU PRUNE:
We recommend you prune during the dormant stage, but you may prune at any time. You may want to prune low-growing branches to encourage growth.

HOW/WHEN YOU FERTILIZE:
Feed your American Beech from November through March with a well-balanced, slow-release granular fertilizer. To promote full coverage, place fertilizer in small holes located generously around the tree's trunk, or you may want to spread fertilizer on the ground under the canopy. In either case, apply at a rate equal to one pound per inch of trunk diameter.

ADDITIONAL ADVICE FOR PROPER CARE:
Common problems for the American Beech are Beechbark disease, Aphids, Beech Scale, Brownwood, Borer, Cankers, and Caterpillar. Consult your garden center or the glossary of this book for assistance in fighting these diseases and insects.

Birch, Heritage River
Betula nigra

This tree will mature at a height of 40-70 feet. It is a vigorous grower that features large, leathery, dark green leaves and salmon colored bark. This tree is a cousin to the White Birch, but unlike the White Birch, it can survive in hot climates and is somewhat resistant to the Brown Birch Borer. As I write this description, I realize that my own landscaping is not complete - simply because I have not planted one of these wonderful specimens.

WHEN TO PLANT:
Plant this tree ONLY in the Spring.

WHY YOU PLANT:
You might consider planting the Heritage River Birch for two reasons. It grows into a wonderful shade tree, and it is truly striking in the Winter when its multiple trunks are most visible.

WHERE YOU PLANT:
Plant this tree 10 feet from decks or patios. The canopy will provide shade for afternoon lounging, and will be close enough to showcase the features of the Winter bark. To guarantee the best growth, try to place these trees in areas with a pH of 6.5 -7.0.

HOW YOU PLANT:
1) Dig a hole that is twice as wide and 30% deeper than the diameter of the root ball. Example: A 24" ball's hole should be 48" wide and 30" deep.
2) Cut the twine from the trunk, but leave the burlap on the ball when you plant. There is no need to loosen the roots.
3) Make a mix of 1/3 course sand, 1/3 soil, and 1/3 peat moss, organic humus or commercial planting mix.
4) Pack firmly around the sides of the root ball.
5) Add 2-3" of mulch on top of the ball.

6) Water well with a root stimulator fertilizer.
Note: Avoid planting when the ground is frozen or muddy.

WHEN YOU WATER:

For a new tree, slowly trickle water from a hose for a period of time equal to one minute per inch of diameter of the root ball. Repeat three times the first week, twice the next week, and weekly thereafter until the tree is firmly established - which is usually one growing season. When in doubt, check the soil's moisture with a moisture meter before watering.

HOW/WHEN YOU PRUNE:

When setting out young trees, thin all cross branches and small center branches. As the tree begins to establish its mature limb structure, trim all limbs that are below 10 feet to allow the sun to enhance the coloring of the bark. You can cut the branches any time during the year, at no risk to the tree.

HOW/WHEN YOU FERTILIZE:

Feed anytime between November and March, using a well-balanced, slow-release granular fertilizer. Apply fertilizer by placing it in holes scattered around the trunk or broadcast under the tree's canopy, to insure an even coverage. Apply fertilizer at the rate of one pound per diameter inch of the tree trunk.

ADDITIONAL ADVICE FOR PROPER CARE:

With this Birch, watch out for Leaf Spot and Birch Borer. If these occur, consult your garden center for proper advice.

D E C I D U O U S T R E E S

Cherry, Japanese Flowering
Prunus serrulata

When mature, your Flowering Cherry will reach 25 feet in height. This tree, while fruitless, comes in both single-and double-blooming varieties. The

canopy is rounded to show flowers that are colored in light and dark pinks. This is really an outstanding tree! The colors are unbelievable and you will be the envy of the neighborhood.

WHEN TO PLANT:

Plant your new tree between November and March for best results, You may plant any time, however, if the tree has been dug during its dormant stage, is healed in, or conditioned for planting. (Consult your garden center to be sure).

WHY YOU PLANT:

Spring brings wonderful colors to the Japanese Cherry. Depending on its variety, your tree may display blooms of white, light pink, pink, to dark pink. Summer will bring an outstanding rich green color, and your Japanese Cherry will round out this visual cycle with Fall colors ranging from light red to yellow.

WHERE YOU PLANT:

This tree is low maintenance and is tolerant of almost any area. This makes it an attractive choice for both residential and commercial projects. Gardeners can let their creative juices flow, since the Japanese Flowering Cherry prospers individually, in rows, or in mass groupings.

HOW YOU PLANT:

1) Dig a hole that is twice as wide and 30% deeper than the diameter of the root ball.
Example: A 24" ball's hole should be 48" wide and 30" deep.
2) Cut the twine from the trunk, but leave the burlap on the ball when you plant. There is no need to loosen the roots.

3) Make a mix of 1/3 course sand, 1/3 soil, and 1/3 peat moss, organic humus or commercial planting mix.

4) Pack firmly around the sides of the root ball.

5) Add 2-3" of mulch on top of the ball.

6) Water well with a root stimulator fertilizer.

Note: Avoid planting when the ground is frozen or muddy.

WHEN YOU WATER:

For a new tree, slowly trickle water from a hose for a period of time equal to one minute per inch of diameter of the root ball. Repeat three times the first week, twice the next week, and weekly thereafter until the tree is firmly established - which is usually one growing season. When in doubt, check the soil's moisture with a moisture meter 2" below the mulch before watering.

HOW/WHEN YOU PRUNE:

Prune during the late Winter or early Spring by pruning inner branches to maintain the desired even shape. You also need to prune the water shoots (or suckers). On weeping varieties, do not cut into the graft union.

HOW/WHEN YOU FERTILIZE:

These trees may be fertilized anytime between November and March. We recommend a well-balanced, slow-release granular fertilizer. You should fertilize at a rate equal to one pound of fertilizer for every inch of diameter of the tree's trunk. Place fertilizer in random holes around the base of the tree or distribute fertilizer on the ground underneath the tree's canopy. Be sure of even distribution to promote the health of your tree.

ADDITIONAL ADVICE FOR PROPER CARE:

The Japanese Flowering Cherry has no major diseases, but borers may attack the trunks and caterpillars do make webs in the trees during the Spring. At night, the caterpillars feed on the foliage of the tree. Otherwise, sit back and enjoy the show of this beautifully colored variety.

Crabapple
Malus

Sizes of this tree vary from dwarf to 30 feet in height. The Crabapple is in the rose family- which explains why there are more than 600 varieties. And like roses, they demand intense maintenance for optimum performance. Noted for its beauty, the Crabapple blooms with flowers that vary from pink to red and in shades that vary from soft to bright. While these trees are maintenance intensive, they will reward you with beautiful flowers and needed shade.

WHEN TO PLANT:
Plant your new Crabapple tree from early Spring through the Fall, but if the tree was dug while it was dormant, was healed in, or conditioned for planting, you may plant anytime. (Consult your garden center to be sure).

WHY YOU PLANT:
Crabapple trees are a challenge, but their bloom, which varies from white to red, makes the effort worthwhile. The trees will produce berries in a variety of sizes, in colors ranging from red to yellow, making a nice complement to the brilliant blooms. If you are considering a Crabapple for your yard, consider our favorite, the 'Donald Wyman' variety.

WHERE YOU PLANT:
We recommend the Crabapple for residential areas and arboretums. This tree will add a certain fullness and maturity to the space where it is planted. Like the rose, Crabapples prefer full sun and a soil that is well drained.

HOW YOU PLANT:

1) Dig a hole that is twice as wide and 30% deeper than the diameter of the root ball. Example: A 24" ball's hole should be 48" wide and 30" deep.

2) Cut the twine from the trunk, but leave the burlap on the ball when you plant. There is no need to loosen the roots.

3) Make a mix of 1/3 course sand, 1/3 soil, and 1/3 peat moss, organic humus or commercial planting mix.

4) Pack firmly around the sides of the root ball.

5) Add 2-3" of mulch on top of the ball.

6) Water well with a root stimulator fertilizer.

Note: Avoid planting when the ground is frozen or muddy.

WHEN YOU WATER:

For a new tree, slowly trickle water from a hose for a period of time equal to one minute per inch of diameter of the root ball. Repeat three times the first week, twice the next week, and weekly thereafter until the tree is firmly established - which is usually one growing season. When in doubt, check the soil's moisture with a moisture meter before watering.

HOW/WHEN YOU PRUNE:

Like roses, pruning is a MUST if your Crabapple is to maintain its best flowering appeal. To prune a Crabapple, you need to remove any low hanging branches. Although it is possible to prune any time, late Winter and early Spring are the preferable times to keep this tree looking its best. Remember, if you prune during the Spring, you will be removing flowering buds.

HOW/WHEN YOU FERTILIZE:

These trees need to be fertilized anytime between November and March, but Spring is best, using a well-balanced, slow-release granular fertilizer. Application of fertilizer should be figured at a rate of one pound per 1" diameter of trunk size. We recommend that you fertilize in holes placed around the tree or spread on the ground under the tree's canopy, being sure to spread evenly.

ADDITIONAL ADVICE FOR PROPER CARE:
Beware of Apple Rust; it is the major threat to the Crabapple. You will recognize this by noticing a splotchy copper-colored area on the leaves. Caterpillars are also a problem with these trees. To those of you who realize anything worth having is worth working for, the Crabapple will reward a keen eye and a dedicated hand.

Dogwood
Cornus florida

Ah, the Dogwood! This is the favorite tree of Tennessee- and with good reason. The Dogwood blooms in white and to a lesser degree, pink. In general, the Dogwood is a small, low branching tree with spreading horizontal limbs, but in the wild it can grow up to 40 feet. When grown in a shady area, the trees will grow flat on top and the blooms will show a layered affect. Most gardeners feel that when the Dogwoods bloom, Spring is really here.

WHEN TO PLANT:
Unlike most deciduous trees, the Dogwood is best planted in the Spring rather than in the Fall.

WHY YOU PLANT:
The Dogwood is probably our most popular flowering tree. Dogwoods make beautiful under-canopy trees that bloom in the Spring in abundant white, and to a lesser extent, pink. Dogwoods are the sign that Spring has sprung in the South, but we also enjoy the Fall color change that slowly occurs from September through October. It could be argued that having a Dogwood in your yard

in Tennessee is just as important as a Southern Magnolia, since the Dogwood distinguishes its landscape as truly Southern.

WHERE YOU PLANT:
Plant your new Dogwood in an area with well-drained, highly organic, acidic soil. If your tree has been nursery grown, it will tolerate full sun or partial shade.

HOW YOU PLANT:
1) Dig a hole that is twice as wide and 30% deeper than the diameter of the root ball. Example: A 24" ball's hole should be 48" wide and 30" deep.
2) Cut the twine from the trunk, but leave the burlap on the ball when you plant. There is no need to loosen the roots.
3) Make a mix of 1/3 course sand, 1/3 soil, and 1/3 peat moss, organic humus or commercial planting mix.
4) Pack firmly around the sides of the root ball.
5) Add 2-3" of mulch on top of the ball.
6) Water well with a root stimulator fertilizer.
Note: Avoid planting when the ground is frozen or muddy.

WHEN YOU WATER:
For a new tree, slowly trickle water from a hose for a period of time equal to one minute per inch of diameter of the root ball. Repeat three times the first week, twice the next week, and weekly thereafter until the tree is firmly established - which is usually one growing season. When in doubt, check the soil's moisture with a moisture meter before watering.

HOW/WHEN YOU PRUNE:
The Dogwood can be pruned at anytime. You may want to prune cross branches and any inner branches to promote an appealing shape and good airflow.

HOW/WHEN YOU FERTILIZE:
You need to feed your trees with a well-balanced, slow-release

granular fertilizer. We suggest that you feed through randomly placed holes around the trunk or on the ground beneath the tree's canopy. Feed at a rate of one pound per 1" of trunk diameter.

ADDITIONAL ADVICE FOR PROPER CARE:
Spotted leaves will indicate the presence of Anthracnose, a disease that is unsightly but not life-threatening. In the higher altitudes around the Plateau and in East Tennessee, Anthracnose Discula attacks limbs and tree trunks. This disease can be fatal. The Dogwood Borer is a major threat to weak or scarred trees under particular stress. Look for holes the size of pencil points to indicate this condition. You need to go to your local garden center and seek professional help if you see these signs.

Fringe Tree, White
Chionanthus virginica

This plant can be considered either a small tree or a large shrub—take your pick. It will mature at about 20 feet and features white, slightly fragrant flowers that bloom in May or early June. The unusual flower formation has given the tree the nickname of 'Granny Grey Beard.' When viewed from across the yard or from a den window, the tree appears to be enveloped in a fuzzy white fog.

WHEN TO PLANT:
This is one of only a very few trees that needs to be planted in the late Winter or early Spring.

WHY YOU PLANT:
Lending a somewhat alternative look, this is a tree/shrub that grows only 12-20 feet, and blooms with a white-grey flower between the early bloomers and the mid-season bloomers.

WHERE YOU PLANT:

Plant this tree along borders with an evergreen background to accentuate the tree's subtle colors. These trees will tolerate most soil conditions, but since the tree is usually found along streams in the wild, we would suggest that you follow the precedent of Mother Nature and place it in an area that is more moist than dry.

HOW YOU PLANT:

1) Dig a hole that is twice as wide and 30% deeper than the diameter of the root ball. Example: A 24" ball's hole should be 48" wide and 30" deep.
2) Cut the twine from the trunk, but leave the burlap on the ball when you plant. There is no need to loosen the roots.
3) Make a mix of 1/3 course sand, 1/3 soil, and 1/3 peat moss, organic humus or commercial planting mix.
4) Pack firmly around the sides of the root ball.
5) Add 2-3" of mulch on top of the ball.
6) Water well with a root stimulator fertilizer.
Note: Avoid planting when the ground is frozen or muddy.

WHEN YOU WATER:

For a new tree, slowly trickle water from a hose for a period of time equal to one minute per inch of diameter of the root ball. Repeat three times the first week, twice the next week, and weekly thereafter until the tree is firmly established - which is usually one growing season. When in doubt, check the soil's moisture with a moisture meter before watering.

HOW/WHEN YOU PRUNE:

Pruning is rarely required for this variety.

HOW/WHEN YOU FERTILIZE:

You need to feed these trees anytime between November and March, using a well-balanced, slow-release granular fertilizer. We recommend you feed by filling holes that have been spread around the trunk or by distributing food over the ground and under the canopy.

ADDITIONAL ADVICE FOR PROPER CARE:
Occasionally, Borers, Scale, and Powdery Mildew will invade. Your garden center can provide proper advice on how to combat these problems.

Ginkgo
Ginkgo biloba

Often called the 'Maidenhair Tree', the Ginkgo will grow to 80 feet. When the tree is young, it will grow in a pyramid shape and be rather sparse, but with age it will develop picturesque spreading branches with outstanding, fan-shaped fleshy leaves that grow in clusters of from 3-5 leaves per shoot. The Ginkgo also has the most outstanding of all the Fall yellow colors.

Don't plant a

$100 tree in a

50¢ hole.

WHEN TO PLANT:
The best time to plant your new Ginkgo tree is from November through March, but a tree that has been dug while dormant, healed in, or conditioned may be planted any time. (Consult your garden center to be sure).

WHY YOU PLANT:
This species of tree is one of the oldest known to man, and remains a perennial favorite today. It is virtually pest and disease-free, and as it ages, the tree produces picturesque spreading branches and an outstanding yellow brilliance.

WHERE YOU PLANT:
Ginkgos are excellent choices for the urban forest since they

will thrive in most any soil conditions. It is important to remember that the Ginkgo's mature size is very impressive and dominant, so it should be placed only in large yards which allow it to spread to fullness. Interestingly, the female Ginkgo produces a fruit that is very messy and somewhat objectionable. Because of this unusual problem, most garden centers only offer male Ginkgo.

HOW YOU PLANT:

1) Dig a hole that is twice as wide and 30% deeper than the diameter of the root ball. Example: A 24" ball's hole should be 48" wide and 30" deep.
2) Cut the twine from the trunk, but leave the burlap on the ball when you plant. There is no need to loosen the roots.
3) Make a mix of 1/3 course sand, 1/3 soil, and 1/3 peat moss, organic humus or commercial planting mix.
4) Pack firmly around the sides of the root ball.
5) Add 2-3" of mulch on top of the ball.
6) Water well with a root stimulator fertilizer.
Note: Avoid planting when the ground is frozen or muddy.

WHEN YOU WATER:

For a new tree, slowly trickle water from a hose for a period of time equal to one minute per inch of diameter of the root ball. Repeat three times the first week, twice the next week, and weekly thereafter until the tree is firmly established - which is usually one growing season. When in doubt, check the soil's moisture with a moisture meter before watering.

HOW/WHEN YOU PRUNE:

The Ginkgo need very little pruning, but when needed, prune in the Spring for proper shape and to encourage fullness.

HOW/WHEN YOU FERTILIZE:

Anytime between November and March is a fine time to fertilize your Ginkgo. We recommend a well-balanced, slow-release granular fertilizer. When feeding, distribute the fertilizer through holes spread around the trunk or on the ground beneath the tree's canopy.

ADDITIONAL ADVICE FOR PROPER CARE:
The best feature of your new Ginkgo is that it is virtually pest and maintenance free! Sit back, kick your feet up, and enjoy!

Hawthorn
Crataegus viridus

This tree will grow to a height of 25 feet. When selecting a Hawthorn, consider one of our favorites, 'The Winter King.' This is a very attractive tree with a silvery bark that exfoliates with age into strong angular lines with a brown pattern. Additionally, the berries that Hawthorns provide us with are exceptional in size and vividly red. These berries will add some color to your Winter landscape.

WHEN TO PLANT:
For best results, plant from late Fall until early Spring, but if the tree was dug in dormancy, is healed in, or conditioned for planting, you may plant any time. (Consult your garden center to be sure).

WHY YOU PLANT:
If you love to plant trees to help the birds, this is the tree for you and your feathered friends. Berries are prevalent and are produced through most of the Winter. Spring brings an abundance of small white-pink blossoms that are a welcome sight after a long, dreary winter. Interesting bark and limb formations add to the desirability of a Hawthorn.

WHERE YOU PLANT:

Your Hawthorn needs full sun and a well-drained soil. This unusual tree is perfect for home or commercial uses because of its detailed beauty. We used this tree in a commercial setting and have received several compliments on the facelift. Try a Hawthorn - it could be the wonderful addition to your yard that gets the whole neighborhood talking!

HOW YOU PLANT:

1) Dig a hole that is twice as wide and 30% deeper than the diameter of the root ball. Example: A 24" ball's hole should be 48" wide and 30" deep.
2) Cut the twine from the trunk, but leave the burlap on the ball when you plant. There is no need to loosen the roots.
3) Make a mix of 1/3 course sand, 1/3 soil, and 1/3 peat moss, organic humus or commercial planting mix.
4) Pack firmly around the sides of the root ball.
5) Add 2-3" of mulch on top of the ball.
6) Water well with a root stimulator fertilizer.
Note: Avoid planting when the ground is frozen or muddy.

WHEN YOU WATER:

For a new tree, slowly trickle water from a hose for a period of time equal to one minute per inch of diameter of the root ball. Repeat three times the first week, twice the next week, and weekly thereafter until the tree is firmly established - which is usually one growing season. When in doubt, check the soil's moisture with a moisture meter before watering

HOW/WHEN YOU PRUNE:

Trim your Hawthorn in late Winter or after it blooms. Pruning is necessary to shape and groom the tree to your personal taste.

HOW/WHEN YOU FERTILIZE:

Fertilize any time between November and March, using a well-balanced, slow-release granular fertilizer. We suggest that you feed by filling various holes around the tree or spreading the fertilizer on the ground underneath the tree's canopy. Use an application rate of one pound per inch of trunk diameter.

ADDITIONAL ADVICE FOR PROPER CARE:
Unfortunately, Hawthorn is susceptible to a number of diseases and insects, including: Leaf Blight, Rust, Leaf Spots, Powdery Mildew, Scab, Borer, Tent Caterpillar, and Lacebug. We have found that 'Winter King' is a resistant variety and can be a help in fighting these diseases and pests. If the problems persist, call your local garden center for assistance.

Linden, Littleleaf
Tilia cordata

A beautiful tree, the Littleleaf Linden will mature to a height of 70 feet. This upright, oval tree has a shiny, dark look due to an abundance of thick, small, waxy leaves. An additional benefit to this tree is that it can be pruned to almost any shape—from formal to fun!

WHEN TO PLANT:
Plant your new tree between November and March. Trees that have been dug while dormant, healed in, or conditioned for planting may be planted at any time of the year. (Consult your garden center to be sure).

WHY YOU PLANT:
If you want a high quality specimen shade tree, plant a Littleleaf Linden. It can be planted in many different soils and pH conditions, and it has a great little name.

WHERE YOU PLANT:

It can be grown in many locations, but it is one of the few trees that can be successfully grown in a planter.

HOW YOU PLANT:

1) Dig a hole that is twice as wide and 30% deeper than the diameter of the root ball. Example: A 24" ball's hole should be 48" wide and 30" deep.
2) Cut the twine from the trunk, but leave the burlap on the ball when you plant. There is no need to loosen the roots.
3) Make a mix of 1/3 course sand, 1/3 soil, and 1/3 peat moss, organic humus or commercial planting mix.
4) Pack firmly around the sides of the root ball.
5) Add 2-3" of mulch on top of the ball.
6) Water well with a root stimulator fertilizer.
Note: Avoid planting when the ground is frozen or muddy.

WHEN YOU WATER:

For a new tree, slowly trickle water from a hose for a period of time equal to one minute per inch of diameter of the root ball. Repeat three times the first week, twice the next week, and weekly thereafter until the tree is firmly established - which is usually one growing season. When in doubt, check the soil's moisture with a moisture meter before watering

HOW/WHEN YOU PRUNE:

This is one of the few shade trees you can shear or shape to a formal hedge. This should be done prior to leafing out in the Spring. It will give your yard a rather regal look.

HOW/WHEN YOU FERTILIZE:

Feed at anytime between November and March, using a well-balanced, slow-release granular fertilizer. Feed through holes spaced around the trunk or spread over the ground under the canopy.

DECIDUOUS TREES

Aphids and Japanese Beetles may be a problem for the Littleleaf Linden. Consult you garden center for proper advice.

Magnolia, Saucer
Magnolia x soulangiana

Maturing to a height of 30 feet, the Saucer Magnolia has multiple trunks and low, spreading branches that spread as far as the tree is tall. It is also one of the earliest blooming large trees to show its Spring colors. When they bloom, the Saucer shows colors that vary from white to pink to purple. The tree is nicknamed the 'Tulip Tree' due to the shape of the flowers that have a knock-out appearance in the early Spring.

WHEN TO PLANT:
The best time to plant this tree is from late Fall until early Spring, but a tree that has been dug in dormancy, healed in, or conditioned for planting can be planted anytime. (Consult your garden center to be sure).

WHY YOU PLANT:
If you need a reminder that Spring is on the way, the Saucer Magnolia is the tree for you! Beautiful pink blooms appear in late February or early March, even before the leaves have appeared. The only downside for Tennesseans is that the bloom display is shortened because of frost one year out of every three, but we feel that risk is worth the early blooms.

WHERE YOU PLANT:
You need to look for an area that has deep, rich, moist soil to plant your Saucer Magnolia. They can be planted in the lawn individually or incorporated with other landscape materials.

HOW YOU PLANT:

1) Dig a hole that is twice as wide and 30% deeper than the diameter of the root ball. Example: A 24″ ball's hole should be 48″ wide and 30″ deep.

2) Cut the twine from the trunk, but leave the burlap on the ball when you plant. There is no need to loosen the roots.

3) Make a mix of 1/3 course sand, 1/3 soil, and 1/3 peat moss, organic humus or commercial planting mix.

4) Pack firmly around the sides of the root ball.

5) Add 2-3″ of mulch on top of the ball.

6) Water well with a root stimulator fertilizer.

Note: Avoid planting when the ground is frozen or muddy.

WHEN YOU WATER:

For a new tree, slowly trickle water from a hose for a period of time equal to one minute per inch of diameter of the root ball. Repeat three times the first week, twice the next week, and weekly thereafter until the tree is firmly established - which is usually one growing season. When in doubt, check the soil's moisture with a moisture meter before watering.

HOW/WHEN YOU PRUNE:

When pruning to shape this tree, prune after the tree has bloomed, and before the new growth appears.

HOW/WHEN YOU FERTILIZE:

To feed your new tree, select a time from November until March and use a well-balanced, slow-release granular fertilizer. Apply at the rate of one pound of fertilizer per 1″ of trunk diameter. We suggest that you feed by placing the fertilizer in holes located randomly around the base of the tree or broadcast it on the ground under the tree's canopy.

ADDITIONAL ADVICE FOR PROPER CARE:

Common diseases for this tree include Leaf Spot, Dieback, Leaf

Scale, Magnolia Scale and Tulip Tree Scale. You may notice a uniform series of holes in the tree's trunk. These are caused by sap-sucker birds. Even though these trees have these problems, Magnolias are very hardy trees and can grow to a ripe old age.

Maple, Japanese
Acer palmatum

This is one of the most universally planted trees for urban landscapes. It can be used as a single specimen or grouped with other varieties as an accent tree. At maturity, the Japanese Maple will grow up to 15 feet and its canopy can spread to 20 feet. This tree's lacy, deep-cut leaves are majestic, and the various cultivars offer characteristics that vary from mounding to erect forms. See your local garden center for more information and to see the wide range of choices.

WHEN TO PLANT:

Plant your new Japanese Maple any time from November through March. Those trees dug while dormant, healed in, or conditioned, may be planted at any time. (Consult your garden center to be sure).

WHY YOU PLANT:

If you need a specimen tree to fit a small area of your landscape, the Japanese Maple is one to consider. The tree has multi-leaf shapes and the Fall colors also kaleidoscope from green to yellow to red. This tree is universally used in landscaping because of its variety and unusual characteristics. If you are looking for a tree that grows taller, ask you garden center for a non-dissectum type Japanese Maple. For a tree that grows in a wider fashion, ask for a dissectum Japanese Maple.

WHERE YOU PLANT:

Plant in a moist, highly organic, well-drained soil. In the heat of Tennessee, you need to plant your Japanese Maple in a partially shaded area and out of as much wind as possible. At times, we may have a late frost that occurs after new growth appears. While this is not lifethreatening, it may slow the growth of the tree.

HOW YOU PLANT:

1) Dig a hole that is twice as wide and 30% deeper than the diameter of the root ball. Example: A 24″ ball's hole should be 48″ wide and 30″ deep.

2) Cut the twine from the trunk, but leave the burlap on the ball when you plant. There is no need to loosen the roots.

3) Make a mix of 1/3 course sand, 1/3 soil, and 1/3 peat moss, organic humus or commercial planting mix.

4) Pack firmly around the sides of the root ball.

5) Add 2-3″ of mulch on top of the ball.

6) Water well with a root stimulator fertilizer.

Note: Avoid planting when the ground is frozen or muddy.

WHEN YOU WATER:

For a new tree, slowly trickle water from a hose for a period of time equal to one minute per inch of diameter of the root ball. Repeat three times the first week, twice the next week, and weekly thereafter until the tree is firmly established - which is usually one growing season. When in doubt, check the soil's moisture with a moisture meter before watering.

HOW/WHEN YOU PRUNE:

You may prune at any time during the year. Japanese Maples benefit greatly from the pruning of smaller and interior branches.

HOW/WHEN YOU FERTILIZE:
Feed your Maple any time between November and March,
using a well-balanced, slow-release granular fertilizer. Try feeding by filling holes that are spread around the trunk, or you may
feed by distributing food over the ground under the canopy.

ADDITIONAL ADVICE FOR PROPER CARE:
Leaf Scorch is the main problem in Japanese Maples.

Maple, Red
Acer rubrum

*What a tree! The Red Maple will grow at a rate that is considered medium to
fast. Expect your new tree to grow 10-12 feet during the first 5 years - maturing to a height of 60 feet with a canopy stretching to 40 feet. While the blaz-
ing reds of the Fall are the best known, don't overlook the Red Maple's Spring
color that is also a red shade. Some of our favorite cultivars are 'October
Glory,' 'Red Sunset,' and 'Autumn Blaze.' If you plant one of each, you will
have foliage that colors early, middle, and late.*

WHEN TO PLANT:
Red Maples should be planted from November 15th through
the middle of March. Those trees that have been dug during
their dormant stage, healed in, or conditioned for planting may
be planted Spring through the Fall. (Consult your garden center
to be sure).

WHY YOU PLANT:
For a brilliant welcome to Fall, there is no better tree than the
Red Maple, with brilliant leaves that turn a lush, bright red. In
addition to Fall color, a Red Maple will announce the coming of
Spring with new red growth dappling its smooth grey bark.
There are few trees that complement like the Red Maple.

WHERE YOU PLANT:

Red Maples prefer a well-drained, moderately moist, fertile soil. They are tolerant to a wide range of soil pH. However, if your goal is faster growth, slightly acidic soil will be of great benefit. Avoid planting near sidewalks, driveways, or patios, because roots may spread and buckle these areas. We recommend that you place a new tree at least 20 feet away from any obstruction to insure that no problems arise.

HOW YOU PLANT:

1) Dig a hole that is twice as wide and 30% deeper than the diameter of the root ball. Example: A 24″ ball's hole should be 48″ wide and 30″ deep.
2) Cut the twine from the trunk, but leave the burlap on the ball when you plant. There is no need to loosen the roots.
3) Make a mix of 1/3 course sand, 1/3 soil, and 1/3 peat moss, organic humus or commercial planting mix.
4) Pack firmly around the sides of the root ball.
5) Add 2-3″ of mulch on top of the ball.
6) Water well with a root stimulator fertilizer.
Note: Avoid planting when the ground is frozen or muddy.

WHEN YOU WATER:

For a new tree, slowly trickle water from a hose for a period of time equal to one minute per inch of diameter of the root ball. Repeat three times the first week, twice the next week, and weekly thereafter until the tree is firmly established - which is usually one growing season. When in doubt, check the soil's moisture with a moisture meter before watering.

HOW/WHEN YOU PRUNE:

To develop a beautiful spreading canopy on your 8-10 feet young trees, "head back" all vertical growth that exceeds the tree's lateral branching, and this can be done at any time during the year. If you will do this consistently, your young tree will develop into the Red Maple you have always dreamed would grace your yard.

HOW/WHEN YOU FERTILIZE:

Fertilize Maples anytime between November and March, using a high nitrogen mix at a rate of one pound of fertilizer for every inch of trunk diameter. Place the fertilizer in random holes around the tree's dripline or broadcast the mix over the ground, under the outer two-thirds of the canopy.

ADDITIONAL ADVICE FOR PROPER CARE:

If you will be diligent in your watering habits, or if there is plentiful rainfall, the tree will be able to resist some diseases that are common to Red Maples, such as Leaf Scorch, or the dying back of leaves or whole limbs. Bark splitting may occur due to rapid growth and extremely hot sun. You may consider wrapping young trees until they start to shade themselves.

Maple, Sugar
Acer saccharum

If you are looking for a great shade tree that produces wonderful Fall foliage, the Sugar Maple is the tree for you! Maturing to a height of 60 feet, the Sugar Maple will turn a beautiful orange or yellow in the Fall. When mature, the canopy of a Sugar Maple is very upright and oval in shape. New cultivars have been developed for Tennessee gardeners. 'Green Mountain' and 'Legacy' are two of these cultivars that have been developed to combat drought and heat.

WHEN TO PLANT:

Plant your new Sugar Maple any time from November through March. Trees that have been dug while dormant, healed in, or conditioned for planting may be planted anytime. (Ask your local garden center to be sure).

WHY YOU PLANT:

These trees, which are native to the Volunteer State, are noted for their brilliant Fall colors, dense shade, and interesting bark. They announce, "It's Football Time In Tennessee" to the faithful. If you choose to adorn your yard with one of these beauties, you should try to purchase a larger specimen, since they are slow growers in their youth.

WHERE YOU PLANT:

Since these trees can grow very large, place them at least 20 feet from any drive or sidewalk. Look for an area that is slightly acidic to encourage faster growth, even though the Sugar Maple is tolerant of a wide range of pH conditions. A well-drained, moderately moist soil will be a great benefit.

HOW YOU PLANT:

1) Dig a hole that is twice as wide and 30% deeper than the diameter of the root ball. Example: A 24" ball's hole should be 48" wide and 30" deep.
2) Cut the twine from the trunk, but leave the burlap on the ball when you plant. There is no need to loosen the roots.
3) Make a mix of 1/3 course sand, 1/3 soil, and 1/3 peat moss, organic humus or commercial planting mix.
4) Pack firmly around the sides of the root ball.
5) Add 2-3" of mulch on top of the ball.
6) Water well with a root stimulator fertilizer.
Note: Avoid planting when the ground is frozen or muddy.

WHEN YOU WATER:

For a new tree, slowly trickle water from a hose for a period of time equal to one minute per inch of diameter of the root ball. Repeat three times the first week, twice the next week, and weekly thereafter until the tree is firmly established - which is usually one growing season. When in doubt, check the soil's moisture with a moisture meter before watering.

How/When you prune:

You may prune at any time to remove any low or undesirable limbs.

How/When you fertilize:

You may feed any time between November and March, using a well-balanced, slow-release granular fertilizer. We recommend that you feed by filling holes spread around the trunk or broadcasting fertilizer on the ground under the tree's canopy to insure even distribution.

Additional advice for proper care:

Droughts are the most common predator of the Sugar Maple. They may bring on Leaf Scorch and the dying back of entire limbs. Verticillium Wilt, called "Maple Decline", is caused by severe drought. The solution is an aggressive and consistent watering campaign. Use a moisture meter to make sure that the tree is getting sufficient water.

Oak, Pin

Quercus palustris

Your new Pin Oak can grow to a height of 70 feet, and when you add the fact that Pin Oaks leaves remain during the Winter, the Pin Oak is a great choice for screening. Pin Oaks are a very formal tree due to their pyramidal shape, and their fast growing patterns give rise to their desirability as a tree for the urban forest.

When to plant:

Plant Pin Oaks from November through March. Trees that have been dug while dormant, healed in, or conditioned for planting may be planted all year long. (Ask your local garden center to be sure).

WHY YOU PLANT:

When a space needs some dressing up, Pin Oaks add a formal shape to the yard that contrasts to more informal shade trees and are widely used in yards and along residential streets. An additional bonus of this variety is a fibrous root system - allowing for easy transplanting.

WHERE YOU PLANT:

Any gardener who is tired of the same old thing, and has soil which is acidic, rich, and well-drained, should consider the Pin Oak. They will tolerate heavy, wet soil (they even will survive long periods under water), but cannot survive in soils that have a pH reading of 7 or above. If your Pin Oaks have yellowing of the leaves (Chlorosis), your soil is probably above 7, and your tree's long-term success is in doubt.

HOW YOU PLANT:

1) Dig a hole that is twice as wide and 30% deeper than the diameter of the root ball. Example: A 24" ball's hole should be 48" wide and 30" deep.
2) Cut the twine from the trunk, but leave the burlap on the ball when you plant. There is no need to loosen the roots.
3) Make a mix of 1/3 course sand, 1/3 soil, and 1/3 peat moss, organic humus or commercial planting mix.
4) Pack firmly around the sides of the root ball.
5) Add 2-3" of mulch on top of the ball.
6) Water well with a root stimulator fertilizer.
Note: Avoid planting when the ground is frozen or muddy.

WHEN YOU WATER:

For a new tree, slowly trickle water from a hose for a period of time equal to one minute per inch of diameter of the root ball. Repeat three times the first week, twice the next week, and weekly thereafter until the tree is firmly established - which is usually one growing season. When in doubt, check the soil's moisture with a moisture meter before watering.

HOW/WHEN YOU PRUNE:

Deciduous trees may be pruned any time, but Pin Oaks are worry free in that they need very little pruning. You will need to prune lower branches to have access to the tree, due to the pendular growth habits of the Pin Oak.

HOW/WHEN YOU FERTILIZE:

You may fertilize your Pin Oak any time from November through March. We recommend that you use a well-balanced, slow-release granular fertilizer and apply it at a rate of one pound for each inch of diameter of the trunk. Feed by filling holes around the trunk, or spread on the soil under the tree's canopy.

ADDITIONAL ADVICE FOR PROPER CARE:

Pin Oaks are susceptible to Galls, Environmental Leaf Scorch and Fall Webworm. High pH levels in the soil may cause Iron Chlorosis. Remedy this by acidifying your soil by placing Ferric Ammonium around the tree trunk.

WALT'S WISDOM

The worst criticism against you can bring out the best in you.

Pear, Bradford
Pyrus calleryana

This tree's popularity has reached almost epidemic proportions in recent years. It blooms in the Spring with an incredible display of white flowers and colors the Fall with vivid reds. The Bradford Pear is easily transplanted and can be pruned to meet your needs. The density of the branches and foliage make it an excellent choice for screening. While we recommend the Bradford Pear, we are concerned about the long-term viability of this tree. We have noticed that it has a tendency to split with age. Consider this when selecting your new tree.

WHEN TO PLANT:
Plant in the Fall, Winter, or Spring when the leaves are absent and soil conditions allow.

WHY YOU PLANT:
If you want a tree that has great flowers, excellent screen, and beautiful Fall colors, the Bradford Pear is for you.

WHERE YOU PLANT:
Plant in full sun and in a well-drained area.

HOW YOU PLANT:
1) Dig a hole that is twice as wide and 30% deeper than the diameter of the root ball. Example: A 24″ ball's hole should be 48″ wide and 30″ deep.
2) Cut the twine from the trunk, but leave the burlap on the ball when you plant. There is no need to loosen the roots.
3) Make a mix of 1/3 course sand, 1/3 soil, and 1/3 peat moss, organic humus or commercial planting mix.
4) Pack firmly around the sides of the root ball.
5) Add 2-3″ of mulch on top of the ball.
6) Water well with a root stimulator fertilizer.
Note: Avoid planting when the ground is frozen or muddy.

WHEN YOU WATER:
For a new tree, slowly trickle water from a hose for a period of time equal to one minute per inch of diameter of the root ball. Repeat three times the first week, twice the next week, and weekly thereafter until the tree is firmly established - which is usually one growing season. When in doubt, check the soil's moisture with a moisture meter before watering.

HOW/WHEN YOU PRUNE:
The Bradford Pear may be pruned any time, but the dormant season is preferable. These trees can be shaped to meet your preferences, but be careful to prune evenly to reduce the chance of tree-splitting.

How/When you fertilize:

These trees may be fertilized any time between November and March, using a well-balanced, slow-release granular fertilizer. Apply your fertilizer at a rate of one pound per inch of the trunk's diameter. Try placing food in holes spaced around the trunk, or distribute on the ground under the tree's canopy.

Additional Advice for proper Care:

Fire Blight may attack new growth during the Spring. If the leaves turn black, this may be terminal.

Poplar, Tulip
Liriodendron tulipifera

The Tennessee state tree, the Tulip Poplar is one of our state's great trees. It can grow to a massive size - some measure as large as 100 feet tall with a canopy that stretches to 75 feet. The tree's green foliage turns a brilliant yellow in the Fall, and like the tree's flowers, the leaves are tulip-shaped. If you want a great shade tree, the Tulip Poplar is for you!

When to plant:

Plant your new Tulip Poplar during the late Winter to early Spring for best results.

Why you plant:

If you have a new yard and want a tree that is fast growing, the Tulip Poplar is a great choice. A mature tree will grow tall, erect, and have a large crown that will provide years of shade for the Tennessee gardener.

Where you plant:

This magnificent tree that may grow to as much as 100 feet

should be planted at least 20 feet or more from your home. We suggest that for optimum growth and success, you place your new tree on the southwest side of your house in a soil with light to medium texture.

HOW YOU PLANT:

1) Dig a hole that is twice as wide and 30% deeper than the diameter of the root ball. Example: A 24" ball's hole should be 48" wide and 30" deep.

2) Cut the twine from the trunk, but leave the burlap on the ball when you plant. There is no need to loosen the roots.

3) Make a mix of 1/3 course sand, 1/3 soil, and 1/3 peat moss, organic humus or commercial planting mix.

4) Pack firmly around the sides of the root ball.

5) Add 2-3" of mulch on top of the ball.

6) Water well with a root stimulator fertilizer.

Note: Avoid planting when the ground is frozen or muddy.

WHEN YOU WATER:

For a new tree, slowly trickle water from a hose for a period of time equal to one minute per inch of diameter of the root ball. Repeat three times the first week, twice the next week, and weekly thereafter until the tree is firmly established - which is usually one growing season. When in doubt, check the soil's moisture with a moisture meter before watering.

HOW/WHEN YOU PRUNE:

Tulip Poplars need very little pruning. As the tree grows, the limbs lower than 6-8 feet may be removed during the Winter. We recommend that you make your first cut upward at a distance of 2-3" from the trunk. After cutting approximately one-third of the limb, finish the cut from above.

HOW/WHEN YOU FERTILIZE:

Feed your Poplars any time from November through March, using a well-balanced, slow-release granular fertilizer. Use a rate of one pound of fertilizer for every inch of trunk diameter. Feed by placing your fertilizer in holes spread around the tree or on the ground under the tree's canopy.

ADDITIONAL ADVICE FOR PROPER CARE:
Poplars may encounter a few problems with diseases and insects. They include: Powdery Mildew, Sooty Mold Fungus, Aphids, and Scale. Consult your garden center if any problems are noticed.

Redbud

Cercis canadensis

There is no more sure sign of Spring than to drive through the countryside of Tennessee and see the blooming Redbuds. Their lavender colored blooms are easily spotted and give the impression that the limbs are on fire. The Redbud has a small vase-shaped form that produces a fairly large crown. The leaves will change slowly in the Fall revealing a brilliant yellow color. Ask your local garden center about a new cultivar, 'Forest Pansy,' that displays maroon foliage throughout the growing season.

WHEN TO PLANT:
For best results and the healthiest trees, Redbuds should be planted between November 15th and March 15th. Redbuds while dormant, healed in, or conditioned for planting, may be planted Spring through Fall. (Consult your local garden center to be sure).

WHY YOU PLANT:
This tree grows wild in the rolling Tennessee countryside, producing lavender flowers which fill the color gap that occurs between the blooming of Forsythia and the Dogwood.

WHERE YOU PLANT:

The Redbud is very tolerant of most conditions, except soil saturated by rainwater. Ideal placement should be in well-drained soil where the tree will be visually appealing. A back-drop of evergreens will effectively accentuate the vivid Redbud colors.

HOW YOU PLANT:

1) Dig a hole that is twice as wide and 30% deeper than the diameter of the root ball. Example: A 24" ball's hole should be 48" wide and 30" deep.

2) Cut the twine from the trunk, but leave the burlap on the ball when you plant. There is no need to loosen the roots.

3) Make a mix of 1/3 course sand, 1/3 soil, and 1/3 peat moss, organic humus or commercial planting mix.

4) Pack firmly around the sides of the root ball.

5) Add 2-3" of mulch on top of the ball.

6) Water well with a root stimulator fertilizer.

Note: Avoid planting when the ground is frozen or muddy.

WHEN YOU WATER:

For a new tree, slowly trickle water from a hose for a period of time equal to one minute per inch of diameter of the root ball. Repeat three times the first week, twice the next week, and weekly thereafter until the tree is firmly established - which is usually one growing season. When in doubt, check the soil's moisture with a moisture meter before watering

HOW/WHEN YOU PRUNE:

You may prune a Redbud at any time of year. Trim out the inner branches to allow light in and to allow air to move throughout.

HOW/WHEN YOU FERTILIZE:

Redbuds should be fertilized anytime between November and March. When fertilizing, use a well-balanced, slow-release granular fertilizer. The amount of fertilizer to be applied can be determined by using the formula of one pound per one inch of trunk diameter.

ADDITIONAL ADVICE FOR PROPER CARE:
Redbuds can be plagued by Verticullium Wilt, but you can prevent this disease by following our pruning tips carefully. Additionally, Tree Hoppers, Scale and Caterpillars may be a problem. If you notice these, or any other problems, consult your garden center for proper advice.

Serviceberry
Amelanchier arborea

If you are looking for an interesting conversation piece you may want to try a Serviceberry. It has a very interesting multi-stem form and cascading 2-4" white flowers that tend to catch the eye. Growing to a height of 25 feet, this is one of the finest small trees for Fall foliage and ranges in color from yellow to orange to a rusty-red.

WHEN TO PLANT:
Plant your new tree between November and March, but if it was dug while dormant, healed in, or conditioned for planting, it may be planted at any time. (Consult your garden center to be sure).

WHY YOU PLANT:
If you want a tree that's for the birds, the Serviceberry may fill the order. The fruit is edible - if you get to it before the birds. In addition, this tree's bark is captivating because of its color, with red streaks on a grey background.

WHERE YOU PLANT:
Place the Serviceberry in a planned, landscaped area. This tree's

relatively small size will nicely complement many of your other plantings, shrubs and trees. Serviceberry will grow vigorously in a moist soil with a pH of 6 - 7.

How you plant:
1) Dig a hole that is twice as wide and 30% deeper than the diameter of the root ball. Example: A 24″ ball's hole should be 48″ wide and 30″ deep.
2) Cut the twine from the trunk, but leave the burlap on the ball when you plant. There is no need to loosen the roots.
3) Make a mix of 1/3 course sand, 1/3 soil, and 1/3 peat moss, organic humus or commercial planting mix.
4) Pack firmly around the sides of the root ball.
5) Add 2-3″ of mulch on top of the ball.
6) Water well with a root stimulator fertilizer.
Note: Avoid planting when the ground is frozen or muddy.

When you water:
For a new tree, slowly trickle water from a hose for a period of time equal to one minute per inch of diameter of the root ball. Repeat three times the first week, twice the next week, and weekly thereafter until the tree is firmly established—which is usually one growing season. When in doubt, check the soil's moisture with a moisture meter before watering.

How/When you prune:
This tree needs little pruning, but the tree's multi-stem quality demands that you trim the under limbs.

How/When you fertilize:
These trees may be fertilized anytime between November and March, using a well-balanced, slow-release granular fertilizer. Apply your fertilizer at a rate of one pound per inch of the trunk's diameter. Try placing food in holes spaced around the trunk, or distribute on the ground under the canopy.

ADDITIONAL ADVICE FOR PROPER CARE:

This tree can be affected by Rust, Powdery Mildew, Fire Blight, Leafminers, and Bark Borers. If any of these become a problem, consult your garden center. If you plant disease-resistant cultivars such as 'Autumn Brilliance', 'Cole', or 'Ballerina', you will have fewer problems.

Silverbell, Carolina
Halesia carolina

This tree is very attractive. Its shape is squatty, broad and slightly round-looking, strikingly similar to our publisher. The main difference in appearance being that the Silverbell freely produces small, white, bell-shaped flowers in the Spring. The Silverbell is a great choice for a shady area since it demands relatively little direct sunlight.

The way we

respond to

temptation

will make or

break us.

WHEN TO PLANT:
Plant your new tree between November and March, but if your tree was dug while dormant, healed-in, or conditioned, it may be planted at any time. (consult your local garden center for proper advice).

WHY YOU PLANT:
A Tennessee native, the Silverbell offers low maintenance and an abundance of beautiful, bell-shaped white flowers in the Spring. At a mature height of 50 feet, the Silverbell will grow to be a towering and impressive addition to your yard.

WHERE YOU PLANT:
You may plant in either full sun or shade. The Silverbell needs

to be planted in a soil that has a pH of 6.5 or lower.

HOW YOU PLANT:

1) Dig a hole that is twice as wide and 30% deeper than the diameter of the root ball. Example: A 24″ ball's hole should be 48″ wide and 30″ deep.

2) Cut the twine from the trunk, but leave the burlap on the ball when you plant. There is no need to loosen the roots.

3) Make a mix of 1/3 course sand, 1/3 soil, and 1/3 peat moss, organic humus or commercial planting mix.

4) Pack firmly around the sides of the root ball.

5) Add 2-3″ of mulch on top of the ball.

6) Water well with a root stimulator fertilizer.

Note: Avoid planting when the ground is frozen or muddy.

WHEN YOU WATER:

For a new tree, slowly trickle water from a hose for a period of time equal to one minute per inch of diameter of the root ball. Repeat three times the first week, twice the next week, and weekly thereafter until the tree is firmly established - which is usually one growing season. When in doubt, check the soil's moisture with a moisture meter before watering.

HOW/WHEN YOU PRUNE:

The only reason you need to prune the Silverbell is for cosmetic reasons and to appeal to your own specific tastes.

HOW/WHEN YOU FERTILIZE:

These trees may be fertilized anytime between November and March, using a well-balanced, slow-release granular fertilizer. Apply your fertilizer at a rate of one pound per inch of the trunk's diameter. Try placing food in holes spaced around the trunk, or distribute it on the ground under the canopy.

ADDITIONAL ADVICE FOR PROPER CARE:

This tree is particularly insect and disease-free. However, if you notice a yellowing of the leaves, check the pH of the soil. It probably means that the pH has dropped below 6.5, and a healthy dose of lime should be applied.

Sourwood

Oxydendrum arboreum

The Sourwood begins the Spring with foliage that is an iridescent green that slowly turns to a lustrous dark green with maturity. The flowers are urn-shaped and literally cover the entire tree with wonderful blossoms. Wow! This tree rivals any tree in our area, but it is not readily available. If you can find a Sourwood - buy it, take it home, and plant it!

WHEN TO PLANT:
Your Sourwood needs to be planted in the late Winter or early Spring for best results.

WHY YOU PLANT:
Described as "The Lily of the Valley," this tree has not been given the attention it deserves, primarily because it grows relatively slowly and is, therefore, difficult to find. Sourwoods dazzle a landscape all year round, as Spring brings urn-shaped white flowers - Summer brings dark green leaves - and the Fall brings the tree to a beautiful, purple hue. Truly an all-season ornamental!

WHERE YOU PLANT:
Sourwoods prefer a dark, rich, moist soil with a pH of 5.5-6.5. If you can find a partial sun location, it is preferred, but they will grow in full sun. We suggest you try to locate Sourwoods in front of larger, more mature trees for the most striking results.

HOW YOU PLANT:

1) Dig a hole that is twice as wide and 30% deeper than the diameter of the root ball. Example: A 24" ball's hole should be 48" wide and 30" deep.

2) Cut the twine from the trunk, but leave the burlap on the ball when you plant. There is no need to loosen the roots.

3) Make a mix of 1/3 course sand, 1/3 soil, and 1/3 peat moss, organic humus or commercial planting mix.

4) Pack firmly around the sides of the root ball.

5) Add 2-3" of mulch on top of the ball.

6) Water well with a root stimulator fertilizer.

Note: Avoid planting when the ground is frozen or muddy.

WHEN YOU WATER:

For a new tree, slowly trickle water from a hose for a period of time equal to one minute per inch of diameter of the root ball. Repeat three times the first week, twice the next week, and weekly thereafter until the tree is firmly established - which is usually one growing season. When in doubt, check the soil's moisture with a moisture meter watering

HOW/WHEN YOU PRUNE:

Minimal pruning is needed, and if required, it should be done after the tree has bloomed.

HOW/WHEN YOU FERTILIZE:

You may feed at any time from November through March with a well-balanced, slow-release granular fertilizer. We suggest you feed by filling holes spread around the trunk or by spreading feed on the ground under the tree's canopy.

ADDITIONAL ADVICE FOR PROPER CARE:

This tree is very easy to maintain, and it is truly an underrated beauty, but you may run across some Leaf Spot or Twig Blight.

Sweet Gum

Liquidambar styraciflua

The Sweet Gum has some of the largest leaves of any Tennessee deciduous tree-reaching a width of 8". These five-pointed leaves are at times referred to as "Star leaves." The Sweet Gum has an excellent rich Autumn color and grows very well if planted in a moist location.

WHEN TO PLANT:
Plant your new tree in the late Winter or early Spring.

WHY YOU PLANT:
If you have an area that is constantly moist, the Sweet Gum is the tree to plant, since it thrives in moist soil. The Fall foliage of the Sweet Gum is the stuff that memories are made of, and the "Sweet Gum Fall" lasts longer than most trees, stretching all the way from September to November.

WHERE YOU PLANT:
The Sweet Gum can tolerate a wide variety of soil conditions, but due to the large size of the tree at maturity, plant at least 20 feet from drives and patios.

HOW YOU PLANT:
1) Dig a hole that is twice as wide and 30% deeper than the diameter of the root ball. Example: A 24" ball's hole should be 48" wide and 30" deep.
2) Cut the twine from the trunk, but leave the burlap on the ball when you plant. There is no need to loosen the roots.
3) Make a mix of 1/3 course sand, 1/3 soil, and 1/3 peat moss, organic humus or commercial planting mix.
4) Pack firmly around the sides of the root ball.
5) Add 2-3" of mulch on top of the ball.
6) Water well with a root stimulator fertilizer.

Note: Avoid planting when the ground is frozen or muddy.

WHEN YOU WATER:

For a new tree, slowly trickle water from a hose for a period of time equal to one minute per inch of diameter of the root ball. Repeat three times the first week, twice the next week, and weekly thereafter until the tree is firmly established - which is usually one growing season. When in doubt, check the soil's moisture with a moisture meter before watering.

HOW/WHEN YOU PRUNE:

A Sweet Gum has strong branching habits, therefore, little pruning is needed to maintain a full, healthy appearance.

HOW/WHEN YOU FERTILIZE:

Feed sometime between November and March, using a well-balanced, slow-release granular fertilizer. Try placing food in holes spaced around the trunk or distribute on the ground under the tree's canopy.

ADDITIONAL ADVICE FOR PROPER CARE:

You may notice Galling, Sweet Gum Webworm, Caterpillar, Cushion Scale, or Walnut Scale. You can fight any of these by consulting with your garden center. If you notice leaf-yellowing, it may be caused by Iron Chlorosis. This is caused by a soil pH of 7 or above, which is too high for Sweet Gum.

Yellowwood, American
Cladrastis kentukea

This tree has been difficult for nurseries to grow, therefore it is scarce at local garden centers. But the Yellowwood was recognized as the state's Bicentennial Tree for 1996. This may make the tree more available. At maturity, the tree

will grow to a height of 30 feet with a white flower that is 1" in size. Interestingly, the Yellowwood blooms more profusely in alternate years. During those years, the tree seems to be completely covered in dripping blooms.

WHEN TO PLANT:

The best time to plant Yellowwood is in the late Winter or early Spring.

WHY YOU PLANT:

The fact that this is a relatively small tree that has a large canopy makes it an excellent choice for smaller yards. The Yellowwood's blooms, which can be 14" long and 6" wide, are absolutely stunning and a great conversation piece. When you smell the lovely fragrance wafting from the blooms, the Yellowwood will win you over.

WHERE YOU PLANT:

The American Yellowwood loves full sun and a well-drained soil. It will also tolerate high pH soils.

HOW YOU PLANT:

1) Dig a hole that is twice as wide and 30% deeper than the diameter of the root ball. Example: A 24" ball's hole should be 48" wide and 30" deep.
2) Cut the twine from the trunk, but leave the burlap on the ball when you plant. There is no need to loosen the roots.
3) Make a mix of 1/3 course sand, 1/3 soil, and 1/3 peat moss, organic humus or commercial planting mix.
4) Pack firmly around the sides of the root ball.
5) Add 2-3" of mulch on top of the ball.
6) Water well with a root stimulator fertilizer.
Note: Avoid planting when the ground is frozen or muddy.

WHEN YOU WATER:
For a new tree, slowly trickle water from a hose for a period of
time equal to one minute per inch of diameter of the root ball.
Repeat three times the first week, twice the next week, and
weekly thereafter until the tree is firmly established - which is
usually one growing season. When in doubt, check the soil's
moisture with a moisture meter before watering.

HOW/WHEN YOU PRUNE:
Prune the Yellowwood ONLY in the Summer. It will bleed profusely if pruned at any other time of year, and may result in the
tree's death.

HOW/WHEN YOU FERTILIZE:
Feed any time between November and March, using a well-
balanced, slow-release granular fertilizer. Feed by filling holes
placed around the trunk or on the ground under the tree's canopy.

ADDITIONAL ADVICE FOR PROPER CARE:
This tree has very few insect and disease problems, making it
fairly trouble free.

Zelkova, Japanese
Zelkova serrata

*The Zelkova matures at a height of 80 feet with a huge, spreading canopy
that resembles the long-gone American Elm. The spreading branches make this
an excellent choice as a shade tree. Bring back some memories of the American
Elm, plant a Zelkova.*

WHEN TO PLANT:
Plant your new tree between November and March, unless your
tree was dug while dormant, healed in, or conditioned for planting, then it may be planted any time. (Check your garden center to be sure).

WHY YOU PLANT:

This tree, which has been compared to the American Elm, features a huge canopy that can shade a 50 feet x 50 feet area. In drought, the Zelkova will stay healthier than most other Tennessee trees.

WHERE YOU PLANT:

Plant your new tree wherever you need shade - perhaps near streets, so that the canopy can shade the sidewalk.

HOW YOU PLANT:

1) Dig a hole that is twice as wide and 30% deeper than the diameter of the root ball. Example: A 24" ball's hole should be 48" wide and 30" deep.
2) Cut the twine from the trunk, but leave the burlap on the ball when you plant. There is no need to loosen the roots.
3) Make a mix of 1/3 course sand, 1/3 soil, and 1/3 peat moss, organic humus or commercial planting mix.
4) Pack firmly around the sides of the root ball.
5) Add 2-3" of mulch on top of the ball.
6) Water well with a root stimulator fertilizer.
Note: Avoid planting when the ground is frozen or muddy.

WHEN YOU WATER:

For a new tree, slowly trickle water from a hose for a period of time equal to one minute per inch of diameter of the root ball. Repeat three times the first week, twice the next week, and weekly thereafter until the tree is firmly established - which is usually one growing season. When in doubt, check the soil's moisture with a moisture meter before watering

HOW/WHEN YOU PRUNE:

This tree prefers to be pruned in the Fall. As the tree grows, prune away all limbs that are lower than 6-8 feet. This will encourage more growth and allow better access for grass cutting and for Summer recreation.

How/When you fertilize:

These trees may be fertilized any time between November and March, using a well-balanced, slow-release granular fertilizer. Apply your fertilizer at a rate of one pound per inch of the trunk's diameter. Try placing food in holes spaced around the trunk, or distribute on the ground under the tree's canopy.

Additional advice for proper care:

Only the Elm Leaf Beetle and the Japanese Beetle pose a threat to the Japanese Zelkova. Otherwise, it is relatively pest and disease free. If you do encounter problems, contact your local garden center for proper advice.

Notes:

D
E
C
I
D
U
O
U
S

T
R
E
E
S

Evergreens

*F*ROM THE SMOKY MOUNTAINS to Memphis, Tennessee's landscape is filled with a wide variety of gorgeous evergreens. Because of the abundance of native trees in Tennessee, gardeners have a wide variety of evergreens from which to choose. We hope you will find a variety from our evergreen selections to enhance your home landscape.

One of our most common evergreen trees is the Eastern Red Cedar. The tree is a rugged specimen that evokes an image of the pioneers who crossed the mountains to settle in our state. While the Cedar may be the most common evergreen in Tennessee, it is probably not the gardener's first choice when planting a tree. Check with your local garden center to get a first hand look at the Eastern Red Cedar and all the available choices.

We think it is both interesting and important to know how and why plants and trees fit into our environment and how these plants have impacted the lives of animals, birds, and

CHAPTER THIRTEEN

humans. Due to the protection provided by branches that keep their needles and leaves, evergreens are responsible for helping animals and birds survive even our coldest Winters. Additionally, the wood of many evergreens, especially the Red Cedar, is used in the manufacture of furniture. Many of us grew up in a time when a cedar chest was an important part of our home's decor. I can smell the inside of that chest now!

While many of the choices for a garden or landscape reflect our desire to create a "pretty picture", the evergreen reflects our past and reminds us that all varieties of flowers, shrubs, and trees have their important place in the landscape.

Evergreens play a major role in your own Tennessee Winter landscape. We believe that at least some of your overall landscaping plan should include evergreen specimens. Not only will they provide an excellent backdrop for your flowering plants and shrubs, but they will also help in reminding us "from whence we came."

Cedar, Eastern Red
Juniperus virginiana

Eastern Red Cedars mature at 40-50 feet in height and 10-20 feet in width. This plant varies from the native Red Cedars found growing wild along East Tennessee roads and in undeveloped fields, to the narrow, upright silver-blue cultivars. When grown from seed, the Eastern Red Cedar varies greatly in size and shape. Rarely will you see two of these plants that are alike.

WHEN TO PLANT:
Because of its resilience as an evergreen, the Eastern Red Cedar can be transplanted year round, as soil conditions permit.

WHY YOU PLANT:
Cedars may be used effectively as wind breaks, in mass group-ings, as topiary forms, and even as specimen plants. They also benefit nature and wildlife in that Eastern Red Cedars consis-tently attract birds because of the dense foliage that provides shelter from the elements.

WHERE YOU PLANT:
This variety prefers a sunny location in well-drained soil. In its natural habitat, this particular Cedar is a prolific re-seeder, hence the many Cedar forests common in the Tennessee coun-tryside.

HOW YOU PLANT:
1) Dig a hole that is twice as wide and 30% deeper than the diameter of the root ball. Example: A 24" ball's hole should be 48" wide and 30" deep.
2) Cut the twine from the trunk, but leave the burlap on the ball when you plant. There is no need to loosen the roots.
3) Make a mix of 1/3 coarse sand, 1/3 soil, and 1/3 peat moss, organic humus or commercial planting mix.

4) Pack firmly around the sides of the root ball.

5) Add 2-3" of mulch on top of the ball.

6) Water well with a root stimulator fertilizer.

*Note: Avoid planting when the ground is frozen or muddy. A key to success-
ful transplanting is moisture management. Do not allow container or ball to
dry out, either before or after planting.*

WHEN YOU WATER:

For a new tree, slowly trickle water from a hose for a period of
time equal to one minute per inch of diameter of the root ball.
Repeat three times the first week, twice the next week, and
weekly thereafter until the tree is firmly established—which is
usually one growing season. When in doubt, check the soil's
moisture with a moisture meter before watering.

HOW/WHEN YOU PRUNE:

Shearing with hedge trimmers is the best method to maintain
optimum size and shape of these trees. Spring is preferable for
pruning, but Eastern Red Cedars may be trimmed any time.

HOW/WHEN YOU FERTILIZE:

Fertilize in the Spring by applying a well-balanced, slow-release
granular fertilizer in holes placed around the trunk or under the
canopy, at a rate of one pound per 1" of trunk diameter. You
may also broadcast fertilizer on the ground under the canopy.

ADDITIONAL ADVICE FOR PROPER CARE:

Common diseases and insects include Cedar Apple Rust and
Bagworms. Look for Bagworms from late March through June.
Remove and destroy these, and consult your garden center for
advice on proper control. Cedar Apple Rust occurs in late Winter
or early Spring and is detected by gelatin-looking orange growth
on tree branches.

Cypress, Leyland

Cupressocyparis leylandii

This magnificent, noble, needled evergreen has taken the South by storm. It displays fine, feathery foliage that grows in a graceful pyramidal form. The Leyland Cypress is a tremendously fast growing tree. A 2 foot specimen can grow up to 7 feet in only two years and accepts a wide range of soil conditions, making it a favorite for the impatient gardener. It has been observed that container grown Leyland Cypress are more successful than the balled and burlaped specimens. NOTE: When considering a site for planting, take into account that this tree can reach 60-70 feet in normal conditions, and up to 100 feet in height under optimum growing conditions.

WHEN TO PLANT:

You may plant nursery grown container stock at anytime. If you desire a larger specimen, balled and burlaped stock is needed. Like container plants, balled and burlaped Leyland Cypress can be planted any time the soil is workable.

WHY YOU PLANT:

If you are looking for a fast growing evergreen, the Leyland Cypress may be the tree for you. This tree provides an excellent screen and a nice backdrop to landscape plantings. Try placing a grouping in the corner of your lawn for excellent backdrop results.

WHERE YOU PLANT:

Leyland Cypress is a particularly effective solution where a fast-growing evergreen visual screen is required. It is often used to identify borders and works quite well in groupings. You may notice Leyland Cypress is used in commercial applications where "instant trees" are needed. We have observed these trees around shopping malls and commercial buildings.

How you plant:

1) Dig a hole that is twice as wide and 30% deeper than the diameter of the root ball. Example: A 24" ball's hole should be 48" wide and 30" deep.

2) Cut the twine from the trunk, but leave the burlap on the ball when you plant. There is no need to loosen the roots.

3) Make a mix of 1/3 coarse sand, 1/3 soil, and 1/3 peat moss, organic humus or commercial planting mix.

4) Pack firmly around the sides of the root ball.

5) Add 2-3" of mulch on top of the ball.

6) Water well with a root stimulator fertilizer.

Note: Avoid planting when the ground is frozen or muddy. A key to successful transplanting is moisture management. Do not allow container or ball to dry out, either before or after planting.

When you water:

For a new tree, slowly trickle water from a hose for a period of time equal to one minute per inch of diameter of the root ball. Repeat three times the first week, twice the next week, and weekly thereafter until the tree is firmly established—which is usually one growing season. When in doubt, check the soil's moisture with a moisture meter before watering.

How/When you prune:

Although there are no horticultural reasons to prune your Leyland Cypress, it can be sheared to shape any time.

How/When you fertilize:

Fertilize in the Spring by applying a well-balanced, slow-release granular fertilizer in holes around the trunk or under the canopy, at a rate of one pound per 1" of trunk diameter. You may also broadcast fertilizer on the ground under the canopy.

ADDITIONAL ADVICE FOR PROPER CARE:

No serious problems exist with Leyland Cypress, although Bagworms may occur. If so, remove and destroy them at your earliest convenience. To inhibit future Bagworm attack, use an insecticide recommended by your garden center. Timing of insecticide application is important for proper control of Bagworms, so follow the advice of your garden center.

Hemlock
Tsuga canadensis

The Hemlock is considered the most graceful of all evergreen conifers. It has a pyramidal growth habit with slender horizontal drooping branches. Soft-textured, flattened needles make this a popular choice for the landscape. The Hemlock can be maintained as a 3-5 foot hedge or it can reach heights of 50-70 feet. In Tennessee, the Hemlock can most often be found growing native in the Eastern region. By comparison, it is almost non-existent in West Tennessee.

WHEN TO PLANT:

Hemlocks have a very fibrous root system that allows them to be transplanted in the Spring and in the Fall.

WHY YOU PLANT:

Hemlocks have two identities. They are quite effective when used as an evergreen screen or hedge where they can be sheared into a formal shape. On the other hand, they can become impressive single specimens that can dominate an area of the lawn.

WHERE YOU PLANT:

Hemlocks can be planted in full sun to full shade. When planting in West Tennessee, some shade is preferred. Hemlocks like soil conditions similar to Rhododendrons and Azaleas. They prefer moist, highly organic, yet extremely well-drained soil. Hemlocks also prefer a pH level from 5.0 - 6.0 and they hate WET FEET!

HOW YOU PLANT:

1) Dig a hole that is twice as wide and 30% deeper than the diameter of the root ball. Example: A 24″ ball's hole should be 48″ wide and 30″ deep.

2) Cut the twine from the trunk, but leave the burlap on the ball when you plant. There is no need to loosen the roots.

3) Make a mix of 1/3 coarse sand, 1/3 soil, and 1/3 peat moss, organic humus or commercial planting mix.

4) Pack firmly around the sides of the root ball.

5) Add 2-3″ of mulch on top of the ball.

6) Water well with a root stimulator fertilizer.

Note: Avoid planting when the ground is frozen or muddy. A key to successful transplanting is moisture management. Do not allow container or ball to dry out, either before or after planting.

WHEN YOU WATER:

For a new tree, slowly trickle water from a hose for a period of time equal to one minute per inch of diameter of the root ball. Repeat three times the first week, twice the next week, and weekly thereafter until the tree is firmly established—which is usually one growing season. When in doubt, check the soil's moisture with a moisture meter before watering.

HOW/WHEN YOU PRUNE:

Canadian Hemlock can be pruned or sheared into the chosen shape during the Spring or the Fall. The Carolina Hemlock is stiffer and less pendulous in growth. It should be pruned by cutting back individual branches to maintain size.

HOW/WHEN YOU FERTILIZE:

Fertilize in the Spring by applying a well-balanced, slow-release granular fertilizer in holes around the trunk or under the canopy, at a rate of one pound per 1" of trunk diameter. You may also broadcast fertilizer on the ground under the canopy.

ADDITIONAL ADVICE FOR PROPER CARE:
Common diseases and insects include Leaf Blight, Blister Rust, Canker, Sapwood Rot, Hemlock Borers, Spider Mites, Bagworms, Hemlock Sourflies, and problems brought on by drought or prolonged dry conditions. In spite of these potential problems, Hemlocks are reliable when given the proper location and horticultural care.

Juniper, Chinese
Juniperus chinensis

Chinese Juniper matures at a height of 50-60 feet and 10-20 feet in width. It is an evergreen conifer that grows in an upright to low-spreading form. Its foliage ranges from blue to green to grey. Chinese Junipers are often planted too close to houses, not allowing for the natural spread of branches. This Juniper should never be sheared. Prune by the reach and cut method where individual branches are removed.

WHEN TO PLANT:
Chinese Juniper may be planted year round, as the soil conditions permit.

WHY YOU PLANT:
The Chinese Juniper is easy to transplant and requires little maintenance. It is very tolerant of a wide range of soil conditions, and can survive in very hot, dry climates.

WHERE YOU PLANT:

Chinese Juniper is quite adaptable and will work well in a variety of situations. It may be used on slopes, as a hedge, a foundation planting, and as a single specimen.

HOW YOU PLANT:

1) Dig a hole that is twice as wide and 30% deeper than the diameter of the root ball. Example: A 24″ ball's hole should be 48″ wide and 30″ deep.
2) Cut the twine from the trunk, but leave the burlap on the ball when you plant. There is no need to loosen the roots.
3) Make a mix of 1/3 coarse sand, 1/3 soil, and 1/3 peat moss, organic humus or commercial planting mix.
4) Pack firmly around the sides of the root ball.
5) Add 2-3″ of mulch on top of the ball.
6) Water well with a root stimulator fertilizer.
Note: Avoid planting when the ground is frozen or muddy. A key to successful transplanting is moisture management. Do not allow container or ball to dry out, either before or after planting.

WHEN YOU WATER:

For a new tree, slowly trickle water from a hose for a period of time equal to one minute per inch of diameter of the root ball. Repeat three times the first week, twice the next week, and weekly thereafter until the tree is firmly established—which is usually one growing season. When in doubt, check the soil's moisture with a moisture meter before watering.
Note: The Chinese Juniper is very tolerant of dry or arid growing conditions.

HOW/WHEN YOU PRUNE:

Prune any time of the year. If a major cutback is contemplated, consider pruning just prior to new growth emerging in the Spring.

How/When you fertilize:

Fertilize in the Spring by applying a well-balanced, slow-release granular fertilizer in holes around the trunk or under the canopy, at a rate of one pound per 1" of trunk diameter. You may also broadcast fertilizer on the ground under the canopy.

Additional advice for proper care:

Phomopsis Blight attacks the young shoots when wet conditions prevail, the Chinese Juniper is very tolerant and is ideal for folks who forget where they put the watering can!

Pine, Eastern White
Pinus strobus

The Eastern White Pine matures at 50-80 feet in height. This tree is widely used in Middle and East Tennessee, but has less acceptance in West Tennessee. It is best grown in moist, fertile, well-draining soils and likes full sun to partial shade areas. When full grown, this tree typifies the pyramidal shape of Christmas trees. Eastern White Pine has needles that are 4-6" in length.

When to plant:

Plant any time except during the late Spring to early Summer when new growth is present and showing a light green color.

Why you plant:

Eastern White Pines are versatile and are used as windbreaks, for screening, and as backdrops for other landscape plantings.

Where you plant:

The Eastern White Pine can be planted almost anywhere, except in soils that stay saturated with moisture. It is best grown in well-drained, moist, fertile soil. You have the option of planting in full sun to partial shade.

How you plant:

1) Dig a hole that is twice as wide and 30% deeper than the ball.

2) Plant tree and backfill with an amended soil, allowing the ball to sit slightly higher than existing soil.

3) Fertilize with a starter fertilizer.

4) Mulch to a 2" thickness, but do not place mulch against tree trunk.

5) Water for a period of time equal to one minute for every inch of the ball's diameter.

6) During the first year, staking is advised for trees over 6 feet in height, to prevent winds from uprooting them.

When you water:

For a new tree, slowly trickle water from a hose for a period of time equal to one minute per inch of diameter of the root ball. Repeat three times the first week, twice the next week, and weekly thereafter until the tree is firmly established—which is usually one growing season. When in doubt, check the soil's moisture with a moisture meter before watering.

How/When you prune:

It is best to let the Eastern White Pine grow naturally. However, if shaping is desired, shear after new growth has hardened-off, during June or July. As your tree grows, the removal of under-limbs is permissible.

How/When you fertilize:

Fertilize in the Spring by applying a well-balanced, slow-release granular fertilizer in holes placed around the trunk or under the canopy, at a rate of one pound per 1" of trunk diameter. You may also broadcast fertilizer on the ground under the canopy.

Additional advice for proper care:

Watch for White Pine Blister Rust and the White Pine Weevil.

If any problems are detected, consult your garden center for proper advice.

Pine, Japanese Black
Pinus thunbergiana

The Japanese Black Pine matures at 20-40 feet in height. This tree is the most overlooked evergreen in the Tennessee landscape and is a great evergreen tree for all areas of the state and works quite well in most landscape conditions. The somewhat irregular growth and lustrous dark green needles, with beautiful white candle-like buds, are very striking. The selection of this tree for screening use will reward the patient gardener for years to come. The Japanese Black Pine must not be overlooked as a single specimen tree. Try it, you'll like it!

WHEN TO PLANT:
Plant any time except during the late Spring to early Summer, when new growth is present and showing a light green color.

WHY YOU PLANT:
This variety works well as a featured specimen tree or in groups for screening and as a backdrop to landscape plantings. The Black Pine shows good tolerance to drought and high temperatures, making it highly suitable for life in our steamy Southern Summers.

WHERE YOU PLANT:
Plant this variety in full sun areas with well-draining, fertile, moist soil. The Japanese Black Pine even shows tolerance to salty soils.

HOW YOU PLANT:

1) Dig a hole that is twice as wide and 30% deeper than the ball.
2) Plant tree and backfill with an amended soil, allowing the ball to sit slightly higher than existing soil.
3) Fertilize with a starter fertilizer.
4) Mulch to a 2" thickness, but do not place mulch against tree trunk.
5) Water for a period of time equal to one minute for every inch of the ball's diameter.
6) During the first year, staking is advised for trees over 6 feet in height, to prevent winds from uprooting them.

WHEN YOU WATER:

For a new tree, slowly trickle water from a hose for a period of time equal to one minute per inch of diameter of the root ball. Repeat three times the first week, twice the next week, and weekly thereafter until the tree is firmly established—which is usually one growing season. When in doubt, check the soil's moisture with a moisture meter before watering.

HOW/WHEN YOU PRUNE:

The Japanese Black Pine should not be subjected to extensive pruning. It is best to let the tree grow naturally. Any necessary trimming should be done during the late Summer or Fall.

HOW/WHEN YOU FERTILIZE:

These trees should be fertilized any time from November through March. Use a well-balanced, slow-release granular fertilizer. Use your rate of fertilizer at one pound per 1" diameter of the tree trunk. Place fertilizer in random holes around the tree trunk or broadcast fertilizer on top of the ground under the outer two-thirds of the tree trunk canopy.

ADDITIONAL ADVICE FOR PROPER CARE:

This is a rather pest-free tree. Just keep those clippers away!

Pine, Loblolly
Pinus taeda

This fast growing evergreen is more often used in West Tennessee because of its tolerance to heat and its ability to adapt to a wide range of soil conditions. The Loblolly Pine matures at 60-90 feet in height. The Loblolly is not fully needled to the base like the Eastern White Pine, but has a high canopy almost like the Palm tree.

WHEN TO PLANT:
Container grown trees of this type may be planted anytime soil conditions allow. If the tree is bareroot, hold off planting until February, March, or April.

WHY YOU PLANT:
The Loblolly Pine is used as a fast-growing screen, particularly in West and Middle Tennessee. It is quite tolerant of most soil conditions, and is the wet one of the evergreens, since it will take root in wet soils.

WHERE YOU PLANT:
Plant your Loblolly in full sun. A distinct mark of this variety is that it can be under-limbed (the pruning of lower limbs) to allow activities under the tree canopy.

HOW YOU PLANT:
1) Dig a hole that is twice as wide and 30% deeper than the ball.
2) Plant tree and backfill with an amended soil, allowing the ball to sit slightly higher than existing soil.
3) Fertilize with a starter fertilizer.
4) Mulch to a 2" thickness, but do not place mulch against tree trunk.
5) Water for a period of time equal to one minute for every inch of the ball's diameter.

6) During the first year, staking is advised for trees over 6ft. in height, to prevent winds from uprooting them.

WHEN YOU WATER:
For a new tree, slowly trickle water from a hose for a period of time equal to one minute per inch of diameter of the root ball. Repeat three times the first week, twice the next week, and weekly thereafter until the tree is firmly established—which is usually one growing season. When in doubt, check the soil's moisture with a moisture meter before watering.

HOW/WHEN YOU PRUNE:
Feel free to prune the Loblolly anytime, except before new growth has had the chance to harden-off.

HOW/WHEN YOU FERTILIZE:
These trees should be fertilized any time from November through March. Use a well-balanced, slow-release granular fertilizer. Use your rate of fertilizer at one pound per 1" diameter of the tree trunk. Place fertilizer in random holes around the tree trunk or broadcast fertilizer on top of the ground under the outer two-thirds of the tree trunk canopy.

ADDITIONAL ADVICE FOR PROPER CARE:
Although the Pine Beetle and Fungal Rust can occur, rarely does the Loblolly Pine suffer any serious problems. Consult your garden center for proper advice if problems do occur.

Magnolia, Southern
Magnolia grandiflora

This Magnolia is a Southern tradition, a Southern heritage. This large evergreen tree matures at 60-80 feet in height. Its trademark dark green shiny leaves are

5-10" in length. During May and June it bears beautiful 8-12" single creamy-white fragrant blossoms. This tree needs space, but is a must to complete a Southern landscape. There are many good cultivars to choose from, 'Bracken's Brown Beauty,' 'Claudia Wannamaker,' and 'D. D. Blancher' are a few that are chosen for their more compact growth and their ability to flower at a younger age. The 'Little Gem' is the smallest of the new cultivars and is almost considered a shrub. It blooms continuously throughout the Summer and the Fall. This is a good choice when limited space is a factor.

WHEN TO PLANT:
Transplant during the Winter, early Spring, or early Fall. Container grown trees may be planted anytime, except during December, as long as they were conditioned for planting.

WHY YOU PLANT:
It is said that Northern gardeners complete their landscaping only after they have planted a Blue Spruce. By the same token, many Southern gardeners feel their landscape is incomplete without a Southern Magnolia. Due to its dense evergreen foliage, the Southern Magnolia is used as a single specimen tree, or as a beautiful screening tree.

WHERE YOU PLANT:
Plant along drives or in large lawn areas. Vanderbilt University, in Nashville, has lined its campus with this traditional Southern tree. The Southern Magnolia lends a feeling of grandeur to any home landscape.

HOW YOU PLANT:
1) Dig a hole that is twice as wide and 30% deeper than the ball.
2) Plant tree and backfill with an amended soil, allowing the ball to sit slightly higher than existing soil.
3) Fertilize with a starter fertilizer.
4) Mulch to a 2" thickness, but do not place mulch against tree trunk.

5) Water for a period of time equal to one minute for every inch of the ball's diameter.

6) During the first year, staking is advised for trees over 6 feet in height, to prevent winds from uprooting them.

Prior to planting, be sure to keep the root ball moist, otherwise, the Southern Magnolia can get shocked and drop leaves.

WHEN YOU WATER:

The Southern Magnolia tolerates highly moist soil. Overwatering is rare. For a new tree, slowly trickle water from a hose for a period of time equal to one minute per inch of diameter of the root ball. Repeat three times the first week, twice the next week, and weekly thereafter until the tree is firmly established- which is usually one growing season. When in doubt, check the soil's moisture with a moisture meter before watering.

HOW/WHEN YOU PRUNE:

Perform selective pruning to shape the tree and if you want, you may cut out underlimbs to open space under the canopy. However, most Southern gardeners prefer the limbs to grow low to the ground, trimming off boughs only for Christmas greenery.

HOW/WHEN YOU FERTILIZE:

These trees should be fertilized any time from November through March. Use a well-balanced, slow-release granular fertilizer. Use your rate of fertilizer at one pound per 1" diameter of the tree trunk. Place fertilizer in random holes around the tree trunk or broadcast fertilizer on top of the ground under the outer two-thirds of the tree trunk canopy.

ADDITIONAL ADVICE FOR PROPER CARE:

No known diseases exist, however, "Shotgun" holes may appear in leaves. These are believed to be the work of the Tulip Poplar Twig Borer. Consult your garden center for proper advice on how to combat this problem should it become apparent.

Spruce, Colorado

Picea pungens

This is normally a dense, narrow to broad, pyramidal evergreen with horizontal, stiff branches reaching to the ground. In Tennessee, the older Colorado Spruce, or Blue Spruce as it is often called, will become open and washed-out in appearance. In selecting a Colorado Spruce, you should consider the grafted cultivars, such as 'Fat Albert,' 'Hoopsii,' and 'Thompsenii.' The Colorado Spruce is very popular due to its striking contrast to other evergreen-needled trees.

WHEN TO PLANT:
With its fibrous root system, the Colorado Spruce is best transplanted from November through March.

WHY YOU PLANT:
Colorado Spruces are used as screens, wind and noise barriers, and as topiary specimens. They are singularly impressive and easily dominate the home landscape.

WHERE YOU PLANT:
Plant in full sun to very light, partial shade. This tree prefers a cold climate, and moderately moist, light acid, well-drained soils. In Tennessee, the Colorado Spruce does best in the Eastern and Plateau regions. It shows moderate performance in Middle Tennessee, but does not do as well in West Tennessee.

HOW YOU PLANT:
1) Dig a hole that is twice as wide and 30% deeper than the ball.
2) Plant tree and backfill with an amended soil, allowing the ball to sit slightly higher than existing soil.

3) Fertilize with a starter fertilizer.

4) Mulch to a 2″ thickness, but do not place mulch against tree trunk.

5) Water for a period of time equal to one minute for every inch of the ball's diameter.

6) During the first year, staking is advised for trees over 6 feet in height, to prevent winds from uprooting them.

WHEN YOU WATER:

For a new tree, slowly trickle water from a hose for a period of time equal to one minute per inch of diameter of the root ball. Repeat three times the first week, twice the next week, and weekly thereafter until the tree is firmly established—which is usually one growing season. When in doubt, check the soil's moisture with a moisture meter before watering.

HOW/WHEN YOU PRUNE:

Prune during early Spring by removing individual branches. If hedging is desired, prune the new growth to shape.

HOW/WHEN YOU FERTILIZE:

These trees should be fertilized any time from November through March. Use a well-balanced, slow-release granular fertilizer. Apply it at the rate of one pound per 1″ diameter of the tree trunk. Place fertilizer in random holes around the tree trunk or broadcast it on top of the ground under the outer two-thirds of the canopy.

ADDITIONAL ADVICE FOR PROPER CARE:

Watch for Cytospora Canker, which causes lower branch die-back, and Spruce Gall Aphid, which causes branch tip die-back. Red Spider Mites are a common problem for Colorado Spruce and should be suspected if needles begin to turn brown. Consult your garden center for proper advice should problems occur.

Spruce, Norway
Picea abies

This evergreen tree grows in pyramidal form holding stiff lateral branches all the way to the ground. These branches are covered by 1/2-1" long needles that are somewhat sharp to the touch. When limbs on older trees reach 15 feet or higher, they tend to droop taking on a more graceful form. This tree performs best in East Tennessee, moderately well in Middle Tennessee, and is questionable as a choice for West Tennessee.

WHEN TO PLANT:

With its fibrous root system, Norway Spruce is best transplanted from November through March.

WHY YOU PLANT:

Norway Spruces are used as screens, wind and noise barriers, and as topiary specimens. Because of its unique branching and dominating size, the Norway Spruce can be an impressive addition to the home landscape.

WHERE YOU PLANT:

Plant in full sun to very light, partial shade. This tree prefers a cold climate, and moderately moist, light acid, well-drained soils. In Tennessee, the Norway Spruce does best in the Eastern and Plateau regions. It shows moderate performance in Middle Tennessee, but does not do as well in West Tennessee.

HOW YOU PLANT:

1) Dig a hole that is twice as deep and 30% wider than the ball.
2) Plant tree and backfill with an amended soil, allowing the ball to sit slightly higher than existing soil.
3) Fertilize with a starter fertilizer.
4) Mulch to a 2" thickness, but do not place mulch against tree trunk.

5) Water for a period of time equal to one minute for every inch of the ball's diameter.

6) During the first year, staking is advised for trees over 6 feet in height, to prevent winds from uprooting them.

WHEN YOU WATER:

For a new tree, slowly trickle water from a hose for a period of time equal to one minute per inch of diameter of the root ball. Repeat three times the first week, twice the next week, and weekly thereafter until the tree is firmly established—which is usually one growing season. When in doubt, check the soil's moisture with a moisture meter before watering.

HOW/WHEN YOU PRUNE:

Prune during the early Spring by removing individual branches. If hedging is desired, prune the new growth to shape.

HOW/WHEN YOU FERTILIZE:

These trees should be fertilized any time from November through March. Use a well-balanced, slow-release granular fertilzer. Use your rate of fertilizer at one pound per 1" diameter of the tree trunk. Place fertilizer in random holes around the tree trunk or broadcast fertilizer on top of the ground under the outer two-thirds of the tree trunk canopy.

ADDITIONAL ADVICE FOR PROPER CARE:

Spruce Gall, Red Spider Mites, Aphids, Bagworms, and Borers can affect Norway Spruce. If you suspect a problem, consult your lawn and garden center for advice.

Acidic - Soil that demonstrates a pH lower than 7.0 on a scale of 1 to 13.

Alkaline - Soil that demonstrates a pH higher than 7.1 on a scale of 1 to 13.

Amended Soil - Soil with texture or structure improved by adding organic matter.

Anthracnose - Bacterial disease causes brown, dead areas on leaves, which turn to black, and extend to leaf margins. May be treated with registered fungicide on a program basis.

Anthracnose Discula - An anthracnose disease attacking Dogwood in higher elevations. Check for enlarged areas on stems and branches where foliage is dying. Beginning in Spring, use registered fungicide on a programmed schedule.

Aphids - Small (1/8″) insects, usually green in color, found in groups or clusters on the underside of leaves. Release ladybugs or use registered insecticide to treat.

Army Worm - Caterpillars in multitudes that defoliate grass, leaving large thin and bare areas, usually in late Summer. Active mostly in West Tennessee. Use registered lawn insecticide to treat.

Backfill - Refilling the planting hole with soil after the plant has been set in place.

Bagworm - Insect with larvae hatching from late May through June. Larvae cover bodies with foliage to create a small, bag-like protective covering. Spray with Bt, between May and June.

Bark Borers - Larvae which pierce bark and create tunnels running under bark surface. Look for pinholes and peel back bark to confirm random tunneling. Use registered insecticide to treat.

Beech Scale - Small dry scab-like spots (scale) on the underside of beech leaves. Use registered horticultural oil spray to treat.

Biennial - Term describing plants with a two-year life cycle. The first year of biennials is typified by seed germination and foliage growth, and the second year (after the plant dies back during the Winter) is typified by foliage growth and flowering, and then the production of seed for species propagation.

Birch Borer - Larvae which bore into trunk bark causing sparse leaves, especially at the top of the crown, leaving swollen ridges in the bark. Treat tree trunks with registered insecticide.

Black Seed Smut - Black, dusty particles found on the seed heads of Bermuda grass. Control by mowing off seed heads, bagging clippings and fertilizing the lawn with a recommended lawn fertilizer.

Bract - A modified leaf at the base of a flower or flower cluster.

Broadcast - Application method of sowing seed or spreading fertilizer over an entire area.

Broadleaf Weed - A broadleaf weed is best described as what it is not. Broadleaf weeds are weeds which do not have blades resembling grass.

Brown Patch - A lawn fungus which is increasing in Tennessee lawns. Starts as a small brown spot and progressively enlarges to several feet in diameter. Fungus is active on the perimeter of the ring, appearing black or a darker brown. When patches begin to run together, treat with a registered fungicide.

Canopy - Refers to the height and width of a tree's branch area.

Cedar Apple Rust - A rust found on apple and cedar trees. Use registered fungicide to treat.

Chlorosis - A yellowing of normal green foliage. Usually a sign of iron or nitrogen deficiency. Supplemental feeding of iron and/or nitrogen suggested.

Complete Soil - Soil that is prepared with the proper ratio of humus, silt, clay and sand.

Conditioned Soil - Planting soil that is not too wet (makes mud balls) or soil that is not too dry (makes dust).

Corm - A solid, bulb-like underground stem.

Crabgrass - An annual grass that grows in lawns during the Summer and dies in the Fall, reseeding itself for next year's growth.

Cultivar - Refers to the variety of plant species. For example, "Red Maple" is a species, and 'October Glory' is a cultivar.

Damping Off - Common name of a soil disease which affects new seedlings and may be prevented by selecting seeds that are treated with a fungicide.

Deadheading - Removing dead flower seed heads by pinching or with scissors, to promote more blooms.

Deciduous - Term used to describe plants that shed their leaves during the Winter season.

Die-back - Fungal disease common to Rhododendron, with scalded or burned appearing new growth Use a registered soil drench fungicide to treat.

Dollar Spot - A lawn fungus named for appearance of small (2-3") round silver-white spots. Treat with a registered fungicide.

Dormant - Resting period in plant life when no growth occurs.

Dormant Oil - A horticultural oil used to control insects, applied while the plant is dormant and at other specific times of the year.

Dripline - Outer fringe or spread of a tree's branches.

Fire Blight - Bacterial disease that attacks tip of branches and progresses toward the trunk. Plants with this disease appear to be burnt. Remove infected limbs or spray with Streptomycin Sulfate.

Fungicide - Product formulated to control the progression of fungal diseases.

Gall - Swollen growth found on limbs or branches, caused by either insects or fungus. Galls are usually harmless and may be pruned out.

Germinate - Term used to describe a seed sprouting (plant birth).

Growing Season - Period of time when a plant is actively growing.

Healed-In - A term used to describe the period when plants are stored prior to transplanting. Roots are protected from drying by covering with loose soil, straw, or mulch.

Horticultural Oil - A refined oil sprayed on plants to help control insects. It works by smothering the pests and their eggs. It can also prevent some fungal diseases. Highly refined types are called summer or superior oils that can be applied during the growing seasons as long as temperatures are below 90°. Heavier oils are called dormant oils and are used during a plant's dormant stage.

Japanese Beetle - Small, leaf-eating beetle with shiny, green body and wings. Usually noticed first on roses and trees. Use registered insecticide or insect traps to treat.

Japanese Beetle Grub - White, legless, C-shaped larval stage of the Japanese beetle, found in lawns (September to May). Treat

soil with a registered soil insecticide or use an organic product called milky spore to control.

Lace Bug - Found primarily on Pyracantha and Azaleas; leaves have yellow specks on upper side and black shiny spots on the underside, and the underside of foliage will appear dirty. Use registered insecticide to treat.

Leaf Miners - Small insects that make zigzag tunnels between the lower and upper surface of leaves for the purpose of harvesting. Use a registered systemic insecticide to treat.

Leaf Scorch - A condition causing leaves to have a burned look. Maple and Oak are susceptible during hot, dry periods. Deep watering is recommended.

Leaf Spot - Black to brown spots on leaf surface, but not a major problem. Black usually indicates a fungal disease and brown usually indicates sunburn.

Lime - Finely-ground limestone rock used to amend soils by raising pH levels. Good source of calcium carbonate.

Liquid Kelp - An organic form of fertilizer derived from seaweed. Excellent for use in vegetable and herb gardens.

Magnolia Scale - Condition causing twigs to have powdery white or tan bumps about half-bean size. Use registered insecticide or dormant oil to treat.

Maple Decline - A disease thought to be associated with several pathogens and with environmental stress. Prune out cankered branches and water deeply.

Moles - Small, blind rodents that burrow randomly, just below the surface of lawns, feeding on insects (particularly grub-worms). Set mole traps or discourage feeding activity by controlling soil insects. Use a registered soil insecticide.

Nitrogen - A gas that makes up the largest percent of breathable atmosphere in the form of NO3 and NH3 (nitrate and ammonium nitrate). The element itself is a plant food stimulating plant growth or cell division.

Overseeding - Process of broadcasting grass seed over an existing lawn.

pH - Measurement of acidity within the soil.

Pinch Back - Process of snipping, cutting or pinching the tips of a plant's new growth in order to encourage bushier growth habit. Potential overall fullness and abundant blooms will occur

Preventer, Weed or Grass - Used in this book to describe weed controls applied to soil prior to seed germination to prevent continual growth of the weed.

Powdery Mildew - A grey-white powdery

growth on leaves and/or stems. Use registered fungicide to treat.

Raceme - A flower cluster with flowers along the stem, blooming from base to tip.

Reach and Cut - The pruning technique of thinning by reaching into the "body" of the plant and selectively pruning by cutting out older limbs individually at the base of the plant.

Scale - A small, dry scab-like spot found on stems and leaves of plants. This can be a protective shell formed by colonies of insects living underneath. Use a registered horticultural oil spray to treat these sap-sucking insects.

Shearing - Pruning process where hedge shears are used to shape shrubs.

Shot Hole Fungus - Fungal disease attacking particular laurels where leaves have holes resembling shot-gun blasts. Good Winter cleanup and well-timed fungicidal sprays are the most effective controls.

Side Dress - Working fertilizer into the soil around the base of the plant.

Soil Moisture Meter - A device used for measuring percentage of moisture in soil.

Sod Webworm - Small (1") worm which feeds on lawn grasses, spinning a web as it feeds at night. Look for small, random patches of webs 3-6" in width. Treat with a registered insecticide.

Sooty Mold Fungus - Black, sooty substance on leaves and branches caused by insect damage, creating sweet sap that ferments, forming mold. Use registered insecticide to treat.

Spider Mites - Very small (pinpoint size) insects that feed on the juices of the foliage of many plants. They thrive in hot, dry weather indoors and out. Infested plants will have overall discoloration of foliage, almost a metalic-look. Also, the plant can become covered with fine spider-type webs. Control with horticultural oils or a registered miticide.

Spurge - A weed found in lawn, with vertical, viney growth habit and small oval leaves.

Starter Fertilizer - Fertilizer formulated to promote quick root development. Formulation contains at least twice the levels of phosphorus as compared to nitrogen or potassium. Example: 10-20-10 to 5-10-5.

Stolon - A prostrate branch from the base of a plant that runs along the ground or just below the surface and takes root, developing a new plant from its tips. Sometimes called a runner.

Supplemental Feeding - The practice of additional feeding of plants after the required initial feeding.

Tulip Tree Scale - A condition causing clusters of bumps on limbs and branches, accompanied by sooty mold. Spray with dormant oil in late Winter to treat.

Twig Blight - A generic term for die-back of small branches and tips of limbs. Some causes are lack of moisture or fungal attack. Check soil moisture and use registered fungicide to treat.

Verticillium Wilt - Characterized by Maple leaves suddenly wilting and turning yellow, then dropping off. Wilt may occur on one side of the tree. Tree may suddenly die, or decline over a period of years. Fertilizing heavily with nitrogen sometimes helps. Water deeply. If tree dies, avoid replanting in same spot.

Winter Dead Spot - Dead spots found in lawns when new Bermuda growth begins in Spring. Control by digging out depth of 3-6" and disposing. Replant or re-sod the affected area.

A Note To The Reader

We hesitate to recommend specific remedies due to climatic, physiological and geographical differences which our readers may face. Therefore, we recommend you seek the advice of garden centers and nurseries which can better supplement and enhance this information with specific knowledge of your local conditions. They are qualified to advise you on the proper solution to any problem, and they sell the products that work best in your own little corner of Tennessee.

I N D E X